C-1081   CAREER EXAMINATION SERIES

*This is your*
*PASSBOOK for...*

# Administrative Secretary

*Test Preparation Study Guide*
*Questions & Answers*

NATIONAL LEARNING CORPORATION®

# COPYRIGHT NOTICE

This book is SOLELY intended for, is sold ONLY to, and its use is RESTRICTED to individual, bona fide applicants or candidates who qualify by virtue of having seriously filed applications for appropriate license, certificate, professional and/or promotional advancement, higher school matriculation, scholarship, or other legitimate requirements of education and/or governmental authorities.

This book is NOT intended for use, class instruction, tutoring, training, duplication, copying, reprinting, excerption, or adaptation, etc., by:

1) Other publishers
2) Proprietors and/or Instructors of "Coaching" and/or Preparatory Courses
3) Personnel and/or Training Divisions of commercial, industrial, and governmental organizations
4) Schools, colleges, or universities and/or their departments and staffs, including teachers and other personnel
5) Testing Agencies or Bureaus
6) Study groups which seek by the purchase of a single volume to copy and/or duplicate and/or adapt this material for use by the group as a whole without having purchased individual volumes for each of the members of the group
7) Et al.

Such persons would be in violation of appropriate Federal and State statutes.

PROVISION OF LICENSING AGREEMENTS – Recognized educational, commercial, industrial, and governmental institutions and organizations, and others legitimately engaged in educational pursuits, including training, testing, and measurement activities, may address request for a licensing agreement to the copyright owners, who will determine whether, and under what conditions, including fees and charges, the materials in this book may be used them. In other words, a licensing facility exists for the legitimate use of the material in this book on other than an individual basis. However, it is asseverated and affirmed here that the material in this book CANNOT be used without the receipt of the express permission of such a licensing agreement from the Publishers. Inquiries re licensing should be addressed to the company, attention rights and permissions department.

All rights reserved, including the right of reproduction in whole or in part, in any form or by any means, electronic or mechanical, including photocopying, recording, or by any information storage and retrieval system, without permission in writing from the Publisher.

Copyright © 2024 by
## National Learning Corporation

212 Michael Drive, Syosset, NY 11791
(516) 921-8888 • www.passbooks.com
E-mail: info@passbooks.com

PUBLISHED IN THE UNITED STATES OF AMERICA

# PASSBOOK® SERIES

THE *PASSBOOK® SERIES* has been created to prepare applicants and candidates for the ultimate academic battlefield – the examination room.

At some time in our lives, each and every one of us may be required to take an examination – for validation, matriculation, admission, qualification, registration, certification, or licensure.

Based on the assumption that every applicant or candidate has met the basic formal educational standards, has taken the required number of courses, and read the necessary texts, the *PASSBOOK® SERIES* furnishes the one special preparation which may assure passing with confidence, instead of failing with insecurity. Examination questions – together with answers – are furnished as the basic vehicle for study so that the mysteries of the examination and its compounding difficulties may be eliminated or diminished by a sure method.

This book is meant to help you pass your examination provided that you qualify and are serious in your objective.

The entire field is reviewed through the huge store of content information which is succinctly presented through a provocative and challenging approach – the question-and-answer method.

A climate of success is established by furnishing the correct answers at the end of each test.

You soon learn to recognize types of questions, forms of questions, and patterns of questioning. You may even begin to anticipate expected outcomes.

You perceive that many questions are repeated or adapted so that you can gain acute insights, which may enable you to score many sure points.

You learn how to confront new questions, or types of questions, and to attack them confidently and work out the correct answers.

You note objectives and emphases, and recognize pitfalls and dangers, so that you may make positive educational adjustments.

Moreover, you are kept fully informed in relation to new concepts, methods, practices, and directions in the field.

You discover that you are actually taking the examination all the time: you are preparing for the examination by "taking" an examination, not by reading extraneous and/or supererogatory textbooks.

In short, this PASSBOOK®, used directedly, should be an important factor in helping you to pass your test.

# ADMINISTRATIVE SECRETARY

**DUTIES**
Performs responsible and frequently confidential secretarial work for an administrative official. Does related work as required.

**SUBJECT OF EXAMINATION**
Written test will cover knowledge, skills, and/or abilities in such areas as:
1. Secretarial practices;
2. English grammar, usage, and punctuation;
3. Spelling;
4. Understanding and interpreting written material; and
5. Administrative supervision.

# HOW TO TAKE A TEST

I. YOU MUST PASS AN EXAMINATION

A. *WHAT EVERY CANDIDATE SHOULD KNOW*

Examination applicants often ask us for help in preparing for the written test. What can I study in advance? What kinds of questions will be asked? How will the test be given? How will the papers be graded?

As an applicant for a civil service examination, you may be wondering about some of these things. Our purpose here is to suggest effective methods of advance study and to describe civil service examinations.

Your chances for success on this examination can be increased if you know how to prepare. Those "pre-examination jitters" can be reduced if you know what to expect. You can even experience an adventure in good citizenship if you know why civil service exams are given.

B. *WHY ARE CIVIL SERVICE EXAMINATIONS GIVEN?*

Civil service examinations are important to you in two ways. As a citizen, you want public jobs filled by employees who know how to do their work. As a job seeker, you want a fair chance to compete for that job on an equal footing with other candidates. The best-known means of accomplishing this two-fold goal is the competitive examination.

Exams are widely publicized throughout the nation. They may be administered for jobs in federal, state, city, municipal, town or village governments or agencies.

Any citizen may apply, with some limitations, such as the age or residence of applicants. Your experience and education may be reviewed to see whether you meet the requirements for the particular examination. When these requirements exist, they are reasonable and applied consistently to all applicants. Thus, a competitive examination may cause you some uneasiness now, but it is your privilege and safeguard.

C. *HOW ARE CIVIL SERVICE EXAMS DEVELOPED?*

Examinations are carefully written by trained technicians who are specialists in the field known as "psychological measurement," in consultation with recognized authorities in the field of work that the test will cover. These experts recommend the subject matter areas or skills to be tested; only those knowledges or skills important to your success on the job are included. The most reliable books and source materials available are used as references. Together, the experts and technicians judge the difficulty level of the questions.

Test technicians know how to phrase questions so that the problem is clearly stated. Their ethics do not permit "trick" or "catch" questions. Questions may have been tried out on sample groups, or subjected to statistical analysis, to determine their usefulness.

Written tests are often used in combination with performance tests, ratings of training and experience, and oral interviews. All of these measures combine to form the best-known means of finding the right person for the right job.

## II. HOW TO PASS THE WRITTEN TEST

### A. NATURE OF THE EXAMINATION

To prepare intelligently for civil service examinations, you should know how they differ from school examinations you have taken. In school you were assigned certain definite pages to read or subjects to cover. The examination questions were quite detailed and usually emphasized memory. Civil service exams, on the other hand, try to discover your present ability to perform the duties of a position, plus your potentiality to learn these duties. In other words, a civil service exam attempts to predict how successful you will be. Questions cover such a broad area that they cannot be as minute and detailed as school exam questions.

In the public service similar kinds of work, or positions, are grouped together in one "class." This process is known as *position-classification*. All the positions in a class are paid according to the salary range for that class. One class title covers all of these positions, and they are all tested by the same examination.

### B. FOUR BASIC STEPS

#### 1) Study the announcement

How, then, can you know what subjects to study? Our best answer is: "Learn as much as possible about the class of positions for which you've applied." The exam will test the knowledge, skills and abilities needed to do the work.

Your most valuable source of information about the position you want is the official exam announcement. This announcement lists the training and experience qualifications. Check these standards and apply only if you come reasonably close to meeting them.

The brief description of the position in the examination announcement offers some clues to the subjects which will be tested. Think about the job itself. Review the duties in your mind. Can you perform them, or are there some in which you are rusty? Fill in the blank spots in your preparation.

Many jurisdictions preview the written test in the exam announcement by including a section called "Knowledge and Abilities Required," "Scope of the Examination," or some similar heading. Here you will find out specifically what fields will be tested.

#### 2) Review your own background

Once you learn in general what the position is all about, and what you need to know to do the work, ask yourself which subjects you already know fairly well and which need improvement. You may wonder whether to concentrate on improving your strong areas or on building some background in your fields of weakness. When the announcement has specified "some knowledge" or "considerable knowledge," or has used adjectives like "beginning principles of…" or "advanced … methods," you can get a clue as to the number and difficulty of questions to be asked in any given field. More questions, and hence broader coverage, would be included for those subjects which are more important in the work. Now weigh your strengths and weaknesses against the job requirements and prepare accordingly.

#### 3) Determine the level of the position

Another way to tell how intensively you should prepare is to understand the level of the job for which you are applying. Is it the entering level? In other words, is this the position in which beginners in a field of work are hired? Or is it an intermediate or advanced level? Sometimes this is indicated by such words as "Junior" or "Senior" in the class title. Other jurisdictions use Roman numerals to designate the level – Clerk I, Clerk II, for example. The word "Supervisor" sometimes appears in the title. If the level is not indicated by the title, check the description of duties. Will you be working under very close supervision, or will you have responsibility for independent decisions in this work?

### 4) Choose appropriate study materials

Now that you know the subjects to be examined and the relative amount of each subject to be covered, you can choose suitable study materials. For beginning level jobs, or even advanced ones, if you have a pronounced weakness in some aspect of your training, read a modern, standard textbook in that field. Be sure it is up to date and has general coverage. Such books are normally available at your library, and the librarian will be glad to help you locate one. For entry-level positions, questions of appropriate difficulty are chosen -- neither highly advanced questions, nor those too simple. Such questions require careful thought but not advanced training.

If the position for which you are applying is technical or advanced, you will read more advanced, specialized material. If you are already familiar with the basic principles of your field, elementary textbooks would waste your time. Concentrate on advanced textbooks and technical periodicals. Think through the concepts and review difficult problems in your field.

These are all general sources. You can get more ideas on your own initiative, following these leads. For example, training manuals and publications of the government agency which employs workers in your field can be useful, particularly for technical and professional positions. A letter or visit to the government department involved may result in more specific study suggestions, and certainly will provide you with a more definite idea of the exact nature of the position you are seeking.

## III. KINDS OF TESTS

Tests are used for purposes other than measuring knowledge and ability to perform specified duties. For some positions, it is equally important to test ability to make adjustments to new situations or to profit from training. In others, basic mental abilities not dependent on information are essential. Questions which test these things may not appear as pertinent to the duties of the position as those which test for knowledge and information. Yet they are often highly important parts of a fair examination. For very general questions, it is almost impossible to help you direct your study efforts. What we can do is to point out some of the more common of these general abilities needed in public service positions and describe some typical questions.

1) General information

Broad, general information has been found useful for predicting job success in some kinds of work. This is tested in a variety of ways, from vocabulary lists to questions about current events. Basic background in some field of work, such as sociology or economics, may be sampled in a group of questions. Often these are principles which have become familiar to most persons through exposure rather than through formal training. It is difficult to advise you how to study for these questions; being alert to the world around you is our best suggestion.

2) Verbal ability

An example of an ability needed in many positions is verbal or language ability. Verbal ability is, in brief, the ability to use and understand words. Vocabulary and grammar tests are typical measures of this ability. Reading comprehension or paragraph interpretation questions are common in many kinds of civil service tests. You are given a paragraph of written material and asked to find its central meaning.

3) Numerical ability

Number skills can be tested by the familiar arithmetic problem, by checking paired lists of numbers to see which are alike and which are different, or by interpreting charts and graphs. In the latter test, a graph may be printed in the test booklet which you are asked to use as the basis for answering questions.

4) Observation

A popular test for law-enforcement positions is the observation test. A picture is shown to you for several minutes, then taken away. Questions about the picture test your ability to observe both details and larger elements.

5) Following directions

In many positions in the public service, the employee must be able to carry out written instructions dependably and accurately. You may be given a chart with several columns, each column listing a variety of information. The questions require you to carry out directions involving the information given in the chart.

6) Skills and aptitudes

Performance tests effectively measure some manual skills and aptitudes. When the skill is one in which you are trained, such as typing or shorthand, you can practice. These tests are often very much like those given in business school or high school courses. For many of the other skills and aptitudes, however, no short-time preparation can be made. Skills and abilities natural to you or that you have developed throughout your lifetime are being tested.

Many of the general questions just described provide all the data needed to answer the questions and ask you to use your reasoning ability to find the answers. Your best preparation for these tests, as well as for tests of facts and ideas, is to be at your physical and mental best. You, no doubt, have your own methods of getting into an exam-taking mood and keeping "in shape." The next section lists some ideas on this subject.

## IV. KINDS OF QUESTIONS

Only rarely is the "essay" question, which you answer in narrative form, used in civil service tests. Civil service tests are usually of the short-answer type. Full instructions for answering these questions will be given to you at the examination. But in case this is your first experience with short-answer questions and separate answer sheets, here is what you need to know:

### 1) Multiple-choice Questions

Most popular of the short-answer questions is the "multiple choice" or "best answer" question. It can be used, for example, to test for factual knowledge, ability to solve problems or judgment in meeting situations found at work.

A multiple-choice question is normally one of three types—
- It can begin with an incomplete statement followed by several possible endings. You are to find the one ending which *best* completes the statement, although some of the others may not be entirely wrong.
- It can also be a complete statement in the form of a question which is answered by choosing one of the statements listed.

- It can be in the form of a problem – again you select the best answer.

Here is an example of a multiple-choice question with a discussion which should give you some clues as to the method for choosing the right answer:

When an employee has a complaint about his assignment, the action which will *best* help him overcome his difficulty is to
- A. discuss his difficulty with his coworkers
- B. take the problem to the head of the organization
- C. take the problem to the person who gave him the assignment
- D. say nothing to anyone about his complaint

In answering this question, you should study each of the choices to find which is best. Consider choice "A" – Certainly an employee may discuss his complaint with fellow employees, but no change or improvement can result, and the complaint remains unresolved. Choice "B" is a poor choice since the head of the organization probably does not know what assignment you have been given, and taking your problem to him is known as "going over the head" of the supervisor. The supervisor, or person who made the assignment, is the person who can clarify it or correct any injustice. Choice "C" is, therefore, correct. To say nothing, as in choice "D," is unwise. Supervisors have and interest in knowing the problems employees are facing, and the employee is seeking a solution to his problem.

## 2) True/False Questions

The "true/false" or "right/wrong" form of question is sometimes used. Here a complete statement is given. Your job is to decide whether the statement is right or wrong.

SAMPLE: A roaming cell-phone call to a nearby city costs less than a non-roaming call to a distant city.

This statement is wrong, or false, since roaming calls are more expensive.

This is not a complete list of all possible question forms, although most of the others are variations of these common types. You will always get complete directions for answering questions. Be sure you understand *how* to mark your answers – ask questions until you do.

## V. RECORDING YOUR ANSWERS

Computer terminals are used more and more today for many different kinds of exams.

For an examination with very few applicants, you may be told to record your answers in the test booklet itself. Separate answer sheets are much more common. If this separate answer sheet is to be scored by machine – and this is often the case – it is highly important that you mark your answers correctly in order to get credit.

An electronic scoring machine is often used in civil service offices because of the speed with which papers can be scored. Machine-scored answer sheets must be marked with a pencil, which will be given to you. This pencil has a high graphite content which responds to the electronic scoring machine. As a matter of fact, stray dots may register as answers, so do not let your pencil rest on the answer sheet while you are pondering the correct answer. Also, if your pencil lead breaks or is otherwise defective, ask for another.

Since the answer sheet will be dropped in a slot in the scoring machine, be careful not to bend the corners or get the paper crumpled.

The answer sheet normally has five vertical columns of numbers, with 30 numbers to a column. These numbers correspond to the question numbers in your test booklet. After each number, going across the page are four or five pairs of dotted lines. These short dotted lines have small letters or numbers above them. The first two pairs may also have a "T" or "F" above the letters. This indicates that the first two pairs only are to be used if the questions are of the true-false type. If the questions are multiple choice, disregard the "T" and "F" and pay attention only to the small letters or numbers.

Answer your questions in the manner of the sample that follows:

32. The largest city in the United States is
    A. Washington, D.C.
    B. New York City
    C. Chicago
    D. Detroit
    E. San Francisco

1) Choose the answer you think is best. (New York City is the largest, so "B" is correct.)
2) Find the row of dotted lines numbered the same as the question you are answering. (Find row number 32)
3) Find the pair of dotted lines corresponding to the answer. (Find the pair of lines under the mark "B.")
4) Make a solid black mark between the dotted lines.

## VI. BEFORE THE TEST

Common sense will help you find procedures to follow to get ready for an examination. Too many of us, however, overlook these sensible measures. Indeed, nervousness and fatigue have been found to be the most serious reasons why applicants fail to do their best on civil service tests. Here is a list of reminders:

- Begin your preparation early – Don't wait until the last minute to go scurrying around for books and materials or to find out what the position is all about.
- Prepare continuously – An hour a night for a week is better than an all-night cram session. This has been definitely established. What is more, a night a week for a month will return better dividends than crowding your study into a shorter period of time.
- Locate the place of the exam – You have been sent a notice telling you when and where to report for the examination. If the location is in a different town or otherwise unfamiliar to you, it would be well to inquire the best route and learn something about the building.
- Relax the night before the test – Allow your mind to rest. Do not study at all that night. Plan some mild recreation or diversion; then go to bed early and get a good night's sleep.
- Get up early enough to make a leisurely trip to the place for the test – This way unforeseen events, traffic snarls, unfamiliar buildings, etc. will not upset you.
- Dress comfortably – A written test is not a fashion show. You will be known by number and not by name, so wear something comfortable.

- Leave excess paraphernalia at home – Shopping bags and odd bundles will get in your way. You need bring only the items mentioned in the official notice you received; usually everything you need is provided. Do not bring reference books to the exam. They will only confuse those last minutes and be taken away from you when in the test room.
- Arrive somewhat ahead of time – If because of transportation schedules you must get there very early, bring a newspaper or magazine to take your mind off yourself while waiting.
- Locate the examination room – When you have found the proper room, you will be directed to the seat or part of the room where you will sit. Sometimes you are given a sheet of instructions to read while you are waiting. Do not fill out any forms until you are told to do so; just read them and be prepared.
- Relax and prepare to listen to the instructions
- If you have any physical problem that may keep you from doing your best, be sure to tell the test administrator. If you are sick or in poor health, you really cannot do your best on the exam. You can come back and take the test some other time.

## VII. AT THE TEST

The day of the test is here and you have the test booklet in your hand. The temptation to get going is very strong. Caution! There is more to success than knowing the right answers. You must know how to identify your papers and understand variations in the type of short-answer question used in this particular examination. Follow these suggestions for maximum results from your efforts:

### 1) Cooperate with the monitor

The test administrator has a duty to create a situation in which you can be as much at ease as possible. He will give instructions, tell you when to begin, check to see that you are marking your answer sheet correctly, and so on. He is not there to guard you, although he will see that your competitors do not take unfair advantage. He wants to help you do your best.

### 2) Listen to all instructions

Don't jump the gun! Wait until you understand all directions. In most civil service tests you get more time than you need to answer the questions. So don't be in a hurry. Read each word of instructions until you clearly understand the meaning. Study the examples, listen to all announcements and follow directions. Ask questions if you do not understand what to do.

### 3) Identify your papers

Civil service exams are usually identified by number only. You will be assigned a number; you must not put your name on your test papers. Be sure to copy your number correctly. Since more than one exam may be given, copy your exact examination title.

### 4) Plan your time

Unless you are told that a test is a "speed" or "rate of work" test, speed itself is usually not important. Time enough to answer all the questions will be provided, but this does not mean that you have all day. An overall time limit has been set. Divide the total time (in minutes) by the number of questions to determine the approximate time you have for each question.

### 5) Do not linger over difficult questions

If you come across a difficult question, mark it with a paper clip (useful to have along) and come back to it when you have been through the booklet. One caution if you do this – be sure to skip a number on your answer sheet as well. Check often to be sure that you have not lost your place and that you are marking in the row numbered the same as the question you are answering.

### 6) Read the questions

Be sure you know what the question asks! Many capable people are unsuccessful because they failed to *read* the questions correctly.

### 7) Answer all questions

Unless you have been instructed that a penalty will be deducted for incorrect answers, it is better to guess than to omit a question.

### 8) Speed tests

It is often better NOT to guess on speed tests. It has been found that on timed tests people are tempted to spend the last few seconds before time is called in marking answers at random – without even reading them – in the hope of picking up a few extra points. To discourage this practice, the instructions may warn you that your score will be "corrected" for guessing. That is, a penalty will be applied. The incorrect answers will be deducted from the correct ones, or some other penalty formula will be used.

### 9) Review your answers

If you finish before time is called, go back to the questions you guessed or omitted to give them further thought. Review other answers if you have time.

### 10) Return your test materials

If you are ready to leave before others have finished or time is called, take ALL your materials to the monitor and leave quietly. Never take any test material with you. The monitor can discover whose papers are not complete, and taking a test booklet may be grounds for disqualification.

## VIII. EXAMINATION TECHNIQUES

1) Read the general instructions carefully. These are usually printed on the first page of the exam booklet. As a rule, these instructions refer to the timing of the examination; the fact that you should not start work until the signal and must stop work at a signal, etc. If there are any *special* instructions, such as a choice of questions to be answered, make sure that you note this instruction carefully.

2) When you are ready to start work on the examination, that is as soon as the signal has been given, read the instructions to each question booklet, underline any key words or phrases, such as *least, best, outline, describe* and the like. In this way you will tend to answer as requested rather than discover on reviewing your paper that you *listed without describing*, that you selected the *worst* choice rather than the *best* choice, etc.

3) If the examination is of the objective or multiple-choice type – that is, each question will also give a series of possible answers: A, B, C or D, and you are called upon to select the best answer and write the letter next to that answer on your answer paper – it is advisable to start answering each question in turn. There may be anywhere from 50 to 100 such questions in the three or four hours allotted and you can see how much time would be taken if you read through all the questions before beginning to answer any. Furthermore, if you come across a question or group of questions which you know would be difficult to answer, it would undoubtedly affect your handling of all the other questions.

4) If the examination is of the essay type and contains but a few questions, it is a moot point as to whether you should read all the questions before starting to answer any one. Of course, if you are given a choice – say five out of seven and the like – then it is essential to read all the questions so you can eliminate the two that are most difficult. If, however, you are asked to answer all the questions, there may be danger in trying to answer the easiest one first because you may find that you will spend too much time on it. The best technique is to answer the first question, then proceed to the second, etc.

5) Time your answers. Before the exam begins, write down the time it started, then add the time allowed for the examination and write down the time it must be completed, then divide the time available somewhat as follows:
    - If 3-1/2 hours are allowed, that would be 210 minutes. If you have 80 objective-type questions, that would be an average of 2-1/2 minutes per question. Allow yourself no more than 2 minutes per question, or a total of 160 minutes, which will permit about 50 minutes to review.
    - If for the time allotment of 210 minutes there are 7 essay questions to answer, that would average about 30 minutes a question. Give yourself only 25 minutes per question so that you have about 35 minutes to review.

6) The most important instruction is to *read each question* and make sure you know what is wanted. The second most important instruction is to *time yourself properly* so that you answer every question. The third most important instruction is to *answer every question*. Guess if you have to but include something for each question. Remember that you will receive no credit for a blank and will probably receive some credit if you write something in answer to an essay question. If you guess a letter – say "B" for a multiple-choice question – you may have guessed right. If you leave a blank as an answer to a multiple-choice question, the examiners may respect your feelings but it will not add a point to your score. Some exams may penalize you for wrong answers, so in such cases *only*, you may not want to guess unless you have some basis for your answer.

7) Suggestions
    a. Objective-type questions
        1. Examine the question booklet for proper sequence of pages and questions
        2. Read all instructions carefully
        3. Skip any question which seems too difficult; return to it after all other questions have been answered
        4. Apportion your time properly; do not spend too much time on any single question or group of questions

5. Note and underline key words – *all, most, fewest, least, best, worst, same, opposite*, etc.
6. Pay particular attention to negatives
7. Note unusual option, e.g., unduly long, short, complex, different or similar in content to the body of the question
8. Observe the use of "hedging" words – *probably, may, most likely*, etc.
9. Make sure that your answer is put next to the same number as the question
10. Do not second-guess unless you have good reason to believe the second answer is definitely more correct
11. Cross out original answer if you decide another answer is more accurate; do not erase until you are ready to hand your paper in
12. Answer all questions; guess unless instructed otherwise
13. Leave time for review

  b. Essay questions
    1. Read each question carefully
    2. Determine exactly what is wanted. Underline key words or phrases.
    3. Decide on outline or paragraph answer
    4. Include many different points and elements unless asked to develop any one or two points or elements
    5. Show impartiality by giving pros and cons unless directed to select one side only
    6. Make and write down any assumptions you find necessary to answer the questions
    7. Watch your English, grammar, punctuation and choice of words
    8. Time your answers; don't crowd material

8) Answering the essay question

Most essay questions can be answered by framing the specific response around several key words or ideas. Here are a few such key words or ideas:

M's: manpower, materials, methods, money, management
P's: purpose, program, policy, plan, procedure, practice, problems, pitfalls, personnel, public relations

  a. Six basic steps in handling problems:
    1. Preliminary plan and background development
    2. Collect information, data and facts
    3. Analyze and interpret information, data and facts
    4. Analyze and develop solutions as well as make recommendations
    5. Prepare report and sell recommendations
    6. Install recommendations and follow up effectiveness

  b. Pitfalls to avoid
    1. *Taking things for granted* – A statement of the situation does not necessarily imply that each of the elements is necessarily true; for example, a complaint may be invalid and biased so that all that can be taken for granted is that a complaint has been registered

2. *Considering only one side of a situation* – Wherever possible, indicate several alternatives and then point out the reasons you selected the best one
3. *Failing to indicate follow up* – Whenever your answer indicates action on your part, make certain that you will take proper follow-up action to see how successful your recommendations, procedures or actions turn out to be
4. *Taking too long in answering any single question* – Remember to time your answers properly

## IX. AFTER THE TEST

Scoring procedures differ in detail among civil service jurisdictions although the general principles are the same. Whether the papers are hand-scored or graded by machine we have described, they are nearly always graded by number. That is, the person who marks the paper knows only the number – never the name – of the applicant. Not until all the papers have been graded will they be matched with names. If other tests, such as training and experience or oral interview ratings have been given, scores will be combined. Different parts of the examination usually have different weights. For example, the written test might count 60 percent of the final grade, and a rating of training and experience 40 percent. In many jurisdictions, veterans will have a certain number of points added to their grades.

After the final grade has been determined, the names are placed in grade order and an eligible list is established. There are various methods for resolving ties between those who get the same final grade – probably the most common is to place first the name of the person whose application was received first. Job offers are made from the eligible list in the order the names appear on it. You will be notified of your grade and your rank as soon as all these computations have been made. This will be done as rapidly as possible.

People who are found to meet the requirements in the announcement are called "eligibles." Their names are put on a list of eligible candidates. An eligible's chances of getting a job depend on how high he stands on this list and how fast agencies are filling jobs from the list.

When a job is to be filled from a list of eligibles, the agency asks for the names of people on the list of eligibles for that job. When the civil service commission receives this request, it sends to the agency the names of the three people highest on this list. Or, if the job to be filled has specialized requirements, the office sends the agency the names of the top three persons who meet these requirements from the general list.

The appointing officer makes a choice from among the three people whose names were sent to him. If the selected person accepts the appointment, the names of the others are put back on the list to be considered for future openings.

That is the rule in hiring from all kinds of eligible lists, whether they are for typist, carpenter, chemist, or something else. For every vacancy, the appointing officer has his choice of any one of the top three eligibles on the list. This explains why the person whose name is on top of the list sometimes does not get an appointment when some of the persons lower on the list do. If the appointing officer chooses the second or third eligible, the No. 1 eligible does not get a job at once, but stays on the list until he is appointed or the list is terminated.

# X. HOW TO PASS THE INTERVIEW TEST

The examination for which you applied requires an oral interview test. You have already taken the written test and you are now being called for the interview test – the final part of the formal examination.

You may think that it is not possible to prepare for an interview test and that there are no procedures to follow during an interview. Our purpose is to point out some things you can do in advance that will help you and some good rules to follow and pitfalls to avoid while you are being interviewed.

*What is an interview supposed to test?*

The written examination is designed to test the technical knowledge and competence of the candidate; the oral is designed to evaluate intangible qualities, not readily measured otherwise, and to establish a list showing the relative fitness of each candidate – as measured against his competitors – for the position sought. Scoring is not on the basis of "right" and "wrong," but on a sliding scale of values ranging from "not passable" to "outstanding." As a matter of fact, it is possible to achieve a relatively low score without a single "incorrect" answer because of evident weakness in the qualities being measured.

Occasionally, an examination may consist entirely of an oral test – either an individual or a group oral. In such cases, information is sought concerning the technical knowledges and abilities of the candidate, since there has been no written examination for this purpose. More commonly, however, an oral test is used to supplement a written examination.

*Who conducts interviews?*

The composition of oral boards varies among different jurisdictions. In nearly all, a representative of the personnel department serves as chairman. One of the members of the board may be a representative of the department in which the candidate would work. In some cases, "outside experts" are used, and, frequently, a businessman or some other representative of the general public is asked to serve. Labor and management or other special groups may be represented. The aim is to secure the services of experts in the appropriate field.

However the board is composed, it is a good idea (and not at all improper or unethical) to ascertain in advance of the interview who the members are and what groups they represent. When you are introduced to them, you will have some idea of their backgrounds and interests, and at least you will not stutter and stammer over their names.

*What should be done before the interview?*

While knowledge about the board members is useful and takes some of the surprise element out of the interview, there is other preparation which is more substantive. It *is* possible to prepare for an oral interview – in several ways:

**1) Keep a copy of your application and review it carefully before the interview**

This may be the only document before the oral board, and the starting point of the interview. Know what education and experience you have listed there, and the sequence and dates of all of it. Sometimes the board will ask you to review the highlights of your experience for them; you should not have to hem and haw doing it.

**2) Study the class specification and the examination announcement**

Usually, the oral board has one or both of these to guide them. The qualities, characteristics or knowledges required by the position sought are stated in these documents. They offer valuable clues as to the nature of the oral interview. For example, if the job involves supervisory responsibilities, the announcement will usually indicate that knowledge of modern supervisory methods and the qualifications of the candidate as a supervisor will be tested. If so, you can expect such questions, frequently in the form of a hypothetical situation which you are expected to solve. NEVER go into an oral without knowledge of the duties and responsibilities of the job you seek.

### 3) Think through each qualification required

Try to visualize the kind of questions you would ask if you were a board member. How well could you answer them? Try especially to appraise your own knowledge and background in each area, *measured against the job sought*, and identify any areas in which you are weak. Be critical and realistic – do not flatter yourself.

### 4) Do some general reading in areas in which you feel you may be weak

For example, if the job involves supervision and your past experience has NOT, some general reading in supervisory methods and practices, particularly in the field of human relations, might be useful. Do NOT study agency procedures or detailed manuals. The oral board will be testing your understanding and capacity, not your memory.

### 5) Get a good night's sleep and watch your general health and mental attitude

You will want a clear head at the interview. Take care of a cold or any other minor ailment, and of course, no hangovers.

*What should be done on the day of the interview?*

Now comes the day of the interview itself. Give yourself plenty of time to get there. Plan to arrive somewhat ahead of the scheduled time, particularly if your appointment is in the fore part of the day. If a previous candidate fails to appear, the board might be ready for you a bit early. By early afternoon an oral board is almost invariably behind schedule if there are many candidates, and you may have to wait. Take along a book or magazine to read, or your application to review, but leave any extraneous material in the waiting room when you go in for your interview. In any event, relax and compose yourself.

The matter of dress is important. The board is forming impressions about you – from your experience, your manners, your attitude, and your appearance. Give your personal appearance careful attention. Dress your best, but not your flashiest. Choose conservative, appropriate clothing, and be sure it is immaculate. This is a business interview, and your appearance should indicate that you regard it as such. Besides, being well groomed and properly dressed will help boost your confidence.

Sooner or later, someone will call your name and escort you into the interview room. *This is it.* From here on you are on your own. It is too late for any more preparation. But remember, you asked for this opportunity to prove your fitness, and you are here because your request was granted.

*What happens when you go in?*

The usual sequence of events will be as follows: The clerk (who is often the board stenographer) will introduce you to the chairman of the oral board, who will introduce you to the other members of the board. Acknowledge the introductions before you sit down. Do not be surprised if you find a microphone facing you or a stenotypist sitting by. Oral interviews are usually recorded in the event of an appeal or other review.

Usually the chairman of the board will open the interview by reviewing the highlights of your education and work experience from your application – primarily for the benefit of the other members of the board, as well as to get the material into the record. Do not interrupt or comment unless there is an error or significant misinterpretation; if that is the case, do not hesitate. But do not quibble about insignificant matters. Also, he will usually ask you some question about your education, experience or your present job – partly to get you to start talking and to establish the interviewing "rapport." He may start the actual questioning, or turn it over to one of the other members. Frequently, each member undertakes the questioning on a particular area, one in which he is perhaps most competent, so you can expect each member to participate in the examination. Because time is limited, you may also expect some rather abrupt switches in the direction the questioning takes, so do not be upset by it. Normally, a board member will not pursue a single line of questioning unless he discovers a particular strength or weakness.

After each member has participated, the chairman will usually ask whether any member has any further questions, then will ask you if you have anything you wish to add. Unless you are expecting this question, it may floor you. Worse, it may start you off on an extended, extemporaneous speech. The board is not usually seeking more information. The question is principally to offer you a last opportunity to present further qualifications or to indicate that you have nothing to add. So, if you feel that a significant qualification or characteristic has been overlooked, it is proper to point it out in a sentence or so. Do not compliment the board on the thoroughness of their examination – they have been sketchy, and you know it. If you wish, merely say, "No thank you, I have nothing further to add." This is a point where you can "talk yourself out" of a good impression or fail to present an important bit of information. Remember, *you close the interview yourself*.

The chairman will then say, "That is all, Mr. _____, thank you." Do not be startled; the interview is over, and quicker than you think. Thank him, gather your belongings and take your leave. Save your sigh of relief for the other side of the door.

*How to put your best foot forward*

Throughout this entire process, you may feel that the board individually and collectively is trying to pierce your defenses, seek out your hidden weaknesses and embarrass and confuse you. Actually, this is not true. They are obliged to make an appraisal of your qualifications for the job you are seeking, and they want to see you in your best light. Remember, they must interview all candidates and a non-cooperative candidate may become a failure in spite of their best efforts to bring out his qualifications. Here are 15 suggestions that will help you:

**1) Be natural – Keep your attitude confident, not cocky**

If you are not confident that you can do the job, do not expect the board to be. Do not apologize for your weaknesses, try to bring out your strong points. The board is interested in a positive, not negative, presentation. Cockiness will antagonize any board member and make him wonder if you are covering up a weakness by a false show of strength.

**2) Get comfortable, but don't lounge or sprawl**

Sit erectly but not stiffly. A careless posture may lead the board to conclude that you are careless in other things, or at least that you are not impressed by the importance of the occasion. Either conclusion is natural, even if incorrect. Do not fuss with your clothing, a pencil or an ashtray. Your hands may occasionally be useful to emphasize a point; do not let them become a point of distraction.

**3) Do not wisecrack or make small talk**

This is a serious situation, and your attitude should show that you consider it as such. Further, the time of the board is limited – they do not want to waste it, and neither should you.

### 4) Do not exaggerate your experience or abilities

In the first place, from information in the application or other interviews and sources, the board may know more about you than you think. Secondly, you probably will not get away with it. An experienced board is rather adept at spotting such a situation, so do not take the chance.

### 5) If you know a board member, do not make a point of it, yet do not hide it

Certainly you are not fooling him, and probably not the other members of the board. Do not try to take advantage of your acquaintanceship – it will probably do you little good.

### 6) Do not dominate the interview

Let the board do that. They will give you the clues – do not assume that you have to do all the talking. Realize that the board has a number of questions to ask you, and do not try to take up all the interview time by showing off your extensive knowledge of the answer to the first one.

### 7) Be attentive

You only have 20 minutes or so, and you should keep your attention at its sharpest throughout. When a member is addressing a problem or question to you, give him your undivided attention. Address your reply principally to him, but do not exclude the other board members.

### 8) Do not interrupt

A board member may be stating a problem for you to analyze. He will ask you a question when the time comes. Let him state the problem, and wait for the question.

### 9) Make sure you understand the question

Do not try to answer until you are sure what the question is. If it is not clear, restate it in your own words or ask the board member to clarify it for you. However, do not haggle about minor elements.

### 10) Reply promptly but not hastily

A common entry on oral board rating sheets is "candidate responded readily," or "candidate hesitated in replies." Respond as promptly and quickly as you can, but do not jump to a hasty, ill-considered answer.

### 11) Do not be peremptory in your answers

A brief answer is proper – but do not fire your answer back. That is a losing game from your point of view. The board member can probably ask questions much faster than you can answer them.

### 12) Do not try to create the answer you think the board member wants

He is interested in what kind of mind you have and how it works – not in playing games. Furthermore, he can usually spot this practice and will actually grade you down on it.

### 13) Do not switch sides in your reply merely to agree with a board member

Frequently, a member will take a contrary position merely to draw you out and to see if you are willing and able to defend your point of view. Do not start a debate, yet do not surrender a good position. If a position is worth taking, it is worth defending.

### 14) Do not be afraid to admit an error in judgment if you are shown to be wrong

The board knows that you are forced to reply without any opportunity for careful consideration. Your answer may be demonstrably wrong. If so, admit it and get on with the interview.

### 15) Do not dwell at length on your present job

The opening question may relate to your present assignment. Answer the question but do not go into an extended discussion. You are being examined for a *new* job, not your present one. As a matter of fact, try to phrase ALL your answers in terms of the job for which you are being examined.

*Basis of Rating*

Probably you will forget most of these "do's" and "don'ts" when you walk into the oral interview room. Even remembering them all will not ensure you a passing grade. Perhaps you did not have the qualifications in the first place. But remembering them will help you to put your best foot forward, without treading on the toes of the board members.

Rumor and popular opinion to the contrary notwithstanding, an oral board wants you to make the best appearance possible. They know you are under pressure – but they also want to see how you respond to it as a guide to what your reaction would be under the pressures of the job you seek. They will be influenced by the degree of poise you display, the personal traits you show and the manner in which you respond.


ABOUT THIS BOOK

This book contains tests divided into Examination Sections. Go through each test, answering every question in the margin. We have also attached a sample answer sheet at the back of the book that can be removed and used. At the end of each test look at the answer key and check your answers. On the ones you got wrong, look at the right answer choice and learn. Do not fill in the answers first. Do not memorize the questions and answers, but understand the answer and principles involved. On your test, the questions will likely be different from the samples. Questions are changed and new ones added. If you understand these past questions you should have success with any changes that arise. Tests may consist of several types of questions. We have additional books on each subject should more study be advisable or necessary for you. Finally, the more you study, the better prepared you will be. This book is intended to be the last thing you study before you walk into the examination room. Prior study of relevant texts is also recommended. NLC publishes some of these in our Fundamental Series. Knowledge and good sense are important factors in passing your exam. Good luck also helps. So now study this Passbook, absorb the material contained within and take that knowledge into the examination. Then do your best to pass that exam.

# EXAMINATION SECTION

# EXAMINATION SECTION

# TEST 1

DIRECTIONS: Each question or incomplete statement is followed by several suggested answers or completions. Select the one that BEST answers the question or completes the statement. *PRINT THE LETTER OF THE CORRECT ANSWER IN THE SPACE AT THE RIGHT.*

1. A supervisor may be required to help train a newly appointed clerk. Which of the following is LEAST important for a newly appointed clerk to know in order to perform his work efficiently?
   A. Acceptable ways of answering and recording telephone calls
   B. The number of files in the storage files unit
   C. The filing methods used by his unit
   D. Proper techniques for handling visitors

   1.____

2. In your agency you have the responsibility of processing clients who have appointments with agency representatives. On a particularly busy day, a client comes to your desk and insists that she must see the person handling her case although she has no appointment.
   Under the circumstances, your FIRST action should be to
   A. show her the full appointment schedule
   B. give her an appointment for another day
   C. ask her to explain the urgency
   D. tell her to return later in the day

   2.____

3. Which of the following practices is BEST for a supervisor to use when assigning work to his staff?
   A. Give workers with seniority the most difficult jobs
   B. Assign all unimportant work to the slower workers
   C. Permit each employee to pick the job he prefers
   D. Make assignments based on the workers' abilities

   3.____

4. In which of the following instances is a supervisor MOST justified in giving commands to people under his supervision? When
   A. they delay in following instructions which have been given to them clearly
   B. they become relaxed and slow about work, and he wants to speed up their production
   C. he must direct them in an emergency situation
   D. he is instructing them on jobs that are unfamiliar to them

   4.____

5. Which of the following supervisory actions or attitudes is MOST likely to result in getting subordinates to try to do as much work as possible for a supervisor? He
   A. shows that his most important interest is in schedules and production goals
   B. consistently pressures his staff to get the work out

   5.____

C. never fails to let them know he is in charge
D. considers their abilities and needs while requiring that production goals be met

6. Assume that a supervisor has been explaining certain regulations to a new clerk under his supervision.
The MOST efficient way for the supervisor to make sure that the clerk has understood the explanation is to
   A. give him written materials on the regulations
   B. ask him if he has any further questions about the regulations
   C. ask him specific questions based on what has just been explained to him
   D. watch the way he handles a situation involving these regulations

7. One of your unit clerks has been assigned to work for a Mr. Jones in another office for several days. At the end of the first day, Mr. Jones, saying the clerk was not satisfactory, asks that she not be assigned to him again. This clerk is one of your most dependable workers, and no previous complaints about her work have come to you from any other outside assignments.
To get to the root of this situation, your FIRST action should be to
   A. ask Mr. Jones to explain in what way her work was unsatisfactory
   B. ask the clerk what she did that Mr. Jones considered unsatisfactory
   C. check with supervisors for whom she previously worked to see if your own rating of her is in error
   D. tell Mr. Jones to pick the clerk he would prefer to have work for him the next time

8. A senior typist, still on probation, is instructed to type, as quickly as possible, one section of a draft of a long, complex report. Her part must be typed and readable before another part of the report can be written. Asked when she can have the report ready, she gives her supervisor an estimate of a day longer than she knows it will actually take. She then finishes the job a day sooner than the date given her supervisor.
The judgment shown by the senior typist in giving an overestimate of time in a situation like this is, in general,
   A. *good*, because it prevents the supervisor from thinking she works slowly
   B. *good*, because it keeps unrealistic supervisors from expecting too much
   C. *bad*, because she should have used the time left to further check and proofread her work
   D. *bad*, because schedules and plans for other parts of the project may have been based on her false estimate

9. Suppose a new clerk, still on probation, is placed under your supervision and refuses to do a job you ask him to do.
What is the FIRST thing you should do?
   A. Explain that you are the supervisor and he must follow your instructions
   B. Tell him he may be suspended if he refuses
   C. Ask someone else to do the job and rate him accordingly
   D. Ask for his reason for objecting to the request

10. As a supervisor of a small group of people, you have blamed worker A for something that you later find out was really done by worker B.
    The BEST thing for you to do now would be to
    A. say nothing to worker A but criticize worker B for his mistake while worker A is near so that A will realize that you know who made the mistake
    B. speak to each worker separately, apologize to worker A for your mistake, and discuss worker B's mistake with him
    C. bring both workers together, apologize to worker A for your mistake, and discuss worker B's mistake with him
    D. say nothing now but be careful about mixing up worker A with worker B in the future

11. You have just learned one of your staff is grumbling that she thinks you are not pleased with her work. As far as you're concerned, this isn't true at all. In fact, you've paid no particular attention to this worker lately because you've been very busy. You have just finished preparing an important report and *breaking in* a new clerk.
    Under the circumstances, the BEST thing to do is
    A. ignore her; after all, it's just a figment of her imagination
    B. discuss the matter with her now to try to find out and eliminate the cause of this problem
    C. tell her not to worry about it; you haven't had time to think about her work
    D. make a note to meet with her at a later date in order to straighten out the situation

12. A most important job of a supervisor is to positively motivate employees to increase their work production.
    Which of the following LEAST indicates that a group of workers has been positively motivated?
    A. Their work output becomes constant and stable.
    B. Their cooperation at work becomes greater.
    C. They begin to show pride in the product of their work.
    D. They show increased interest in their work

13. Which of the following traits would be LEAST important in considering a person for a merit increase?
    A. Punctuality
    B. Using initiative successfully
    C. High rate of production
    D. Resourcefulness

14. Of the following, the action LEAST likely to gain a supervisor the cooperation of his staff is for him to
    A. give each person consideration as an individual
    B. be as objective as possible when evaluating work performance
    C. rotate the least popular assignments
    D. expect subordinates to be equally competent

15. It has been said that, for the supervisor, nothing can beat the *face-to-face* communication of talking to one subordinate at a time.
    This method is, however, LEAST appropriate to use when
    A. supervisor is explaining a change in general office procedure
    B. subject is of personal importance
    C. supervisor is conducting a yearly performance evaluation of all employees
    D. supervisor must talk to some of his employees concerning their poor attendance and punctuality

    15.____

16. While you are on the telephone answering a question about your agency, a visitor comes to your desk and starts to ask you a question. There is no emergency or urgency in either situation, that of the phone call or that of answering the visitor's question.
    In this case, you should
    A. continue to answer the person on the telephone until you are finished and then tell the visitor you are sorry to have kept him waiting
    B. excuse yourself to the person on the telephone and tell the visitor that you will be with him as soon as you have finished on the phone
    C. explain to the person on the telephone that you have a visitor and must shorten the conversation
    D. continue to answer the person on the phone while looking up occasionally at the visitor to let him know that you know he is waiting

    16.____

17. While speaking on the telephone to someone who called, you are disconnected.
    The FIRST thing you should do is
    A. hang up but try to keep your line free to receive the call back
    B. immediately get the dial tone and continually dial the person who called you until you reach him
    C. signal the switchboard operator and ask her to re-establish the connection
    D. dial O for Operator and explain that you were disconnected

    17.____

18. The type of speech used by an office worker in telephone conversations greatly affects the communicator.
    Of the following, the BEST way to express your ideas when telephoning is with a vocabulary that consists mainly of _____ words.
    A. formal, intellectual sounding   B. often used colloquial
    C. technical, emphatic             D. simple, descriptive

    18.____

19. Suppose a clerk under your supervision has taken a personal phone call and is at the same time needed to answer a question regarding an assignment being handled by another member of your office. He appears confused as to what he should do. How should you instruct him later as to how to handle a similar situation?
    You should tell him to
    A. tell the caller to hold on while he answers the question
    B. tell the caller to call back a little later

    19.____

C. return the call during an assigned break
D. finish the conversation quickly and answer the question

20. You are asked to place a telephone call by your supervisor.  When you place the call, you receive what appears to be a wrong number.
    Of the following, you should FIRST
    A. check the number with your supervisor to see if the number he gave you is correct
    B. ask the person on the other end what his number is and who he is
    C. check with the person on the other end to see if the number you dialed is the number you received
    D. apologize to the person on the other end for disturbing him and hang up

20._____

Questions 21-30.

DIRECTIONS: WORD MEANING
Each of Questions 21 through 30 contains a word in capitals followed by four suggested meanings of the word.  For each question, choose the BEST meaning and write the letter of the best meaning in the space at the right.

21. ACCURATE
    A. correct    B. useful    C. afraid    D. careless

21._____

22. ALTER
    A. copy    B. change    C. repeat    D. agree

22._____

23. DOCUMENT
    A. outline    B. agreement    C. blueprint    D. record

23._____

24. INDICATE
    A. listen    B. show    C. guess    D. try

24._____

25. INVENTORY
    A. custom    B. discovery    C. warning    D. list

25._____

26. ISSUE
    A. annoy    B. use up    C. give out    D. gain

26._____

27. NOTIFY
    A. inform    B. promise    C. approve    D. strength

27._____

28. ROUTINE
    A. path    B. mistake    C. habit    D. journey

28._____

29. TERMINATE
    A. rest    B. start    C. deny    D. end

29._____

30. TRANSMIT
    A. put in    B. send    C. stop    D. go across

30._____

Questions 31-35.

DIRECTIONS: READING COMPREHENSION
Questions 31 through 35 test how well you understand what you read. It will be necessary for you to read carefully because your answers to these questions should be based SOLELY on the information given in the following paragraphs.

The recipient gains an impression of a typewritten letter before he begins to read the message. Factors which provide for a good first impression include margins and spacing that are visually pleasing, formal parts of the letter which are correctly placed according to the style of the letter, copy which is free of obvious erasures and over-strikes, and transcript that is even and clear. The problem for the typist is that of how to produce that first, positive impression of her work.

There are several general rules which a typist can follow when she wishes to prepare a properly spaced letter on a sheet of letterhead. Ordinarily, the width of a letter should not be less than four inches nor more than six inches. The side margins should also have a desirable relation to the bottom margin and the space between the letterhead and the body of the letter. Usually the most appealing arrangement is when the side margins are even and the bottom margin is slightly wider than the side margins. In some offices, however, standard line length is used for all business letters, and the secretary then varies the spacing between the date line and the inside address according to the length of the letter.

31. The BEST title for the above paragraphs would be                                31._____
    A. Writing Office Letters
    B. Making Good First Impressions
    C. Judging Well-Typed Letters
    D. Good Placing and Spacing for Office Letters

32. According to the above paragraphs, which of the following might be considered    32._____
    the way in which people very quickly judge the quality of work which has been
    typed?
    By
    A. measuring the margins to see if they are correct
    B. looking at the spacing and cleanliness of the typescript
    C. scanning the body of the letter for meaning
    D. reading the date line and address for errors

33. What, according to the above paragraphs, would be definitely UNDESIRABLE        33._____
    as the average line length of a typed letter?
    A. 4"           B. 5"           C. 6"           D. 7"

34. According to the above paragraphs, when the line length is kept standard,       34._____
    the secretary
    A. does not have to vary the spacing at all since this also is standard
    B. adjusts the spacing between the date line and inside address for different
       lengths of letters
    C. uses the longest line as a guideline for spacing between the date line and
       inside address
    D. varies the number of spaces between the lines

35. According to the above paragraphs, side margins are MOST pleasing when they  35._____
    A. are even and somewhat smaller than the bottom margin
    B. are slightly wider than the bottom margin
    C. vary with the length of the letter
    D. are figured independently from the letterhead and the body of the letter

Questions 36-40.

DIRECTIONS: CODING

| | |
|---|---|
| Name of Applicant | H A N G S B R U K E |
| Test Code | c o m p l e x i t y |
| File Number | 0 1 2 3 4 5 6 7 8 9 |

Assume that each of the above capital letters is the first letter of the name of an applicant, that the small letter directly beneath each capital letter is the test code for the applicant, and that the number directly beneath each code letter is the file number for the applicant.

In each of the following Questions 36 through 40, the test code letters and the file numbers in Columns 2 and 3 should correspond to the capital letters in Column 1. For each question, look at each column carefully and mark your answer as follows:
  If there is an error only in Column 2, mark your answer A.
  If there is an error only in Column 3, mark your answer B.
  If there is an error in both Columns 2 and 3, mark your answer C.
  If both Columns 2 and 3 are correct, mark your answer D.

The following sample question is given to help you understand the procedure.

SAMPLE QUESTION

| Column 1 | Column 2 | Column 3 |
|---|---|---|
| AKEHN | otyci | 18902 |

In Column 2, the final test code letter *i* should be *m*. Column 3 is correctly coded in Column 1. Since there is an error only in Column 2, the answer is A.

| | Column 1 | Column 2 | Column 3 | |
|---|---|---|---|---|
| 36. | NEKKU | mytti | 29987 | 36._____ |
| 37. | KRAEB | txlye | 86095 | 37._____ |
| 38. | ENAUK | ymoit | 92178 | 38._____ |
| 39. | REANA | xeomo | 69121 | 39._____ |
| 40. | EKHSE | ytcxy | 97049 | |

Questions 41-50.

DIRECTIONS: ARITHMETICAL REASONING
Solve the following problems.

41. If a secretary answered 28 phone calls and typed the addresses for 112 credit statements in one morning, what is the RATIO of phone calls answered to credit statements typed for that period of time?
    A. 1:4    B. 1:7    C. 2:3    D. 3:5

    41.____

42. According to a suggested filing system, no more than 10 folders should be filed behind any one file guide, and from 15 to 25 file guides should be used in each file drawer for easy finding and filing.
    The MAXIMUM number of folders that a five-drawer file cabinet can hold to allow easy finding and filing is
    A. 550    B. 750    C. 1,100    D. 1,250

    42.____

43. An employee had a starting salary of $32,902. He received a salary increase at the end of each year, and at the end of the seventh year, his salary was $36,738.
    What was his AVERAGE annual increase in salary over these seven years?
    A. $510    B. $538    C. $548    D. $572

    43.____

44. The 55 typists and 28 senior clerks in a certain agency were paid a total of $1,943,200 in salaries for the year.
    If the average annual salary of a typist was $22,400, the average annual salary of a senior clerk was
    A. $25,400    B. $26,600    C. $26,800    D. $27,000

    44.____

45. A typist has been given a three-page report to type. She has finished typing the first two pages. The first page has 283 words, and the second page has 366 words.
    If the total report consists of 954 words, how many words will she have to type on the third page of the report?
    A. 202    B. 287    C. 305    D. 313

    45.____

46. In one day, Clerk A processed 30% more forms than Clerk B, and Clerk C processed 11/4 as many forms as Clerk A.
    If Clerk B processed 40 forms, how many MORE forms were processed by Clerk C?
    A. 12    B. 13    C. 21    D. 25

    46.____

47. A clerk who earns a gross salary of $452 every week has the following deductions taken from her paycheck: 17½% for City, State, Federal taxes, and for Social Security, $1.20 for health insurance, and $6.10 for union dues.
    The amount of her take-home pay is
    A. $286.40    B. $312.40    C. $331.60    D. $365.60

    47.____

8

48. In 2022 an agency spent $400 to buy pencils at a cost of $1 a dozen. If the agency used ¾ of these pencils in 2022 and used the same number of pencils in 2023, how many MORE pencils did it have to buy to have enough pencils for all of 2023?
   A. 1,200     B. 2,400     C. 3,600     D. 4,800

49. A clerk who worked in Agency X earned the following salaries: $30,070 the first year, $30,500 the second year, and $30,960 the third year. Another clerk who worked in Agency Y for three years earned $30,550 a year for two years and $30,724 the third year.
The DIFFERENCE between the average salaries received by both clerks over a three-year period is
   A. $98     B. $102     C. $174     D. $282

50. An employee who works over 40 hours in any week receives overtime payment for the extra hours at time and one-half (1½ times) his hourly rate of pay. An employee who earns $15.60 an hour works a total of 45 hours during a certain week.
His TOTAL pay for that week would be
   A. $624.00     B. $702.00     C. $741.00     D. $824.00

## KEY (CORRECT ANSWERS)

| | | | | | | | | | |
|---|---|---|---|---|---|---|---|---|---|
| 1. | B | 11. | B | 21. | A | 31. | D | 41. | A |
| 2. | C | 12. | A | 22. | B | 32. | B | 42. | D |
| 3. | D | 13. | A | 23. | D | 33. | D | 43. | C |
| 4. | C | 14. | D | 24. | B | 34. | B | 44. | A |
| 5. | D | 15. | A | 25. | D | 35. | A | 45. | C |
| 6. | C | 16. | B | 26. | C | 36. | B | 46. | D |
| 7. | A | 17. | A | 27. | A | 37. | C | 47. | D |
| 8. | D | 18. | D | 28. | C | 38. | D | 48. | B |
| 9. | D | 19. | C | 29. | D | 39. | A | 49. | A |
| 10. | B | 20. | C | 30. | B | 40. | C | 50. | C |

# TEST 2

DIRECTIONS: Each question or incomplete statement is followed by several suggested answers or completions. Select the one that BEST answers the question or completes the statement. *PRINT THE LETTER OF THE CORRECT ANSWER IN THE SPACE AT THE RIGHT.*

1. To tell a newly employed clerk to fill a top drawer of a four-drawer cabinet with heavy folders which will be often used and to keep lower drawers only partly filled is
   A. *good*, because a tall person would have to bend unnecessarily if he had to use a lower drawer
   B. *bad*, because the file cabinet may tip over when the top drawer is opened
   C. *good*, because it is the most easily reachable drawer for the average person
   D. *bad*, because a person bending down at another drawer may accidentally bang his head on the bottom of the drawer when he straightens up

1.____

2. If you have requisitioned a ream of paper in order to duplicate a single page office announcement, how many announcements can be printed from the one package of paper?
   A. 200    B. 500    C. 700    D. 1,000

2.____

3. In the operations of a government agency, a voucher is ORDINARILY used to
   A. refer someone to the agency for a position or assignment
   B. certify that an agency's records of financial transactions are accurate
   C. order payment from agency funds of a stated amount to an individual
   D. enter a statement of official opinion in the records of the agency

3.____

4. Of the following types of cards used in filing systems, the one which is generally MOST helpful in locating records which might be filed under more than one subject is the _____ card.
   A. cut
   B. tickler
   C. cross-reference
   D. visible index

4.____

5. The type of filing system in which one does NOT need to refer to a card index in order to find the folder is called
   A. alphabetic    B. geographic    C. subject    D. locational

5.____

6. Of the following, records management is LEAST concerned with
   A. the development of the best method for retrieving important information
   B. deciding what records should be kept
   C. deciding the number of appointments a client will need
   D. determining the types of folders to be used

6.____

7. If records are continually removed from a set of files without *charging* them to the borrower, the filing system will soon become ineffective.
Of the following terms, the one which is NOT applied to a form used in a charge-out system is a
   A. requisition card
   B. out-folder
   C. record retrieval form
   D. substitution card

8. A new clerk has been told to put 500 cards in alphabetical order. Another clerk suggests that she divide the cards into four groups such as A to F, G to L, M to R, and S to Z, and then alphabetize these four smaller groups.
The suggested method is
   A. *poor*, because the clerk will have to handle the sheets more than once and will waste time
   B. *good*, because it saves time, is more accurate, and is less tiring
   C. *good*, because she will not have to concentrate on it so much when it is in smaller groups
   D. *bad*, because this method is much more tiring than straight alphabetizing

9. The term that describes the equipment attached to an office computer is
   A. interface   B. network   C. hardware   D. software

10. Suppose a clerk has been given pads of pre-printed forms to use when taking phone messages for others in her office. The clerk is then observed using scraps of paper and not the forms for writing her messages.
It should be explained that the BEST reason for using the forms is that
   A. they act as a checklist to make sure that the important information is taken
   B. she is expected to do her work in the same way as others in the office
   C. they make sure that unassigned paper is not wasted on phone messages
   D. learning to use these forms will help train her to use more difficult forms

11. Of the following, the one which is spelled INCORRECTLY is
   A. alphabetization
   B. reccommendation
   C. redaction
   D. synergy

12. Of the following, the MAIN reason a stock clerk keeps a perpetual inventory of supplies in the storeroom is that such an inventory will
   A. eliminate the need for a physical inventory
   B. provide a continuous record of supplies on hand
   C. indicate whether a shipment of supplies is satisfactory
   D. dictate the terms of the purchase order

13. As a supervisor, you may be required to handle different types of correspondence.
Of the following types of letters, it would be MOST important to promptly seal which kind of letters?

A. One marked *confidential*
B. Those containing enclosures
C. Any letter to be sent airmail
D. Those in which carbons will be sent along with the original

14. While opening incoming mail, you notice that one letter indicates that an enclosure was to be included but, even after careful inspection,, you are not able to find the information to which this refers.
Of the following, the thing that you should do FIRST is
    A. replace the letter in its envelope and return it to the sender
    B. file the letter until the sender's office mails the missing information
    C. type out a letter to the sender informing them of their error
    D. make a notation in the margin of the letter that the enclosure was omitted

14.____

15. You have been given a checklist and assigned the responsibility of inspecting certain equipment in the various offices of your agency.
Which of the following is the GREATEST advantage of the checklist?
    A. It indicates which equipment is in greatest demand.
    B. Each piece of equipment on the checklist will be checked only once.
    C. It helps to insure that the equipment listed will not be overlooked.
    D. The equipment listed suggests other equipment you should look for.

15.____

16. Your supervisor has asked you to locate a telephone number for an attorney named Jones, whose office is located at 311 Broadway and whose name is not already listed in your files.
The BEST method for finding the number would be for you to
    A. call the information operator and have her get it for you
    B. look in the alphabetical directory (white pages) under the name Jones at 311 Broadway
    C. refer to the heading Attorney in the yellow pages for the name Jones at 311 Broadway
    D. ask your supervisor who referred her to Mr. Jones, then call that person for the number

16.____

17. An example of material that should NOT be sent by first class mail is a
    A. carbon copy of a letter      B. postcard
    C. business reply card           D. large catalogue

17.____

18. Which of the following BEST describes *office work simplification*?
    A. An attempt to increase the rate of production by speeding up the movements of employees
    B. Eliminating wasteful steps in order to increase efficiency
    C. Making jobs as easy as possible for employees so they will not be overworked
    D. Eliminating all difficult tasks from an office and leaving only simple ones

18.____

19. The duties of a supervisor who is assigned the job of timekeeper may include all of the following EXCEPT    19.____
    A. computing and recording regular hours worked each day in accordance with the normal work schedule
    B. approving requests for vacation leave, sick leave, and annual leave
    C. computing and recording overtime hours worked beyond the normal schedule
    D. determining the total regular hours and total extra hours worked during the week

20. Suppose a clerk under your supervision accidentally opens a personal letter while handling office mail.    20.____
    Under such circumstances, you should tell the clerk to put the letter back in the envelope and
    A. take the letter to the person to whom it belongs and make sure he understands that the clerk did not read it
    B. try to seal the envelope so it won't appear to have been opened
    C. write on the envelope *Sorry, opened by mistake*, and put his initials on it
    D. write on the envelope *Sorry, opened by mistake*, but not put his initials on it

Questions 21-25.

DIRECTIONS:  SPELLING
Each Question 21 through 25 consists of three words. In each question, one of the words may be spelled incorrectly or all three may be spelled correctly. For each question, if one of the words is spelled incorrectly, write the letter of the incorrect word in the space at the right. If all three words are spelled correctly, write the letter D in the space at the right.

SAMPLE I:  (A) guide      (B) departmint     (C) stranger
SAMPLE II: (A) comply     (B) valuable       (C) window

In Sample Question I, *departmint* is incorrect. It should be spelled *department*. Therefore, B is the answer to Sample Question 1.
In Sample Question II, all three words are spelled correctly. Therefore D is the answer to Sample Question II.

| 21. | A. argument   | B. reciept    | C. complain  | 21.____ |
| 22. | A. sufficient | B. postpone   | C. visible   | 22.____ |
| 23. | A. expirience | B. dissatisfy | C. alternate | 23.____ |
| 24. | A. occurred   | B. noticable  | C. appendix  | 24.____ |
| 25. | A. anxious    | B. guarantee  | C. calender  | 25.____ |

Questions 26-30.

DIRECTIONS: ENGLISH USAGE
Each Question 26 through 30 contains a sentence. Read each sentence carefully to decide whether it is correct. Then, in the space at the right, mark your answer:
A. if the sentence is incorrect because of bad grammar or sentence structure
B. of the sentence is incorrect because of bad punctuation
C. if the sentence is incorrect because of bad capitalization
D. if the sentence is correct

Each incorrect sentence has only one type of error. Consider a sentence correct if it has no errors, although there may be other correct ways of saying the same thing.

SAMPLE QUESTION I: One of our clerks were promoted yesterday.
The subject of this sentence is *one*, so the verb should be *was promoted* instead of *were promoted*. Since the sentence is incorrect because of bad grammar, the answer to Sample Question I is A.

SAMPLE QUESTION II: Between you and me, I would prefer not going there.
Since this sentence is correct, the answer to Sample Question II is D.

26. The National alliance of Businessmen is trying to persuade private businesses to hire youth in the summertime.  26._____

27. The supervisor who is on vacation, is in charge of processing vouchers.  27._____

28. The activity of the committee at its conferences is always stimulating.  28._____

29. After checking the addresses again, the letters went to the mailroom.  29._____

30. The director, as well as the employees, are interested in sharing the dividends.  30._____

Questions 31-40.

DIRECTIONS: FILING
Each Question 31 through 40 contains four names. For each question, choose the name that should be FIRST if the four names are to be arranged in alphabetical order in accordance with the Rules for Alphabetical Filing given below. Read these rules carefully. Then, for each question, indicate in the correspondingly numbered space at the right the letter before the name that should be FIRST in alphabetical order.

## RULES FOR ALPHABETICAL FILING

### Names of People

1. The names of people are filed in strict alphabetical order, first according to the last name, then according to first name or initial, and finally according to middle name or initial. For example: George Allen comes before Edward Bell, and Leonard P. Reston comes before Lucille B. Reston.

2. When last names are the same, for example A. Green and Agnes Green, the one with the initial comes before the one with the name written out when the first initials are identical.

3. When first and last names are alike and the middle initial is given, for example John David Doe and John Devoe Doe, the names should be filed in the alphabetical order of the middle names.

4. When first and last names are the same, a name without a middle initial comes before one with a middle name or initial. For example, John Doe comes before both John A. Doe and John Alan Doe.

5. When first and last names are the same, a name with a middle initial comes before one with a middle name beginning with the same initial. For example: Jack R. Herts comes before Jack Richard Hertz.

6. Prefixes such as De, O', Mac, Mc, and Van are filed as written and are treated as part of the names to which they are connected. For example: Robert O'Dea is filed before David Olsen.

7. Abbreviated names are treated as if they were spelled out. For example: Chas. is filed as Charles and Thos. is filed as Thomas.

8. Titles and designations such as Dr., Mr., and Prof. are disregarded in filing.

### Names of Organizations

1. The names of business organizations are filed according to the order in which each word in the name appears. When an organization name bears the name of a person, it is filed according to the rules for filing names of people as given above. For example, William Smith Service Co. comes before Television Distributors, Inc.

2. Where bureau, board, office or department appears as the first part of the title of a governmental agency, that agency should be filed under the word in the title expressing the chief function of the agency. For example: Bureau of the Budget would be filed as if written Budget, (Bureau of the). The Department of Personnel would be filed as if written Personnel (Department of).

3. When the following words are part of an organization, they are disregarded: the, of, and.

7 (#2)

4. When there are numbers in a name, they are treated as if they were spelled out. For example: 10th Street Bootery is filed as Tenth Street Bootery.

SAMPLE QUESTION:  A. Jane Earl      (2)
                  B. James A. Earle (4)
                  C. James Earl     (1)
                  D. J. Earle       (3)

The numbers in parentheses show the proper alphabetical order in which these names should be filed. Since the name that should be filed FIRST is James Earl, the answer to the sample question is C.

31. A. Majorca Leather Goods          B. Robert Majorca and Sons        31._____
    C. Maintenance Management Corp.   D. Majestic Carpet Mills

32. A. Municipal Telephone Service    B. Municipal Reference Library    32._____
    C. Municipal Credit Union         D. Municipal Broadcasting System

33. A. Robert B. Pierce               B. R. Bruce Pierce                33._____
    C. Ronald Pierce                  D. Robert Bruce Pierce

34. A. Four Seasons Sports Club       B. 14 Street Shopping Center      34._____
    C. Forty Thieves Restaurant       D. 42nd St. Theaters

35. A. Franco Franceschini            B. Amos Franchini                 35._____
    C. Sandra Franceschia             D. Lilie Franchinesca

36. A. Chas. A. Levine                B. Kurt Levene                    36._____
    C. Charles Levine                 D. Kurt E. Levene

37. A. Prof. Geo. Kinkaid             B. Mr. Alan Kinkaid               37._____
    C. Dr. Albert A. Kinkade          D. Kincade Liquors Inc.

38. A. Department of Public Events    B. Office of the Public Administrator   38._____
    C. Queensborough Public Library   D. Department of Public Health

39. A. Martin Luther King, Jr. Towers B. Metro North Plaza              39._____
    C. Manhattanville Houses          D. Marble Hill Houses

40. A. Dr. Arthur Davids              B. The David Check Cashing Service   40._____
    C. A.C. Davidsen                  D. Milton Davidoff

Questions 41-45.

DIRECTIONS: READING COMPREHENSION
Questions 41 through 45 test how well you understand what you read. It will be necessary for you to read carefully because your answers to these questions should be based SOLELY on the information given in the following paragraph.

Work standards presuppose an ability to measure work. Measurement in office management is needed for several reasons. First, it is necessary to evaluate the overall efficiency of the office itself. It is then essential to measure the efficiency of each particular section or unit and that of the individual worker. To plan and control the work of sections and units, one must have measurement. A program of measurement goes hand in hand with a program of standards. One can have measurement without standards, but one cannot have work standards without measurement. Providing data on amount of work done and time expended, measurement does not deal with the amount of energy expended by an individual although in many cases such energy may be in direct proportion to work output. Usually from two-thirds to three fourths of all work can be measured. However, less than two-thirds of all work is actually measured because measurement difficulties are encountered when office work is non-repetitive and irregular, or when it is primarily mental rather than manual. These obstacles are often used as excuses for non-measurement far more frequently than is justified.

41. According to the paragraph, an office manager cannot set work standards unless he can
    A. plan the amount of work to be done
    B. control the amount of work that is done
    C. estimate accurately the quantity of work done
    D. delegate the amount of work to be done to efficient workers

42. According to the paragraph, the type of office work that would be MOST difficult to measure would be
    A. checking warrants for accuracy of information
    B. recording payroll changes
    C. processing applications
    D. making up a new system of giving out supplies

43. According to the paragraph, the actual amount of work that is measured is _____ of all work.
    A. less than two-thirds
    B. two-thirds to three-fourths
    C. less than three-sixths
    D. more than three-fourths

44. Which of the following would be MOST difficult to determine by using measurement techniques?
    A. The amount of work that is accomplished during a certain period of time
    B. The amount of work that should be planned for a period of time
    C. How much time is needed to do a certain task
    D. The amount of incentive a person must have to do his job

45. The one of the following which is the MOST suitable title for the paragraph is:
    A. How Measurement of Office Efficiency Depends on Work Standards
    B. Using Measurement for Office Management and Efficiency
    C. Work Standards and the Efficiency of the Office Worker
    D. Managing the Office Using Measured Work Standards

Questions 46-50.

DIRECTIONS: INTERPRETING STATISTICAL DATA
Questions 46 through 50 are to be answered using the information given in the following table.

AGE COMPOSITION IN THE LABOR FORCE IN CITY A
(2010-2020)

|  | Age Group | 2010 | 2015 | 2020 |
|---|---|---|---|---|
| Men | 14-24 | 8,430 | 10,900 | 14,340 |
|  | 25-44 | 22,200 | 22,350 | 26,065 |
|  | 45+ | 17,550 | 19,800 | 21,970 |
| Women | 14-24 | 4,450 | 6,915 | 7,680 |
|  | 25-44 | 9,080 | 10,010 | 11,550 |
|  | 45+ | 7,325 | 9,470 | 13,180 |

46. The GREATEST increase in the number of people in the labor force between 2010 and 2015 occurred among
   A. men between the ages of 14 and 24
   B. men age 45 and over
   C. women between the ages of 14 and 24
   D. women age 45 and over

46.____

47. If the total number of women of all ages in the labor force increases from 2020 to 2025 by the same number as it did from 2015 to 2020, the TOTAL number of women of all ages in the labor force in 2025 will be
   A. 27,425   B. 29,675   C. 37,525   D. 38,425

47.____

48. The total increase in number of women in the labor force from 2010 to 2015 differs from the total increase of men in the same years by being _____ than that of men.
   A. 770 less   B. 670 more   C. 770 more   D. 1,670 more

48.____

49. In the year 2010, the proportion of married women in each group was as follows: 1/5 of the women in the 14-24 age group, 1/4 of those in the 25-44 age group, and 2/5 of those 45 and over.
   How many married women were in the labor force in 2010?
   A. 4,625   B. 5,990   C. 6,090   D. 7,910

49.____

50. The 14-24 age group of men in the labor force from 2010 to 2020 increased by APPROXIMATELY
   A. 40%   B. 65%   C. 70%   D. 75%

50.____

## KEY (CORRECT ANSWERS)

| | | | | |
|---|---|---|---|---|
| 1. B | 11. B | 21. B | 31. C | 41. C |
| 2. B | 12. B | 22. D | 32. D | 42. D |
| 3. C | 13. A | 23. A | 33. B | 43. A |
| 4. C | 14. D | 24. B | 34. D | 44. D |
| 5. A | 15. C | 25. C | 35. C | 45. B |
| 6. C | 16. C | 26. C | 36. B | 46. A |
| 7. C | 17. D | 27. B | 37. D | 47. D |
| 8. B | 18. B | 28. D | 38. B | 48. B |
| 9. C | 19. B | 29. A | 39. A | 49. C |
| 10. A | 20. C | 30. A | 40. B | 50. C |

# EXAMINATION SECTION
## TEST 1

DIRECTIONS: Each question or incomplete statement is followed by several suggested answers or completions. Select the one that BEST answers the question or completes the statement. *PRINT THE LETTER OF THE CORRECT ANSWER IN THE SPACE AT THE RIGHT.*

1. The MOST important reason for a supervisor to encourage his staff to make suggestions for improving the work of the unit is that such suggestions may

    A. indicate who is the most efficient employee in the unit
    B. increase the productivity of the unit
    C. raise the morale of the employees who make the suggestions
    D. reduce the amount of supervision necessary to perform the work of the unit

    1._____

2. The PRIMARY purpose of a probationary period for a new employee is to

    A. thoroughly train the new employee in his job duties
    B. permit the new employee to become adjusted to his duties
    C. determine the fitness of the new employee for the job
    D. acquaint the new employee fully with the objectives of his agency

    2._____

3. A unit supervisor finds that he is spending too much time on routine tasks, and not enough time on coordinating the work of his employees.
It would be MOST advisable for this supervisor to

    A. delegate the task of work coordination to a capable subordinate
    B. eliminate some of the routine tasks that the unit is required to perform
    C. assign some of the routine tasks to his subordinates
    D. postpone the performance of routine tasks until he has achieved proper coordination of his employees' work

    3._____

4. Of the following, the MOST important reason for having an office manual in looseleaf form rather than in permanent binding is that the looseleaf form

    A. facilitates the addition of new material and the removal of obsolete material
    B. permits several people to use different sections of the manual at the same time
    C. is less expensive to prepare than permanent binding
    D. is more durable than permanent binding

    4._____

5. In his first discussion with an employee newly appointed to the title of Clerk in an agency, the LEAST important of the following topics for a supervisor of a clerical unit to include is the

    A. duties the subordinate is expected to perform on the job
    B. functions of the unit
    C. methods of determining standards of clerical performance
    D. nature and duration of the training the subordinate will receive on the job

    5._____

6. Assume that you have been assigned to organize the files so that all the records now located in the various units in your bureau will be centrally located in a separate files unit. In setting up this system of centrally located files, you should be concerned LEAST with making certain that

   A. the material stored in the files has been checked for accuracy of content
   B. the filing system will be flexible enough to allow for possible future expansion
   C. material stored in the files can be located readily when needed
   D. the filing system will be readily understood by employees assigned to maintaining the files

7. A supervisor of a unit in a city department has just been told by a subordinate, Mr. Jones, that another employee, Mr. Smith, deliberately disobeyed an important rule of the department by taking home some confidential departmental material.
Of the following courses of action, it would be MOST advisable for the supervisor first to

   A. discuss the matter privately with both Mr. Jones and Mr. Smith at the same time
   B. call a meeting of the entire unit and discuss the matter generally without mentioning any employee by name
   C. arrange to supervise Mr. Smith's activities more closely
   D. discuss the matter privately with Mr. Smith

8. A clerk who has the choice of sending a business letter either by certified mail or by registered mail should realize that

   A. it is less expensive to send letters by certified mail than by registered mail
   B. it is safer to send letters by certified mail than by registered mail
   C. letters sent by certified mail reach their destinations faster than those sent by registered mail
   D. the person to whom a certified letter is sent is not asked to acknowledge receipt of the letter

9. If the management of a public agency wishes to retain the elasticity of youth among employees who have been with the agency for a long time, it must furnish variety and novelty of work.
To carry out the above recommendation, the BEST course of action for an agency to take is to

   A. encourage older employees to retire at the minimum retirement age
   B. vary its employees' assignments from time to time
   C. assign the routine tasks to newer and younger employees
   D. provide its employees with varied recreational activities

10. The one of the following actions which would be MOST efficient and economical for a supervisor to take to minimize the effect of seasonal fluctuations in the work load of his unit is to

    A. increase his permanent staff until it is large enough to handle the work of the busy season
    B. request the purchase of time and labor saving equipment to be used primarily during the busy season

C. lower, temporarily, the standards for quality of work performance during peak loads
D. schedule for the slow season work that it is not essential to perform during the busy season

11. A clerk in an agency should realize that each letter he sends out in response to a letter of inquiry from the public represents an expenditure of time and money by his agency. The one of the following which is the MOST valid implication of this statement is that such a clerk should

    A. use the telephone to answer letters of inquiry directly and promptly
    B. answer mail inquiries with lengthy letters to eliminate the need for further correspondence
    C. prevent the accumulation of a large number of similar inquiries by answering each of these letters promptly
    D. use simple, concise language in answer to letters of inquiry

12. The forms and methods of discipline used in public agencies are as varied as the offenses which prompt disciplinary action, and range in severity from a frown of disapproval to dismissal from the service and even to prosecution in the courts.
On the basis of this sentence, the MOST accurate of the following statements is that

    A. the severity of disciplinary measures varies directly with the seriousness of the offenses
    B. dismissal from the service is the most severe action that can be taken by a public agency
    C. public agencies use a variety of disciplinary measures to cope with offenses
    D. public agencies sometimes administer excessive punishments

13. A well-planned training program can assist new employees to acquire the information they need to work effectively. Of the following, the information that a newly-appointed clerk would need LEAST in order to perform his work effectively is knowledge of the

    A. acceptable ways of taking and recording telephone messages
    B. techniques of evaluating the effectiveness of office forms used in the agency
    C. methods of filing papers used in his bureau
    D. proper manner of handling visitors to the agency

14. A supervisor of a unit who is not specific when making assignments creates a dangerous source of friction, misunderstanding, and inefficiency.
The MOST valid implication of this statement is that

    A. supervisors are usually unaware that they are creating sources of friction
    B. it is often difficult to remove sources of friction and misunderstanding
    C. a competent supervisor attempts to find a solution to each problem facing him
    D. employees will perform more efficiently if their duties are defined clearly

15. The employees' interest in the subject matter of a training course must be fully aroused if they are to derive the maximum benefits from the training.
Of the following, the LEAST effective method of arousing such interest is to

    A. state to the employees that the subject matter of the training course will be of interest to mature, responsible workers
    B. point out to the employees that the training course may help them to win promotion

C. explain to the employees how the training course will help them to perform their work better
D. relate the training course to the employees' interests and previous experiences

16. The control of clerical work in a public agency appears impossible if the clerical work is regarded merely as a series of duties unrelated to the functions of the agency. However, this control becomes feasible when it is realized that clerical work links and coordinates the functions of the agency.
On the basis of this statement, the MOST accurate of the following statements is that the

   A. complexity of clerical work may not be fully understood by those assigned to control it
   B. clerical work can be readily controlled if it is coordinated by other work of the agency
   C. number of clerical tasks may be reduced by regarding coordination as the function of clerical work
   D. purposes of clerical work must be understood to make possible its proper control

17. Assume that as supervisor of a unit you are to prepare a vacation schedule for the employees in your unit.
Of the following, the factor which is LEAST important for you to consider in setting up this schedule is

   A. the vacation preferences of each employee in the unit
   B. the anticipated work load in the unit during the vacation period
   C. how well each employee has performed his work
   D. how essential a specific employee's services will be during the vacation period

18. In order to promote efficiency and economy in an agency, it is advisable for the management to systematize and standardize procedures and relationships insofar as this can be done; however, excessive routinizing which does not permit individual contributions or achievements should be avoided.
On the basis of this statement, it is MOST accurate to state that

   A. systematized procedures should be designed mainly to encourage individual achievements
   B. standardized procedures should allow for individual accomplishments
   C. systematization of procedures may not be possible in organizations which have a large variety of functions
   D. individual employees of an organization must fully accept standardized procedures if the procedures are to be effective

19. Trained employees work most efficiently and with a minimum expenditure of time and energy. Suitable equipment and definite, well-developed procedures are effective only when employees know how to use the equipment and procedures. This statement means MOST NEARLY that

   A. employees can be trained most efficiently when suitable equipment and definite procedures are used
   B. training of employees is a costly but worthwhile investment

C. suitable equipment and definite procedures are of greatest value when employees have been properly trained to use them
D. the cost of suitable equipment and definite procedures is negligible when the saving in time and energy that they bring is considered

20. Assume that your supervisor has asked you to present to him comprehensive, periodic reports on the progress that your unit is making in meeting its work goals.
    For you to give your superior oral reports rather than written ones is

    A. *desirable*; it will be easier for him to transmit your oral report to his superiors
    B. *undesirable*; the oral reports will provide no permanent record to which he may refer
    C. *undesirable;* there will be less opportunity for you to discuss the oral reports with him than the written ones
    D. *desirable;* the oral reports will require little time and effort to prepare

21. Assume that an employee under your supervision complains to you that your evaluation of his work is too low.
    The MOST appropriate action for you to take FIRST is to

    A. explain how you arrived at the evaluation of his work
    B. encourage him to improve the quality of his work by pointing out specifically how he can do so
    C. suggest that he appeal to an impartial higher authority if he disagrees with your evaluation
    D. point out to him specific instances in which his work has been unsatisfactory

22. The nature of the experience and education that are made a prerequisite to employment determines in large degree the training job to be done after employment begins.
    On the basis of this statement, it is MOST accurate to state that

    A. the more comprehensive the experience and education required for employment the more extensive the training that is usually given after appointment
    B. the training that is given to employees depends upon the experience and education required of them before appointment
    C. employees who possess the experience and education required for employment should need little additional training after appointment
    D. the nature of the work that employees are expected to perform determines the training that they will need

23. Assume that you are preparing a report evaluating the work of a clerk who was transferred to your unit from another unit in the agency about a year ago.
    Of the following, the method that would probably be MOST helpful to you in making this evaluation is to

    A. consult the evaluations this employee received from his former supervisors
    B. observe this employee at his work for a week shortly before you prepare the report
    C. examine the employee's production records and compare them with the standards set for the position
    D. obtain tactfully from his fellow employees their frank opinions of his work

24. Of the following, the CHIEF value of a flow-of-work chart to the management of an organization is its usefulness in

    A. locating the causes of delay in carrying out an operation
    B. training new employees in the performance of their duties
    C. determining the effectiveness of the employees in the organization
    D. determining the accuracy of its organization chart

25. Assume that a procedure for handling certain office forms has just been extensively revised. As supervisor of a small unit, you are to instruct your subordinates in the use of the new procedure, which is rather complicated.
    Of the following, it would be LEAST helpful to your subordinates for you to

    A. compare the revised procedure with the one it has replaced
    B. state that you believe the revised procedure to be better than the one it has replaced
    C. tell them that they will probably find it difficult to learn the new procedure
    D. give only a general outline of the revised procedure at first and then follow with more detailed instructions

26. A supervisor may make assignments to his subordinates in the form of a command, a request, or a call for volunteers. It is LEAST desirable for a supervisor to make an assignment in the form of a command when

    A. a serious emergency has risen
    B. an employee objects to carrying out an assignment
    C. the assignment must be completed immediately
    D. the assignment is an unpleasant one

27. For an office supervisor to confer periodically with his subordinates in order to anticipate job problems which are likely to arise is desirable MAINLY because

    A. there will be fewer problems for which hasty decisions will have to be made
    B. some problems which are anticipated may not arise
    C. his subordinates will learn to refer the problems arising in the unit to him
    D. constant anticipation of future problems tends to raise additional problems

28. A methods improvement program might be called a war against habit.
    The MOST accurate implication of this statement is that

    A. routine handling of routine office assignments should be discouraged
    B. standardization of office procedures may encourage employees to form inefficient work habits
    C. employees tend to continue the use of existing procedures, even when such procedures are inefficient
    D. procedures should be changed constantly to prevent them from becoming habits

29. An office supervisor may give either a written or an oral order to his subordinates when making an assignment.
    Of the following, it would be MOST appropriate for a supervisor to issue an order in writing when

    A. a large number of two-page reports must be stapled together before the end of the day
    B. the assignment is to be completed within two hours after it is issued to his subordinates

C. his subordinates have completed an identical assignment the day before
D. several entries must be made on a form at varying intervals of time by different clerks

30. A supervisor should always remember that the instruction or training of new employees is most effective if it is given when and where it is needed.
On the basis of this statement, it is MOST appropriate to conclude that

   A. the new employee should be trained to handle any aspect of his work at the time he starts his job
   B. the new employee should be given the training essential to get him started and additional training when he requires it
   C. an employee who has received excessive training will be just as ineffective as one who has received inadequate training
   D. a new employee is trained most effectively by his own supervisor

31. Some employees see an agency training program as a threat. Of the following, the MOST likely reason for such an employee attitude toward training is that the employees involved feel that

   A. some trainers are incompetent
   B. training rarely solves real work-a-day problems
   C. training may attempt to change comfortable behavior patterns
   D. training sessions are boring

32. Of the following, the CHIEF characteristic which distinguishes a good supervisor from a poor supervisor is the good supervisor's

   A. ability to favorably impress others
   B. unwillingness to accept monotony or routine
   C. ability to deal constructively with problem situations
   D. strong drive to overcome opposition

33. Of the following, the MAIN disadvantage of on-the-job training is that, generally,

   A. special equipment may be needed
   B. production may be slowed down
   C. the instructor must maintain an individual relationship with the trainee
   D. the on-the-job instructor must be better qualified than the classroom instructor

34. All of the following are correct methods for a supervisor to use in connection with employee discipline EXCEPT:

   A. Trying not to be too lenient or too harsh
   B. Informing employees of the rules and the penalties for violations of the rules
   C. Imposing discipline immediately after the violation is discovered
   D. Making sure, when you apply discipline, that the employee understands that you do not want to do it

35. Of the following, the MAIN reason for a supervisor to establish standard procedures for his unit is to

   A. increase the motivation of his subordinates
   B. make it easier for the subordinates to submit to authority

C. reduce the number of times that his subordinates have to consult him
D. reduce the number of mistakes that his subordinates will make

36. When delegating responsibility for an assignment to a subordinate, it is MOST important that you

    A. retain all authority necessary to complete the assignment
    B. make yourself generally available for consultation with the subordinate
    C. inform your superiors that you are no longer responsible for the assignment
    D. decrease the number of subordinates whom you have to supervise

37. You, as a unit head, have been asked to submit budget estimates of staff, equipment, and supplies in terms of programs for your unit for the coming fiscal year.
In addition to their use in planning, such unit budget estimates can be BEST used to

    A. reveal excessive costs in operations
    B. justify increases in the debt limit
    C. analyze employee salary adjustments
    D. predict the success of future programs

38. Because higher status is important to many employees, they will often make an effort to achieve it as an end in itself.
Of the following, the BEST course of action for the supervisor to take on the basis of the preceding statement is to

    A. attach higher status to that behavior of subordinates which is directed toward reaching the goals of the organization
    B. avoid showing sympathy toward subordinates' wishes for increased wages, improved working conditions, or other benefits
    C. foster interpersonal competitiveness among subordinates so that personal friendliness is replaced by the desire to protect individual status
    D. reprimand subordinates whenever their work is in some way unsatisfactory in order to adjust their status accordingly

39. Assume that a large office in a certain organization operates long hours and is thus on two shifts with a slight overlap. Those employees, including supervisors, who are most productive are given their choice of shifts. The earlier shift is considered preferable by most employees.
As a result of this method of assignment, which of the following is MOST likely to result?

    A. Most non-supervisory employees will be assigned to the late shift; most supervisors will be assigned to the early shift.
    B. Most supervisors will be assigned to the late shift; most non-supervisory employees will be assigned to the early shift.
    C. The early shift will be more productive than the late shift.
    D. The late shift will be more productive than the early shift.

40. Assume that a supervisor of a unit in which the employees are of average friendliness tells a newly hired employee on her first day that her co-workers are very friendly. The other employees hear his remarks to the new employee. Which of the following is the MOST likely result of this action of the supervisor? The

A. newly hired employee will tend to feel less friendly than if the supervisor had said nothing
B. newly hired employee will tend to believe that her co-workers are very friendly
C. other employees will tend to feel less friendly toward one another
D. other employees will tend to see the newly hired employee as insincerely friendly

41. A recent study of employee absenteeism showed that, although unscheduled absence for part of a week is relatively high for young employees, unscheduled absence for a full week is low. However, although full-week unscheduled absence is least frequent for the youngest employees, the frequency of such absence increases as the age of employees increases.
Which of the following statements is the MOST logical explanation for the greater full-week absenteeism among older employees?

A. Older employees are more likely to be males.
B. Older employees are more likely to have more relatively serious illnesses.
C. Younger employees are more likely to take longer vacations.
D. Younger employees are more likely to be newly hired.

42. An employee can be motivated to fulfill his needs as he sees them. He is not motivated by what others think he ought to have, but what he himself wants.
Which of the following statements follows MOST logically from the foregoing viewpoint?

A. A person's different traits may be separately classified, but they are all part of one system comprising a whole person.
B. Every job, however simple, entitles the person who does it to proper respect and recognition of his unique aspirations and abilities.
C. No matter what equipment and facilities an organization has, they cannot be put to use except by people who have been motivated.
D. To an observer, a person's needs may be unrealistic, but they are still controlling.

43. Assume that you are a supervisor of a unit which is about to start work on an urgent job. One of your subordinates starts to talk to you about the urgent job but seems not to be saying what is really on his mind.
What is the BEST thing for you to say under these circumstances?

A. I'm not sure I understand. Can you explain that?
B. Please come to the point. We haven't got all day.
C. What is it? Can't you see I'm busy?
D. Haven't you got work to do? What do you want?

44. Assume that you have recently been assigned to a new subordinate. You have explained to this subordinate how to fill out certain forms which will constitute the major portion of her job. After the first day, you find that she has filled out the forms correctly but has not completed as many as most other workers normally complete in a day.
Of the following, the MOST appropriate action for you to take is to

A. tell the subordinate how many forms she is expected to complete
B. instruct the subordinate in the correct method of filling out the forms
C. monitor the subordinate's production to see if she improves
D. reassign the job of filling out the forms to a more experienced worker in the unit

45. One of the problems commonly met by the supervisor is the *touchy* employee who imagines slights when none is intended.
    Of the following, the BEST way to deal with such an employee is to

    A. ignore him until he sees the error of his behavior
    B. frequently reassure him of his value as a person
    C. advise him that oversensitive people rarely get promoted
    D. issue written instructions to him to avoid misinterpretation

46. The understanding supervisor should recognize that a certain amount of anxiety is common to all newly hired employees.
    If you are a supervisor of a unit and a newly-hired employee has been assigned to you, you can usually assume that the LEAST likely worry that the new employee has is worry about

    A. the job and the standards required in the job
    B. his acceptance by the other people in your unit
    C. the difficulty of advancing to top positions in the agency
    D. your fairness in evaluating his work

47. In assigning work to subordinates, it is often desirable for you to tell them the overall or ultimate objective of the assignment.
    Of the following, the BEST reason for telling them the objective is that it will

    A. assure them that you know what you are doing
    B. eliminate most of the possible complaints about the assignment
    C. give them confidence in their ability to do the assignment
    D. help them to make decisions consistent with the objective

48. Assume that the regular 8-hour working day of a laborer is from 8 A.M. to 5 P.M., with an hour off for lunch. He earns a regular hourly rate of pay for these 8 hours and is paid at the rate of time-and-a-half for each hour worked after his regular working day.
    If, on a certain day, he works from 8 A.M. to 6 P.M., with an hour off for lunch, and earns $99.76, his regular hourly rate of pay is

    A. $8.50  B. $9.00  C. $10.50  D. $11.50

49. Two clerical units, X and Y, each having a different number of clerks, are assigned to file registration cards. It takes Unit X, which contains 8 clerks, 21 days to file the same number of cards that Unit Y can file, in 28 days. It is also a fact that Unit X can file 174,528 cards in 72 days.
    Assuming that all the clerks in both units work at the same rate of speed, the number of cards which can be filed by Unit Y in 144 days, if 4 more clerks are added to the staff of Unit Y, is MOST NEARLY

    A. 349,000  B. 436,000  C. 523,000  D. 669,000

50. Each side of a square room which is being used as an office measures 66 feet. The floor of the room is divided by six traffic aisles, each aisle being six feet wide. Three of the aisles run parallel to the east and west sides of the room and the other three run parallel to the north and south sides of the room, so that the remaining floor space is divided into 16 equal sections.
If all of the floor space which is not being used for traffic aisles is occupied by desk and chair sets, and each set takes up 24 square feet of floor space, the number of desk and chair sets in the room is

   A. 80        B. 64        C. 36        D. 96

50.____

# KEY (CORRECT ANSWERS)

| | | | | |
|---|---|---|---|---|
| 1. B | 11. D | 21. A | 31. C | 41. B |
| 2. C | 12. C | 22. B | 32. C | 42. D |
| 3. C | 13. B | 23. C | 33. B | 43. A |
| 4. A | 14. D | 24. A | 34. D | 44. C |
| 5. C | 15. A | 25. C | 35. C | 45. B |
| 6. A | 16. B | 26. D | 36. B | 46. C |
| 7. D | 17. C | 27. A | 37. A | 47. D |
| 8. A | 18. B | 28. C | 38. A | 48. C |
| 9. B | 19. C | 29. D | 39. C | 49. B |
| 10. D | 20. B | 30. B | 40. B | 50. D |

# TEST 2

DIRECTIONS: Each question or incomplete statement is followed by several suggested answers or completions. Select the one that BEST answers the question or completes the statement. *PRINT THE LETTER OF THE CORRECT ANSWER IN THE SPACE AT THE RIGHT.*

Questions 1-6.

DIRECTIONS: Each of Questions 1 through 6 consists of statements which contains one word that is incorrectly used because it is not in keeping with the meaning that the statement is evidently intended to convey. For each of these questions, you are to select the incorrectly used word and substitute for it one of the words lettered A, B, C, D, or E, which helps BEST to convey the meaning of the quotation. In the space at the right, write the letter preceding the word which should be substituted for the incorrectly used word.

1. The determination of the value of the employees in an organization is fundamental not only as a guide to the administration of salary schedules, promotion, demotion, and transfer, but also as a means of keeping the working force on its toes and of checking the originality of selection methods.    1.____

   A. effectiveness  B. initiation  C. increasing
   D. system  E. none of these

2. No training course can operate to full advantage without job descriptions which indicate training requirements so that those parts of the job requiring the most training can be carefully analyzed before the training course is completed.    2.____

   A. improved  B. started  C. least
   D. meet  E. predict

3. The criticism that supervisors are discriminatory in their treatment of subordinates is to some extent untrue, for the subjective nature of many supervisory decisions makes it probable that many employees who have not progressed will attribute their lack of success to supervisory favoritism.    3.____

   A. knowledge  B. unavoidable  C. detrimental
   D. deny  E. indifferent

4. Some demands of employees will, if satisfied, result in a decrease in production. Some supervisors largely ignore such demands on the part of their subordinates, and instead, concentrate on the direction and production of work; others yield to such requests and thereby emphasize the production goals and objectives set by higher levels of authority.    4.____

   A. responsibility  B. increase  C. neglect
   D. value  E. morale

5. It is generally accepted that when a supervisor is at least as well informed about the work of his unit as are his subordinates, he will fail to win their approval, which is essential to him if he is to supervise the unit effectively.    5.____

   A. unimportant  B. preferable  C. unless
   D. attention  E. poorly

6. The laws of almost every state permit certain classes of persons to vote despite their absence from home at election time. Sometimes this privilege is given only to members of the armed forces of the United States, though more commonly it is extended to all voters whose occupations make absence preventable.

    A. prohibition      B. sanction      C. intangible
    D. avoidable      E. necessary

6.____

Questions 7-25.

DIRECTIONS: Each of Questions 7 through 25 consists of a word in capitals followed by four suggested meanings of the word. Print in the space at the right the number preceding the word which means MOST NEARLY the same as the word in capitals.

7. ALLEVIATE

    A. soothe      B. make difficult
    C. introduce gradually      D. complicate

7.____

8. OSTENSIBLE

    A. intelligent      B. successful
    C. necessary      D. apparent

8.____

9. REDUNDANT

    A. excessive      B. sufficient
    C. logical      D. unpopular

9.____

10. TANTAMOUNT

    A. superior      B. opposed
    C. equivalent      D. disturbing

10.____

11. EXPUNGE

    A. leap over      B. erase
    C. exploit      D. concede fully

11.____

12. VESTIGE

    A. ancestor      B. basis      C. choice      D. remnant

12.____

13. CONTENTION

    A. modification      B. controversy
    C. cooperation      D. sight

13.____

14. PROSCRIBE

    A. recommend      B. avoid      C. provide      D. prohibit

14.____

15. URBANE

    A. polite      B. adjacent to a city
    C. modern      D. common

15.____

16. INADVERTENT

    A. unknown  B. public
    C. deliberate  D. unintentional

17. EVINCE

    A. enlarge  B. conceal  C. display  D. evade

18. SIMULATE

    A. attempt  B. imitate  C. elude  D. arouse

19. PRECLUDE

    A. prevent  B. contribute generously
    C. simplify  D. prepare gradually

20. REMISS

    A. careless  B. absent  C. guilty  D. thorough

21. CONTRIVE

    A. contract  B. restrict  C. scheme  D. contribute

22. MALIGN

    A. mislead deliberately  B. slander
    C. flatter excessively  D. disturb

23. CONTINGENT

    A. loose  B. intentional
    C. dependent  D. forceful

24. SPORADIC

    A. quick  B. alert  C. destroyed  D. scattered

25. COALESCE

    A. unite  B. reveal  C. abate  D. freeze

Questions 26-33.

DIRECTIONS: Each of Questions 26 through 33 consists of three sentences lettered A, B, and C. In each of these questions, one of the sentences may contain an error in grammar, sentence structure, or punctuation, or all three sentences may be correct. If one of the sentences in a question contains an error in grammar, sentence structure, or punctuation, write in the space at the right, the letter preceding the sentence which contains the error. If all three sentences are correct, write the letter D.

26. A. Mr. Smith appears to be less competent than I in performing these duties.
    B. The supervisor spoke to the employee, who had made the error, but did not reprimand him.
    C. When he found the book lying on the table, he immediately notified the owner.

27. A. Being locked in the desk, we were certain that the papers would not be taken.   27._____
    B. It wasn't I who dictated the telegram; I believe it was Eleanor.
    C. You should interview whoever comes to the office today.

28. A. The clerk was instructed to set the machine on the table before summoning the manager.   28._____
    B. He said that he was not familiar with those kind of activities.
    C. A box of pencils, in addition to erasers and blotters, was included in the shipment of supplies.

29. A. The supervisor remarked, "Assigning an employee to the proper type of work is not always easy."   29._____
    B. The employer found that each of the applicants were qualified to perform the duties of the position.
    C. Any competent student is permitted to take this course if he obtains the consent of the instructor.

30. A. The prize was awarded to the employee whom the judges believed to be most deserving.   30._____
    B. Since the instructor believes this book is the better of the two, he is recommending it for use in the school.
    C. It was obvious to the employees that the completion of the task by the scheduled date would require their working overtime.

31. A. These reports have been typed by employees who were trained by a capable supervisor.   31._____
    B. This employee is as old, if not older, than any other employee in the department.
    C. Running rapidly down the street, the manager soon reached the office.

32. A. It is believed, that if these terms are accepted, the building can be constructed at a reasonable cost.   32._____
    B. The typists are seated in the large office; the stenographers, in the small office.
    C. Either the operators or the machines are at fault.

33. A. Mr. Jones, who is the head of the agency, will come today to discuss the plans for the new training program.   33._____
    B. The reason the report is not finished is that the supply of paper is exhausted.
    C. It is now obvious that neither of the two employees is able to handle this type of assignment.

Questions 34-40.

DIRECTIONS: Each of Questions 34 through 40 consists of four words. In each question, one of the words may be spelled incorrectly or all four words may be spelled correctly. If one of the words in a question is spelled incorrectly, print in the space at the right the letter preceding the word which is spelled incorrectly. If all four words are spelled correctly, print the letter E.

34. A. guarantee         B. committment         34._____
    C. mitigate          D. publicly

| | | | | | |
|---|---|---|---|---|---|
| 35. | A. prerogative | | B. apprise | | 35.____ |
| | C. extrordinary | | D. continual | | |
| 36. | A. arrogant | | B. handicapped | | 36.____ |
| | C. judicious | | D. perennial | | |
| 37. | A. permissable | | B. deceive | | 37.____ |
| | C. innumerable | | D. retrieve | | |
| 38. | A. notable | | B. allegiance | | 38.____ |
| | C. reimburse | | D. illegal | | |
| 39. | A. interceed | | B. benefited | | 39.____ |
| | C. analogous | | D. altogether | | |
| 40. | A. seizure | | B. irrelevant | | 40.____ |
| | C. inordinate | | D. dissapproved | | |

Questions 41-50.

DIRECTIONS: Questions 41 through 50 are based on the Production Record table shown on the following page for the Information Unit in Agency X for the work week ended Friday, December 6. The table shows, for each employee, the quantity of each type of work performed and the percentage of the work week spent in performing each type of work.

NOTE: Assume that each employee works 7 hours a day and 5 days a week, making a total of 35 hours for the work week.

PRODUCTION RECORD - INFORMATION UNIT IN AGENCY X
(For the work week ended Friday, December 6)

Number of

| | Papers Filed | Sheets Proofread | Visitors Received | Envelopes Addressed |
|---|---|---|---|---|
| Miss Agar | 3120 | 33 | 178 | 752 |
| Mr. Brun | 1565 | 59 | 252 | 724 |
| Miss Case | 2142 | 62 | 214 | 426 |
| Mr. Dale | 4259 | 29 | 144 | 1132 |
| Miss Earl | 2054 | 58 | 212 | 878 |
| Mr. Farr | 1610 | 69 | 245 | 621 |
| Miss Glen | 2390 | 57 | 230 | 790 |
| Mr. Hope | 3425 | 32 | 176 | 805 |
| Miss Iver | 3736 | 56 | 148 | 650 |
| Mr. Joad | 3212 | 55 | 181 | 495 |

## Percentage of Work Week Spent On

|  | Filing Papers | Proof-reading | Receiving Visitors | Addressing Envelopes | Performing Miscellaneous Work |
|---|---|---|---|---|---|
| Miss Agar | 30% | 9% | 34% | 11% | 16% |
| Mr. Brun | 13% | 15% | 52% | 10% | 10% |
| Miss Case | 23% | 18% | 38% | 6% | 15% |
| Mr. Dale | 50% | 7% | 17% | 16% | 10% |
| Miss Earl | 24% | 14% | 37% | 14% | 11% |
| Mr. Farr | 16% | 19% | 48% | 8% | 9% |
| Miss Glen | 27% | 12% | 42% | 12% | 7% |
| Mr. Hope | 38% | 8% | 32% | 13% | 9% |
| Miss Iver | 43% | 13% | 24% | 9% | 11% |
| Mr. Joad | 33% | 11% | 36% | 7% | 13% |

41. For the week, the average amount of time which the employees spent in proofreading was MOST NEARLY _____ hours.

    A. 3.1   B. 3.6   C. 4.4   D. 5.1

42. The average number of visitors received daily by an employee was MOST NEARLY

    A. 40   B. 57   C. 198   D. 395

43. Of the following employees, the one who addressed envelopes at the FASTEST rate was

    A. Miss Agar        B. Mr. Brun
    C. Miss Case        D. Mr. Dale

44. Mr. Farr's rate of filing papers was MOST NEARLY _____ pages per minute.

    A. 2   B. 1.7   C. 5   D. 12

45. The average number of hours that Mr. Brun spent daily on receiving visitors exceeded the average number of hours that Miss Iver spent daily on the same type of work by MOST NEARLY _____ hours.

    A. 2   B. 3   C. 4   D. 5

46. Miss Earl worked at a faster rate than Miss Glen in

    A. filing papers         B. proofreading sheets
    C. receiving visitors    D. addressing envelopes

47. Mr. Joad's rate of filing papers _____ Miss Iver's rate of filing papers by approximately _____ %.

    A. was less than; 10      B. exceeded; 33
    C. C. was less than; 16   D. exceeded; 12

48. Assume that in the following week, Miss Case is instructed to increase the percentage of her time spent in filing papers to 35%.
    If she continued to file papers at the same rate as she did for the week ended December 6, the number of additional papers that she filed the following week was MOST NEARLY

    A. 3260        B. 5400        C. 250        D. 1120

49. Assume that in the following week, Mr. Hope increased his weekly total of envelopes addressed to 1092.
    If he continued to spend the same amount of time on this assignment as he did for the week ended December 6, the increase in his rate of addressing envelopes the following week was MOST NEARLY _____ envelopes per hour.

    A. 15          B. 65          C. 155         D. 240

50. Assume that in the following week, Miss Agar and Mr. Dale spent 3 and 9 hours less, respectively, on filing papers than they had spent for the week ended December 6, without changing their rates of work.
    The total number of papers filed during the following week by both Miss Agar and Mr. Dale was MOST NEARLY

    A. 4235        B. 4295        C. 4315        D. 4370

## KEY (CORRECT ANSWERS)

| | | | | |
|---|---|---|---|---|
| 1. A | 11. B | 21. C | 31. B | 41. C |
| 2. B | 12. D | 22. B | 32. A | 42. A |
| 3. B | 13. B | 23. C | 33. D | 43. B |
| 4. C | 14. D | 24. D | 34. B | 44. C |
| 5. C | 15. A | 25. A | 35. C | 45. A |
| 6. E | 16. D | 26. B | 36. E | 46. C |
| 7. A | 17. C | 27. A | 37. A | 47. D |
| 8. D | 18. B | 28. B | 38. E | 48. D |
| 9. A | 19. A | 29. B | 39. A | 49. B |
| 10. C | 20. A | 30. D | 40. D | 50. B |

# EXAMINATION SECTION
# TEST 1

DIRECTIONS: Each question or incomplete statement is followed by several suggested answers or completions. Select the one that BEST answers the question or completes the statement. *PRINT THE LETTER OF THE CORRECT ANSWER IN THE SPACE AT THE RIGHT.*

1. Records of one type or another are kept in every office. The MOST important of the following reasons for the supervisor of a clerical or stenographic unit to keep statistical records of the work done in his unit is generally to
    A. supply basic information needed in planning the work of the unit
    B. obtain statistics for comparison with other units
    C. serve as the basis for unsatisfactory employee evaluation
    D. provide the basis for special research projects on program budgeting

    1.____

2. It is better for an employee to report and be responsible directly to several supervisors than to report and be responsible to only one supervisor.
    This statement directly CONTRADICTS the supervisory principle generally known as
    A. span of control
    B. unity of command
    C. delegation of authority
    D. accountability

    2.____

3. The one of the following which would MOST likely lead to friction among clerks in a unit is for the unit supervisor to
    A. defend the actions of his clerks when discussing them with his own supervisor
    B. praise each of his clerks in confidence as the best clerk in the unit
    C. get his men to work together as a team in completing the work of the unit
    D. consider the point of view of the rank and file clerks when assigning unpleasant tasks

    3.____

4. You become aware that one of the employees you supervise has failed to follow correct procedure and has been permitting various reports to be prepared, typed, and transmitted improperly.
    The BEST action for you to take FIRST in this situation is to
    A. order the employee to review all departmental procedures and reprimand him for having violated them
    B. warn the employee that he must obey regulations because uniformity is essential for effective departmental operation
    C. confer with the employee both about his failure to follow regulations and his reasons for doing so
    D. watch the employee's work very closely in the future but say nothing about this violation

    4.____

5. The supervisory clerk who would be MOST likely to have poor control over his subordinates is the one who
   A. goes to unusually great lengths to try to win their approval
   B. pitches in with the work they are doing during periods of heavy workload when no extra help can be obtained
   C. encourages and helps his subordinates toward advancement
   D. considers suggestions from his subordinates before establishing new work procedures involving them

6. Suppose that a clerk who has been transferred to your office from another division in your agency because of difficulties with his supervisor has been placed under your supervision.
   The BEST course of action for you to take FIRST is to
   A. instruct the clerk in the duties he will be performing in your office and make him feel wanted in his new position
   B. analyze the clerk's past grievance to determine if the transfer was the best solution to the problem
   C. advise him of the difficulties his former supervisor had with other employees and encourage him not to feel bad about the transfer
   D. warn him that you will not tolerate any nonsense and that he will be under continuous surveillance while assigned to you

7. A certain office supervisor takes the initiative to represent his employees' interests related to working conditions, opportunities for advancement, etc. to his own supervisor and the administrative levels of the agency.
   This supervisor's actions will MOST probably have the effect of
   A. preventing employees from developing individual initiative in their work goals
   B. encouraging employees to compete openly for the special attention of their supervisor
   C. depriving employees of the opportunity to be represented by persons and/or unions of their own choosing
   D. building employee confidence in their supervisor and a spirit of cooperation in their work

8. Suppose that you have been promoted, assigned as a supervisor of a certain unit, and asked to reorganize its functions so that specific routine procedures can be established.
   Before deciding which routines to establish, the FIRST of the following steps you should take is to
   A. decide who will perform each task in the routine
   B. determine the purpose to be served by each routine procedure
   C. outline the sequence of steps in each routine to be established
   D. calculate if more staff will be needed to carry out the new procedures

9. When routine procedures covering the ordinary work of an office are established, the supervisor of the office tends to be relieved of the need to
   A. make repeated decisions on the handling of recurring similar situations
   B. check the accuracy of the work completed by his subordinates
   C. train his subordinates in new work procedures
   D. plan and schedule the work of his office

9.____

10. Of the following, the method which would be LEAST helpful to a supervisor in effectively applying the principles of on-the-job safety to the daily work of his unit is for him to
    A. initiate corrections of unsafe layouts of equipment and unsafe work processes
    B. take charge of operations that are not routine to make certain that safety precautions are established and observed
    C. continue to talk safety and promote safety consciousness in his subordinates
    D. figure the cost of all accidents which could possibly occur on the job

10.____

11. A clerk is assigned to serve as receptionist for a large and busy office. Although many members of the public visit this office, the clerk often experiences periods of time in which he has nothing to do.
    In these circumstances, the MOST advisable of the following actions for the supervisor to take is to
    A. assign a number of relatively low priority clerical jobs to the receptionist to do in the slow periods
    B. regularly rotate this assignment so that all of the clerks experience this lighter work load
    C. assign the receptionist job as part of the duties of a number of clerks whose desks are nearest the reception room
    D. overlook the situation since most of the receptionist's time is spent in performing a necessary and meaningful function

11.____

12. For a supervisor to require all stenographers in a stenographic pool to produce the same amount of work on a particular day is
    A. advisable since it will prove that the supervisor plays no favorites
    B. fair since all stenographers are receiving approximately the same salary, their output should be equivalent
    C. not necessary since the fast workers will compensate for the slow workers
    D. not realistic since individual differences in abilities and work assignment must be taken into consideration

12.____

13. The establishment of a centralized typing pool to service the various units in an organization is MOST likely to be worthwhile when there is
    A. wide fluctuation from time to time in the needs of the various units for typing service
    B. a large volume of typing work to be done in each of the units
    C. a need by each unit for different kinds of typing service
    D. a training program in operation to develop and maintain typing skills

13.____

14. A newly appointed supervisor should learn as much as possible about the backgrounds of his subordinates. This statement is GENERALLY correct because
    A. knowing their backgrounds assures they will be treated objectively, equally, and without favor
    B. effective handling of subordinates is based upon knowledge of their individual differences
    C. subordinates perform more efficiently under one supervisor than under another
    D. subordinates have confidence in a supervisor who knows all about them

15. The use of electronic computers in modern businesses has produced many changes in office and information management.
    Of the following, it would NOT be correct to state that computer utilization
    A. broadens the scope of managerial and supervisory authority
    B. establishes uniformity in the processing and reporting of information
    C. cuts costs by reducing the personnel needed for efficient office operation
    D. supplies management rapidly with up-to-date data to facilitate decision-making

16. The CHIEF advantage of having a single, large open office instead of small partitioned ones for a clerical unit or stenographic pool is that the single, large open office
    A. afford privacy without isolation for all office workers not directly dealing with the public
    B. assures the smoother, more continuous inter-office flow of work that is essential for efficient work production
    C. facilitates the office supervisor's visual control over and communication with his subordinates
    D. permits a more decorative and functional arrangement of office furniture and machines

17. When a supervisor provides a new employee with the information necessary for a basic knowledge and a general understanding of practices and procedures of the agency, he is applying the type of training generally known as _____ training.
    A. pre-employment            B. induction
    C. on-the-job                D. supervisory

18. Many government agencies require the approval by a central forms control unit of the design and reproduction of new office forms.
    The one of the following results of this procedure that is a DISADVANTAGE is that requiring prior approval of a central forms control unit usually
    A. limits the distribution of forms to those offices with justifiable reasons for receiving them
    B. permits checking whether existing forms or modifications of them are in line with current agency needs

C. encourages reliance on only the central office to set up all additional forms when needed
D. provides for someone with a specialized knowledge of forms design to review and criticize new and revised forms

19. Suppose that a large quantity of information is in the files which are located a good distance from your desk. Almost every worker in your office must use these files constantly. Your duties in particular require that you refer daily to about 25 of the same items. They are short, one-page items distributed throughout the files.
In this situation, your BEST course would be to
   A. take the items that you use daily from the files and keep them on your desk, inserting out cards in their place
   B. go to the files each time you need the information so that the items will be there when other workers need them
   C. make Xerox copies of the information you use most frequently and keep them in your desk for ready reference
   D. label the items you use most often with different colored tabs for immediate identification

19._____

20. Of the following, the MOST important advantage of preparing manuals of office procedures in loose-leaf form is that this form
   A. permits several employees to use different sections simultaneously
   B. facilitates the addition of new material and the removal of obsolete material
   C. is more readily arranged in alphabetical order
   D. reduces the need for cross-references to locate material carried under several headings

20._____

21. Suppose that you establish a new clerical procedure for the unit you supervise. Your keeping a close check on the time required by your staff to handle the new procedure is WISE mainly because such a check will find out
   A. whether your subordinates know how to handle the new procedure
   B. whether a revision of the unit's work schedule will be necessary as a result of the new procedure
   C. what attitude your employees have toward the new procedure
   D. what alterations in job descriptions will be necessitated by the new procedure

21._____

22. From the viewpoint of an office supervisor, the BEST of the following reasons for distributing the incoming mail before the beginning of the regular work day is that
   A. distribution can be handled quickly and most efficiently at that time
   B. distribution later in the day may be distracting to or interfere with other employees
   C. the employees who distribute the mail can then perform other tasks during the rest of the day
   D. office activities for the day based on the mail may then be started promptly

22._____

23. Suppose you are the head of a unit with ten staff members who are located in several different rooms.
   If you want to inform your staff of a minor change in procedure, the BEST and LEAST expensive way of doing so would usually be to
   A. send a copy to each staff member
   B. call a special staff meeting and announce the change
   C. circulate a memo, having each staff member initial it
   D. have a clerk tell each member of the staff about the change

24. The numbered statements below relate to the stenographic skill of taking dictation. According to authorities on secretarial practices, which of these are generally recommended guides to development of efficient stenographic skills?
   I. A stenographer should date her notebook daily to facilitate locating certain notes at a later time.
   II. A stenographer should make corrections of grammatical mistakes while her boss is dictating to her.
   III. A stenographer should draw a line through the dictated matter in her notebook after she has transcribed it
   IV. A stenographer should write in longhand unfamiliar names and addresses dictated to her.

   The CORRECT answer is:
   A. Only Statements I, II, and III are generally recommended guides.
   B. Only Statements II, III, and IV are generally recommended guides.
   C. Only Statements I, III, and IV are generally recommended guides.
   D. All four statements are generally recommended guides.

25. A bureau of a city agency is about to move to a new location.
   Of the following, the FIRST step that should be taken in order to provide a good layout for the office at the new location is to
   A. decide the exact amount of space to be assigned to each unit of the bureau
   B. decide whether to lay out a single large open office or one consisting of small partitioned units
   C. ask each unit chief in the bureau to examine the new location and submit a request for the amount of space he needs
   D. prepare a detailed plan of the dimensions of the floor space to be occupied by the bureau at the new location

26. Of the following, the BEST reason for discarding a sheet of carbon paper is that
   A. some carbon rubs off on your fingers when handled
   B. there are several creases in the sheet
   C. the short edge of the sheet is curled
   D. the finish on the sheet is smooth and shiny

27. Suppose you are the supervisor of a mailroom of a large city agency where the mail received daily is opened by machine, sorted by hand for delivery, and time-stamped. Letters and any enclosures are removed from envelopes and stapled together before distribution. One of your newest clerks asks you what should be done when a letter makes reference to an enclosure but no enclosure is in the envelope.
You should tell him that, in this situation, the BEST procedure is to
    A. make an entry of the sender's name and address in the missing enclosures file and forward the letter to its proper destination
    B. return the letter to its sender, attaching a request for the missing enclosure
    C. put the letter aside until a proper investigation may be made concerning the missing enclosure
    D. route the letter to the person for whom it is intended, noting the absence of the enclosure on the letter-margin

28. The term *work flow*, when used in connection with office management or the activities in an office, GENERALLY means the
    A. use of charts in the analysis of various office functions
    B. rate of speed at which work flows through a single section of an office
    C. step-by-step physical routing of work through its various procedures
    D. number of individual work units which can be produced by the average employee

29. Physical conditions can have a definite effect on the efficiency and morale of an office. Which of the following statements about physical conditions in an office is CORRECT?
    A. Hard, non-porous surfaces reflect more noise than linoleum on the top of a desk.
    B. Painting in tints of bright yellow is more appropriate for sunny, well-lit offices than for dark, poorly-lit offices.
    C. Plate glass is better than linoleum for the top of a desk.
    D. The central typing room needs less light than a conference room does.

30. In a certain filing system, documents are consecutively numbered as they are filed, a register is maintained of such consecutively numbered documents, and a record is kept of the number of each document removed from the files and its destination.
This system will NOT help in
    A. finding the present whereabouts of a particular document
    B. proving the accuracy of the data recorded on a certain document
    C. indicating whether observed existing documents were ever filed
    D. locating a desired document without knowing what its contents are

31. In deciding the kind and number of records an agency should keep, the administrative staff must recognize that records are of value in office management PRIMARILY as
    A. informational bases for agency activities
    B. data for evaluating the effectiveness of the agency
    C. raw material on which statistical analyses are to be based
    D. evidence that the agency is carrying out its duties and responsibilities

32. Complaints are often made by the public about the government's procedures. Although in most cases such procedures cannot be changed since various laws and regulations require them, it may still be possible to reduce the number of complaints.
    Which one of the following actions by personnel dealing with applicants for city services is LEAST likely to reduce complaints concerning city procedures?
    A. Treating all citizens alike and explaining to them that no exceptions to required procedures can be made.
    B. Explaining briefly to the citizen why he should comply with regulations.
    C. Being careful to avoid mistakes which may make additional interviews or correspondence necessary.
    D. Keeping the citizen informed of the progress of his correspondence when immediate disposition cannot be made.

33. Persons whose native language is not English sometimes experience difficulty in communication when visiting public offices.
    The MOST common method used by such persons to overcome the difficulty in communication is to
    A. write in their own language whatever they wish to say
    B. hire a professional interpreter
    C. ask a patrolman for assistance
    D. bring with them an English-speaking friend or relative

34. In answering a complaint made by a member of the public that a certain essential procedure required by your agency is difficult to follow, it would be BEST for you to stress most
    A. that a change in the rules may be considered if enough complaints are received
    B. why the operation of a large agency sometimes proves a hardship in individual cases
    C. the necessity for the procedure
    D. the origin of the procedure

35. When talking to a citizen, it is BEST for an employee of government to
    A. use ordinary conversational phrases and a natural manner
    B. try to copy the pronunciation and level of education shown by the citizen
    C. try to speak in a very cultured manner and tone
    D. use technical terms to show his familiarity with his own work

36. Employees who service the public should maintain an attitude which is both sympathetic and objective. An unsympathetic and subjective attitude would be shown by a public employee who
    A. says *no* with a smile when a citizen's request must be denied
    B. listens attentively to a long complaint from a citizen about government's *red tape*
    C. responds with sarcasm when a citizen asks a question which has an obvious manner
    D. suggests a definite solution to a citizen's problems

37. Of the following methods of conducting an interview, the BEST is to
    A. ask questions with *yes* or *no* answers
    B. listen carefully and ask only questions that are pertinent
    C. fire questions at the interviewee so that he must answer sincerely and briefly
    D. read standardized questions to the person being interviewed

38. An interviewer should begin with topics which are easy to talk about and which are not threatening. This procedure is useful MAINLY because it
    A. allows the applicant a little time to get accustomed to the situation and leads to freer communication
    B. distracts the attention of the person being interviewed from the main purpose of the questioning
    C. is the best way for the interviewer to show that he is relaxed and confident on the job
    D. causes the interviewee to feel that the interviewer is apportioning valuable questioning time

39. The initial interview will normally be more of a problem to the interviewer than any subsequent interviews he may have with the same person because
    A. the interviewee is likely to be hostile
    B. there is too much to be accomplished in one session
    C. he has less information about the client than he will have later
    D. some information may be forgotten when later making record of this first interview

40. You are a supervisor in an agency and are holding your first interview with a new employee. In this interview, you should strive MAINLY to
    A. show the new employee that you are an efficient and objective supervisor, with a completely impersonal attitude toward your subordinate
    B. complete the entire orientation process including the giving of detailed job-duty instructions
    C. make it clear to the employee that all your decisions are based on your many years of experience
    D. lay the groundwork for a good employee-supervisor relationship by gaining the new employee's confidence

41. Most successful interviews are those in which the interviewer shows a genuine interest in the person he is questioning. This attitude would MOST likely cause the individual being interviewed to
    A. feel that the interviewer already knows all the facts in his case
    B. act more naturally and reveal more of his true feelings
    C. request that the interviewer give more attention to his problems, not his personality
    D. react defensively, suppress his negative feelings, and conceal the real facts in his case

42. Questions worded so that the person being interviewed has some hint of the desired answer can modify the person's response. The result of the inclusion of such questions in an interview, even when they are used inadvertently, is to
    A. have no effect on the basic content of the information given by the person interviewed
    B. have value in convincing the person that the suggested plan is the best for him
    C. cause the person to give more meaningful information
    D. reduce the validity of the information obtained from the person

43. The person MOST likely to be a good interviewer is one who
    A. is able to outguess the person being interviewed
    B. tries to change the attitudes of the persons he interviews
    C. controls the interview by skillfully dominating the conversation
    D. is able to imagine himself in the position of the person being interviewed

44. The *halo effect* is an overall impression on the interviewer, whether favorable or unfavorable, usually created by a single trait. This impression then influences the appraisal of all other factors.
    A *halo effect* is LEAST likely to be created at an interview where the interviewee is a
    A. person of average appearance and ability
    B. rough-looking man who uses abusive language
    C. young attractive woman being interviewed by a man
    D. person who demonstrates an exceptional ability to remember facts

45. Of the following, the BEST way for an interviewer to calm a person who seems to have become emotionally upset as a result of a question asked is for the interviewer to
    A. talk to the person about other things for a short time
    B. ask that the person control himself
    C. probe for the cause of his emotional upset
    D. finish the questioning as quickly as possible

46. Of the following, a centralized filing system is LEAST suitable for filing
    A. material which is confidential in nature
    B. routine correspondence
    C. periodic reports of the divisions of the department
    D. material used by several divisions of the department

47. Form letters should be used MAINLY when
    A. an office has to reply to a great many similar inquiries
    B. the type of correspondence varies widely
    C. it is necessary to have letters which are well-phrased and grammatically correct
    D. letters of inquiry have to be answered as soon as possible after they are received

48. Suppose that you are assigned to prepare a form from which certain information will be posted in a ledger. It would be MOST helpful to the person posting the information in the ledger is, in designing the form, you were to
    A. use the same color paper for both the form and the ledger
    B. make the form the same size as the pages of the ledger
    C. have the information on the form in the same order as that used in the ledger
    D. include in the form a box which is to be initialed when the data on the form have been posted in the ledger

49. A misplaced record is a lost record. Of the following, the MOST valid implication of this statement in regard to office work is that
    A. all records in an office should be filed in strict alphabetical order
    B. accuracy in filing is essential
    C. only one method of filing should be used throughout the office
    D. files should be locked when not in use

50. James Jones is applying for a provisional appointment as a clerk in your department. He presents a letter of recommendation from a former employer stating: *James Jones was rarely late or absent; he has a very pleasing manner and never got into an argument with his fellow employees.*
    The above information concerning this applicant
    A. proves clearly that he produces more work than the average employee
    B. indicates that he was probably attempting to conceal his inefficiency from his former employer
    C. presents no conclusive evidence of his ability to do clerical work
    D. indicates clearly that with additional training he will make a good supervisor

## KEY (CORRECT ANSWERS)

| | | | | |
|---|---|---|---|---|
| 1. A | 11. A | 21. B | 31. A | 41. B |
| 2. B | 12. D | 22. D | 32. A | 42. D |
| 3. B | 13. A | 23. C | 33. D | 43. D |
| 4. C | 14. B | 24. C | 34. C | 44. A |
| 5. A | 15. A | 25. D | 35. A | 45. A |
| 6. A | 16. C | 26. B | 36. C | 46. A |
| 7. D | 17. B | 27. D | 37. B | 47. A |
| 8. B | 18. C | 28. C | 38. A | 48. C |
| 9. A | 19. C | 29. A | 39. C | 49. B |
| 10. D | 20. B | 30. B | 40. D | 50. C |

# TEST 2

DIRECTIONS: Each question or incomplete statement is followed by several suggested answers or completions. Select the one that BEST answers the question or completes the statement. *PRINT THE LETTER OF THE CORRECT ANSWER IN THE SPACE AT THE RIGHT.*

Questions 1-10.

DIRECTIONS: In each of Questions 1 through 10, there is a quotation which contains a word (one of those underlined) that is either incorrectly used because it is not in keeping with the meaning the quotation is evidently intended to convey, or is misspelled. There is only one incorrect word in each quotation. Of the four underlined words in each question, determine if the first one should be replaced by the word lettered A, the second replaced by the word lettered B, the third replaced by the word lettered C, or the fourth replaced by the word lettered D. Print the letter of the replacement word you have selected in the space at the right.

1. Whether one depends on flourescent or artificial light or both, adequate standards should be maintained by means of systematic tests.
   A. natural  B. safeguards  C. established  D. routine

2. A policeman has to be prepared to assume his knowledge as a social scientist in the community.
   A. forced  B. role  C. philosopher  D. street

3. It is practically impossible to tell whether a sentence is very long simply by measuring its length.
   A. almost  B. mark  C. too  D. denoting

4. By using carbon paper, the typist easily is able to insert as many as six copies of a report.
   A. adding  B. seldom  C. make  D. forms

5. Although all people have many traits in common, a receptionist in her agreements with people learns quickly how different each person is from every other person.
   A. impressions  B. associations  C. decides  D. various

6. Strong leaders are required to organize a community for delinquency prevention and for dissemination of organized crime and drug addiction.
   A. tactics  B. important  C. control  D. meetings

7. The demonstrators, who were taken to the Criminal Courts building in Manhattan (because it was large enough to accommodate them), contended that the arrests were unwarrented.
   A. demonstraters  B. Manhatten  C. accomodate  D. unwarranted

8. When two or more forms for spelling a word exist, it is advisable to use the preferred spelling indicated in the dictionary, and to use it consistently.
   A. adviseable   B. prefered   C. dictionery   D. consistently

8.____

9. If you know the language of the foreign country you are visiting, your embarassment will disappear and you will learn a lot more about the customs and characteristics.
   A. foriegn        B. embarrassment
   C. dissappear     D. charactaristics

9.____

10. Material consisting of government bulletins, adverticements, catalogues, announcements of address changes and any other periodical material of this nature, may be filed alphabetically according to subject.
    A. advertisements    B. cataloges
    C. announcments      D. pereodical

10.____

Questions 11-14.

DIRECTIONS: Each of the two sentences in Questions 11 through 14 may contain errors in punctuation, capitalization, or grammar.
If there is an error in only Sentence I, mark your answer A.
If there is an error in only Sentence II, mark you answer B.
If there is an error in both Sentences I and II, mark your answer C.
If both Sentences I and II are correct, mark your answer D.

11. I. It is very annoying to have a pencil sharpener, which is not in proper working order.
    II. The building watchman checked the door of Charlie's office and found that the lock has been jammed.

11.____

12. I. Since he went on the New York City council a year ago, one of his primary concerns has been safety in the streets.
    II. After waiting in the doorway for about 15 minutes, a black sedan appeared.

12.____

13. I. When you are studying a good textbook is important.
    II. He said he would divide the money equally between you and me.

13.____

14. I. The question is, "How can a large number of envelopes be sealed rapidly without the use of a sealing machine?"
    II. The administrator assigned two stenographers, Mary and I, to the new bureau.

14.____

52

Questions 15-16.

DIRECTIONS: In each of Questions 15 and 16, the four sentences are from a paragraph in a report. They are not in the right order. Which of the following arrangements is the BEST one?

15.  I. An executive may answer a letter by writing his reply on the face of the letter itself instead of having a return letter typed.
II. This procedure is efficient because it saves the executive's time, the typist's time, and saves office file space.
III. Copying machines are used in small offices as well as large offices to save time and money in making brief replies to business letters.
IV. A copy is made on a copying machine to go into the company files, while the original is mailed back to the sender.

15.____

The CORRECT answer is:
A. I, II, IV, III     B. I, IV, II, III     C. III, I, IV, II     D. III, IV, II, I

16.  I. Most organizations favor one of the types but always include the others to a lesser degree.
II. However, we can detect a definite trend toward greater uses of symbolic control.
III. We suggest that our local police agencies are today primarily utilizing material control.
IV. Control can be classified into three types: physical, material, and symbolic.

16.____

The CORRECT answer is:
A. IV, II, III, I     B. II, I, IV, III     C. III, IV, II, I     D. IV, I, III, II

17. Of the following, the MOST effective report writing style is usually characterized by
   A. covering all the main ideas in the same paragraph
   B. presenting each significant point in a new paragraph
   C. placing the least important points before the most important points
   D. giving all points equal emphasis throughout the report

17.____

18. Of the following, which factor is COMMON to all types of reports?
   A. Presentation of information
   B. Interpretation of findings
   C. Chronological ordering of the information
   D. Presentation of conclusions and recommendations

18.____

19. When writing a report, the one of the following which you should do FIRST is
   A. set up a logical work schedule
   B. determine your objectives in writing the report
   C. select your statistical material
   D. obtain the necessary data from the files

19.____

20. Generally, the frequency with which reports are to be submitted or the length of the interval which they cover should depend MAINLY on the
    A. amount of time needed to prepare the reports
    B. degree of comprehensiveness required in the reports
    C. availability of the data to be included in the reports
    D. extent of the variations in the data with the passage of time

21. The objectiveness of a report is its unbiased presentation of the facts. If this be so, which of the following reports listed below is likely to be the MOST objective?
    A. The Best Use of an Electronic Computer in Department Z
    B. The Case for Raising the Salaries of Employees in Department A
    C. Quarterly Summary of Production in the Duplicating Unit of Department Y
    D. Recommendation to Terminate Employee X's Services Because of Misconduct

Questions 22-27.

DIRECTIONS: Questions 22 through 27 are to be answered SOLELY on the basis of the information contained in the charts below which relate to the budget allocations of City X, a small suburban community. The charts depict the annual budget allocations by Department and by Expenditures over a five-year period.

## CITY X BUDGET IN MILLIONS OF DOLLARS

### TABLE I. Budget Allocations By Department

| Department | 2012 | 2013 | 2014 | 2015 | 2016 |
| --- | --- | --- | --- | --- | --- |
| Public Safety | 30 | 45 | 50 | 40 | 50 |
| Health and Welfare | 50 | 75 | 90 | 60 | 70 |
| Engineering | 5 | 8 | 10 | 5 | 8 |
| Human Resources | 10 | 12 | 20 | 10 | 22 |
| Conversation and Environment | 10 | 15 | 20 | 20 | 15 |
| Education and Development | 15 | 25 | 35 | 15 | 15 |
| TOTAL BUDGET | 120 | 180 | 225 | 150 | 180 |

### TABLE II. Budget Allocations by Expenditures

| Category | 2012 | 2013 | 2014 | 2015 | 2016 |
| --- | --- | --- | --- | --- | --- |
| Raw Materials and Machinery | 36 | 63 | 68 | 30 | 98 |
| Capital Outlay | 12 | 27 | 56 | 15 | 18 |
| Personal Services | 72 | 90 | 101 | 105 | 65 |
| TOTAL BUDGET | 120 | 180 | 225 | 150 | 180 |

22. The year in which the SMALLEST percentage of the total annual budget was allocated to the Department of Education and Development is
    A. 2012    B. 2013    C. 2015    D. 2016

5 (#2)

23. Assume that, in 2015, the Department of Conservation and Environment divided its annual budget into the three categories of expenditures and in exactly the same proportion as the budget shown in Table II for the year 2015. The amount allocated for capital outlay in the Department of Conservation and Environment's 2015 budget was MOST NEARLY _____ million.
    A. $2     B. $4     C. $6     D. $10

24. From the year 2013 to the year 2015, the sum of the annual budgets for the Departments of Public Safety and Engineering showed an overall _____ of _____ million.
    A. decline; $8     B. increase; $7     C. decline; $15     D. increase; $22

25. The LARGEST dollar increase in departmental budget allocations from one year to the next was in
    A. Public Safety from 2012 to 2013
    B. Health and Welfare from 2012 to 2013
    C. Education and Development from 2014 to 2015
    D. Human Resources from 2014 to 2015

26. During the five-year period, the annual budget of the Department of Human Resources was GREATER than the annual budget for the Department of Conservation and Environment in _____ of the years.
    A. none     B. one     C. two     D. three

27. If the total City X budget increases at the same rate from 2016 to 2017 as it did from 2015 to 2016, the total City X budget for 2017 will be MOST NEARLY _____ million.
    A. $180     B. $200     C. $210     D. $215

Questions 28-34.

DIRECTIONS: Questions 28 through 34 are to be answered SOLELY on the basis of the information contained in the graph below which relates to the work of a public agency.

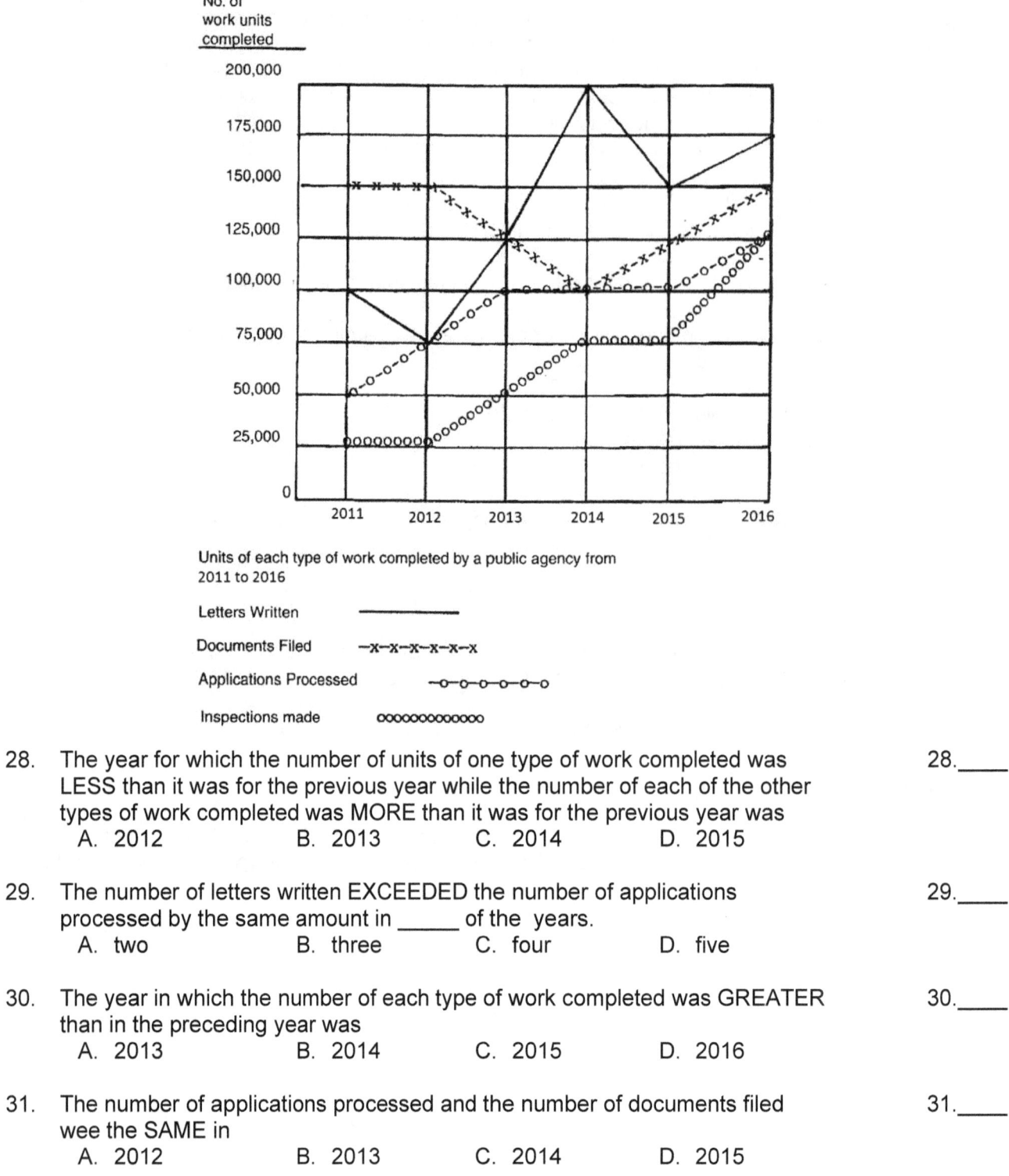

Units of each type of work completed by a public agency from 2011 to 2016

Letters Written ─────────
Documents Filed ─x─x─x─x─x─x
Applications Processed ─o─o─o─o─o─o
Inspections made ∞∞∞∞∞∞∞

28. The year for which the number of units of one type of work completed was LESS than it was for the previous year while the number of each of the other types of work completed was MORE than it was for the previous year was
 A. 2012   B. 2013   C. 2014   D. 2015

29. The number of letters written EXCEEDED the number of applications processed by the same amount in _____ of the years.
 A. two   B. three   C. four   D. five

30. The year in which the number of each type of work completed was GREATER than in the preceding year was
 A. 2013   B. 2014   C. 2015   D. 2016

31. The number of applications processed and the number of documents filed wee the SAME in
 A. 2012   B. 2013   C. 2014   D. 2015

32. The TOTAL number of units of work completed by the agency   32.____
    A. increased in each year after 2011
    B. decreased from the prior year in two of the years after 2011
    C. was the same in two successive years from 2011 to 2016
    D. was less in 2011 than in any of the following years

33. For the year in which the number of letters written was twice as high as it   33.____
    was in 2011, the number of documents filed was _____ it was in 2011.
    A. the same as              B. two-thirds of what
    C. five-sixths of what      D. 1½ times what

34. The variable which was the MOST stable during the period 2011 through   34.____
    2016 was
    A. Inspections Made         B. Letters Written
    C. Documents Filed          D. Applications Processed

Questions 35-41.

DIRECTIONS:  Questions 35 through 41 are to be answered SOLELY on the basis of the information in the following passage.

Job evaluation and job rating systems are intended to introduce scientific procedures. Any type of approach, when properly used, will give satisfactory results. The Point System, when properly validated by actual use, is more likely to be suitable for general use than the ranking system. In many aspects, the Factor Comparison Plan is a point system tied to money values. Of course, there may be another system that combines the ranking system with the point system, especially during the initial stages of the development of the program. After the program has been in use for some time, the tendency is to drop off the ranking phrase and continue the use of the point system.

In the ranking system of rating of jobs, every job within the plant is arranged in some order, either from the one with the simplest qualifications to the one with maximum requirements, or in the reverse order. This system should be preceded by careful job analysis and the writing of accurate job descriptions before the rating process is undertaken. It is possible, of course, to take the jobs as they are found in the business enterprise and use the names as they are without any attempt at standardization, and merely rank them according to the general overall impression of the raters. Such a procedure is certain to fall short of what may reasonably be expected of job rating. Another procedure that is in reality merely a modification of the simple rating described above is to establish a series of grades or zones and arrange all the jobs in the plant into groups within these grades and zones. The practice in most common use is to arrange all the jobs in the plant according to their requirements by rating them and then to establish the classifications or groups.

The actual ranking of jobs may be done by one individual, several individuals, or a committee. If several individuals are working independently on the task, it will usually be found that, in general, they agree but that their rankings vary in certain details. A conference between the individuals, with each person giving his reasons why he rated one way or another, usually produces agreement. The detailed job descriptions are particularly helpful when there is disagreement among raters as to the rating of certain jobs. It is not only possible but desirable to have workers participate in the construction of the job description and in rating the job.

8 (#2)

35. The MAIN theme of this passage is
    A. the elimination of bias in job rating
    B. the rating of jobs by the ranking system
    C. the need for accuracy in allocating points in the point system
    D. pitfalls to avoid in selecting key jobs in the Factor Comparison Plan

36. The ranking system of rating jobs consists MAINLY of
    A. attaching a point value to each ratable factor of each job prior to establishing an equitable pay scale
    B. arranging every job in the organization in descending order and then following this up with a job analysis of the key jobs
    C. preparing accurate job descriptions after a job analysis and then arranging all jobs either in ascending or descending order based on job requirements
    D. arbitrarily establishing a hierarchy of job classes and grades and then fitting each job into a specific class and grade based on the opinions of unit supervisors

37. The above passage states that the system of classifying jobs MOST used in an organization is to
    A. organize all jobs in the organization in accordance with their requirements and then create categories or clusters of jobs
    B. classify all jobs in the organization according to the titles and ranks by which they are currently known in the organization
    C. establish a pre-arranged series of grades or zones and then fit all jobs into one of the grades or zones
    D. determine the salary currently being paid for each job, and then rank the jobs in order according to salary

38. According to the above passage, experience has shown that when a group of raters is assigned to the job evaluation task and each individual rates independently of the others, the raters GENERALLY
    A. *agree* with respect to all aspects of their rankings
    B. *disagree* with respect to all or nearly all aspects of the rankings
    C. *disagree* on overall ratings but agree on specific rating factors
    D. *agree* on overall rankings but have some variance in some details

39. The above passage states that the use of a detailed job description is of SPECIAL value when
    A. employees of an organization have participated in the preliminary steps involved in actual preparation of the job description
    B. labor representatives are not participating in ranking of the jobs
    C. an individual rater who is unsure of himself is ranking the jobs
    D. a group of raters is having difficulty reaching unanimity with respect to ranking a certain job

9 (#2)

40. A comparison of the various rating systems as described in the above passage shows that
    A. the ranking system is not as appropriate for general use as a properly validated point system
    B. the point system is the same as the Factor Comparison Plan except that it places greater emphasis on money
    C. no system is capable of combining the point system and the Factor Comparison Plan
    D. the point system will be discontinued last when used in combination with the Factor Comparison System

41. The above passage implies that the PRINCIPAL reason for creating job evaluation and rating systems was to help
    A. overcome union opposition to existing salary plans
    B. base wage determination on a more objective and orderly foundation
    C. eliminate personal bias on the part of the trained scientific job evaluators
    D. management determine if it was overpricing the various jobs in the organizational hierarchy

42. As a general rule, in a large office it is desirable to have more than one one employee who is able to operate any one machine and more than one office machine capable of performing any one type of required operation. According to this statement, there USUALLY should be
    A. fewer office machines in an office than are necessary for efficient job performance
    B. more office machines in an office than there are employees able to operate them
    C. more types of required operations to be performed than there are machines necessary to their performance
    D. fewer types of required operations to be performed than there are machines capable of performing them

43. The plan of an organization's structure and procedures may appear to be perfectly sound, but the organization may still operate wastefully and with a great amount of friction because of the failure of the people in the organization to work together.
    The MOST valid implication of this statement is that
    A. inefficiency within an organization may be caused by people being directed to do the wrong things
    B. an organization which operates inefficiently might be improved by revising its systems and methods of operations
    C. use of the best methods an organization can devise may not prevent an organization from being inefficient
    D. the people in an organization may not have an appreciation of the high quality of the organization's plan of operations

44. If an employee is to be held responsible for obtaining results, he should be given every reasonable freedom to exercise his own intelligence and initiative to achieve the results expected.
The MOST valid implication of this statement is that
   A. the authority delegated should match the responsibility assigned
   B. achieving results depends upon the individual's willingness to work
   C. the most important aspect of getting a job done is to know how to do it
   D. understanding the requirements of a task is essential to its accomplishment

45. Essentially, an organization is defined as any group of individuals who are cooperating under the direction of executive leadership in an attempt to accomplish certain common objectives.
The one of the following which this statement does NOT include as an essential characteristic of an organization is _____ the members of the group.
   A. cooperation among
   B. proficiency of
   C. authoritative guidance of
   D. goals common to

46. A supervisor, in organizing the work activities of the staff of an office, should recognize that one of the conditions which is expected to promote a high level of interest on the part of an office worker in his job is to assign him to perform a variety of work.
The MOST valid implication of this statement is that
   A. each worker should be taught to perform each type of work in the office
   B. workers should be assigned to perform types of work in which they have expressed interest
   C. a worker who is assigned to perform a single type of work is likely to become bored
   D. some workers are likely to perform several types of work better than other workers are able to

47. Of the following basic guides to effective letter writing, which one would NOT be recommended as a way of improving the quality of business letters?
   A. Use emphatic phrases like *close proximity* and *first and foremost* to round out sentences.
   B. Break up complicated sentences by making short sentences out of dependent clauses.
   C. Replace old-fashioned phrases like *enclosed please find* and *recent date* with a more direct approach.
   D. Personalize letters by using your reader's name at least once in the body of the message.

48. Suppose that you must write a reply letter to a citizen's request for a certain pamphlet printed by your agency. The pamphlet is temporarily unavailable but a new supply will be arriving by December 8 or 9.
Of the following four sentences, which one expresses the MOST positive business letter writing approach?
    A. We cannot send the materials you requested until after December 8.
    B. May we assure you that the materials you requested will be sent as quickly as possible.
    C. We will be sending the materials you requested as soon as our supply is replenished.
    D. We will mail the materials you requested on or shortly after December 8.

49. Using form letters in business correspondence is LEAST effective when
    A. answering letters on a frequently recurring subject
    B. giving the same information to many addresses
    C. the recipient is only interested in the routine information contained in the form letter
    D. a replay must be keyed to the individual requirements of the intended reader

50. The ability to write memos and letters is very important in clerical and administrative work. Methodical planning of a reply letter usually involves the following basic steps which are arranged in random order:
    I. Determine the purpose of the letter you are about to write.
    II. Make an outline of what information your reply letter should contain.
    III. Read carefully the letter to be answered to find out its main points.
    IV. Assemble the facts to be included in your reply letter.
    V. Visualize your intended reader and adapt your letter writing style to him.
    If the above-numbered steps were arranged in their proper logical order, the one which would be THIRD in the sequence is
    A. II        B. III        C. IV        D. V

## KEY (CORRECT ANSWERS)

| | | | | |
|---|---|---|---|---|
| 1. A | 11. C | 21. C | 31. C | 41. B |
| 2. B | 12. C | 22. D | 32. C | 42. D |
| 3. C | 13. A | 23. A | 33. B | 43. C |
| 4. C | 14. B | 24. A | 34. D | 44. A |
| 5. B | 15. C | 25. B | 35. B | 45. B |
| 6. C | 16. D | 26. B | 36. C | 46. C |
| 7. D | 17. B | 27. D | 37. A | 47. A |
| 8. D | 18. A | 28. B | 38. D | 48. D |
| 9. B | 19. B | 29. B | 39. D | 49. D |
| 10. A | 20. D | 30. D | 40. A | 50. A |

# EXAMINATION SECTION
## TEST 1

DIRECTIONS: Each question or incomplete statement is followed by several suggested answers or completions. Select the one that BEST answers the question or completes the statement. *PRINT THE LETTER OF THE CORRECT ANSWER IN THE SPACE AT THE RIGHT.*

1. When you select someone to serve as supervisor of your unit during your absence on vacation and at other times, it would generally be BEST to choose the employee who is

    A. able to move the work along smoothly without friction
    B. on staff longest
    C. liked best by the rest of the staff
    D. able to perform the work of each employee to be supervised

2. Successful supervision of handicapped persons employed in a department depends MOST on providing them with a work place and work climate

    A. which is safe and accident-free
    B. that requires close and direct supervision by others
    C. that requires the performance of routine, repetitive tasks under a minimum of pressure
    D. where they will be accepted by the other employees

3. Studies have indicated that when employees feel that their work is aimless and unchallenging, the allocation or payment of more money for this type of work is LIKELY to

    A. contribute little to increased production
    B. bring more status to this work
    C. increase employees' feelings of security
    D. give employees greater motivation

4. An employee's performance has fallen below established minimum standards of quantity and quality.
   The threat of monetary or other disciplinary action as a device for improving this employee's performance would PROBABLY be acceptable and most effective

    A. only if applied as soon as the performance fell below standard
    B. only after more constructive techniques have failed
    C. at any time provided the employee understands that the punishment will be carried out
    D. at no time

5. A supervisor must, on short notice, ask his staff to work overtime.
   Of the following, a technique that is MOST likely to win their willing cooperation would be to

    A. explain that occasional overtime is part of the job requirement
    B. explain that they will be doing him a personal favor which he will appreciate very much
    C. explain why the overtime is necessary
    D. promise them that they can take the extra time off in the near future

6. On checking a completed work assignment of an employee, the supervisor finds that the work was not done correctly because the employee had not understood his instructions. Of the following, the BEST way to prevent repetition of this situation next time is for the supervisor to

    A. ask the employee whether he fully understood the instructions and tell him to ask questions in the future whenever anything is unclear
    B. ask the employee to repeat the instructions given and test his understanding with several key questions
    C. give the instructions a second time, emphasizing the more complicated aspects of the job
    D. give work instructions in writing

7. If, as a supervisor, you find yourself pressured for time to handle all of your job responsibilities, the one of the following tasks which it would be MOST appropriate for you to delegate to a subordinate is

    A. attending a staff conference of unit supervisors to discuss the implementation of a new departmental policy
    B. making staff work assignments
    C. interviewing a new employee
    D. checking work of certain employees for accuracy

8. Suppose you are unavoidably late for work one morning. When you arrive at 10 o'clock, you find there are several matters demanding your attention.
    Which one of the following matters should you handle LAST?

    A. A visitor who had a 9:30 appointment with you has been waiting to see you since 9 o'clock
    B. An employee on an assignment which should have been completed that morning is absent, and the work will have to be reassigned
    C. Several letters which you dictated at the end of the previous day have been typed and are on your desk for signature and mailing
    D. Your superior called asking you to get certain information for him when you come in and to call him back

9. Suppose that you have assigned a typist to type a report containing considerable statistical and tabular material and have given her specific instructions as to how this material is to be laid out on each page. When she returns the completed report, you find that it was not prepared according to your instructions, but you may possibly be able to use it the way it was typed. When you question her, she states that she thought her layout was better, but you were unavailable for consultation when she began the work.
    Of the following, the BEST action for you to take is to

    A. criticize her for not doing the work according to your instructions
    B. have her retype the report
    C. praise her for her work but tell her she could have waited until she could consult you
    D. praise her for using initiative

10. Of the following, the MOST effective way for a supervisor to correct poor working habits of an employee which result in low and poor quality output is to give the employee

A. additional training
B. less demanding assignments until his work improves
C. continuous supervision
D. more severe criticism

11. Of the following, the BEST way for a supervisor to teach an employee how to do a new and somewhat complicated job is to

    A. assign him to observe another employee who is already skilled in this work and instruct him to consult this employee if he has any questions
    B. explain to him how to do it, then demonstrate how it is done, then observe and correct the employee as he does it, then follow up
    C. give him a written, detailed, step-by-step explanation of how to do the job and instruct him to ask questions if anything is unclear when he does the work
    D. teach him the easiest part of the job first, then the other parts one at a time, in order of their difficulty, as the employee masters the easier parts

12. After an employee has completed telling his supervisor about a grievance against a co-worker, the supervisor tells the employee that he will take action to remove the cause of the grievance.
    The action of the supervisor was

    A. *good* because ill feeling between subordinates interferes with proper performance
    B. *poor* because the supervisor should give both employees time to *cool off*
    C. *good* because grievances that appear petty to the supervisor are important to subordinates
    D. *poor* because the supervisor should tell the employee that he will investigate the matter before he comes to any conclusion

13. During work on an important project, one employee in a secretarial pool turns in several pages of typed copy, one page of which contains several errors.
    Of these four comments which her supervisor might possibly make, which one would be MOST constructive?

    A. "You did such a poor job on this; I'll have to have it done over."
    B. "You will have to do better more consistently than this if you want to be in charge of a secretarial pool yourself someday."
    C. "How come you made so many mistakes here? Your other pages were all right."
    D. "If my boss saw this, he'd be very displeased with you."

14. A supervisor has general supervision over a large, complex project with many employees. The work is subdivided among small units of employees, each with a senior clerk or senior stenographer in charge. At a staff meeting, after all work assignments have been made, the supervisor tells all the employees that they are to take orders only from their immediate supervisor and instructs them to let him know if any one else tries to give them orders.
    This instruction by the supervisor is

    A. *good* because it may prevent the issuance of orders by unauthorized persons which would interfere with the accomplishment of the assignment
    B. *poor* because employees should be instructed to take up such problems with their immediate supervisor

C. *good* because orders issued by immediate supervisors would be precise and directly related to the tasks of the assignments while those issued by others would not be
D. *poor* because it places upon all employees a responsibility which should not normally be theirs

15. A supervisor who is to direct a team of senior clerks and clerks and senior stenographers and stenographers in a complex project calls them together beforehand to inform them of the tasks each employee will perform on this job. Of the following, the CHIEF value of this action by the supervisor is that each member of this team will be able to

    A. work independently in the absence of the supervisor
    B. understand what he will do and how this will fit into the total picture
    C. share in the process of decision-making as an equal participant
    D. judge how well the plans for this assignment have been made

16. A supervisor who has both younger and older employees under his supervision may sometimes find that employee absenteeism seriously interferes with accomplishment of goals.
    Studies of such employee absenteeism have shown that the absences of employees

    A. under 35 years of age are usually unexpected and the absences of employees over 45 years of age are usually unnecessary
    B. of all age groups show the same characteristics as to length of absence
    C. under 35 years of age are for frequent, short periods while the absences of employees over 45 years of age are less frequent but of longer duration
    D. under 35 years of age are for periods of long duration and the absences of employees over 45 years of age are for periods of short duration

17. Suppose you have a long-standing procedure for getting a certain job done by your subordinates that is apparently a good one. Changes in some steps of the procedure are made from time to time to handle special problems that come up.
    For you to review this procedure periodically is desirable MAINLY because

    A. the system is working well
    B. checking routines periodically is a supervisor's chief responsibility
    C. subordinates may be confused as to how the procedure operates as a result of the changes made
    D. it is necessary to determine whether the procedure has become outdated or is in need of improvement

18. In conducting an interview, the BEST types of questions with which to begin the interview are those which the person interviewed is _____ to answer.

    A. willing and able            B. willing but unable
    C. able to but unwilling       D. unable and unwilling

19. In order to determine accurately a child's age, it is BEST for an interviewer to rely on

    A. the child's grade in school    B. what the mother says
    C. birth records                  D. a library card

20. In his first interview with a new employee, it would be LEAST appropriate for a unit supervisor to

    A. find out the employee's preference for the several types of jobs to which he is able to assign him
    B. determine whether the employee will make good promotion material
    C. inform the employee of what his basic job responsibilities will be
    D. inquire about the employee's education and previous employment

21. If an interviewer takes care to phrase his questions carefully and precisely, the result will MOST probably be that

    A. he will be able to determine whether the person interviewed is being truthful
    B. the free flow of the interview will be lost
    C. he will get the information he wants
    D. he will ask stereotyped questions and narrow the scope of the interview

22. When, during an interview, is the person interviewed LEAST likely to be cautious about what he tells the interviewer?

    A. Shortly after the beginning when the questions normally suggest pleasant associations to the person interviewed
    B. As long as the interviewer keeps his questions to the point
    C. At the point where the person interviewed gains a clear insight into the area being discussed
    D. When the interview appears formally ended and goodbyes are being said

23. In an interview held for the purpose of getting information from the person interviewed, it is sometimes desirable for the interviewer to repeat the answer he has received to a question.
    For the interviewer to rephrase such an answer in his own words is good practice MAINLY because it

    A. gives the interviewer time to make up his next question
    B. gives the person interviewed a chance to correct any possible misunderstanding
    C. gives the person interviewed the feeling that the interviewer considers his answer important
    D. prevents the person interviewed from changing his answer

24. There are several methods of formulating questions during an interview. The particular method used should be adapted to the interview problems presented by the person being questioned.
    Of the following methods of formulating questions during an interview, the ACCEPTABLE one is for the interviewer to ask questions which

    A. incorporate several items in order to allow a cooperative interviewee freedom to organize his statements
    B. are ambiguous in order to foil a distrustful interviewee
    C. suggest the correct answer in order to assist an interviewee who appears confused
    D. would help an otherwise unresponsive interviewee to become more responsive

25. For an interviewer to permit the person being interviewed to read the data the interviewer writes as he records the person's responses on a routine departmental form is

   A. *desirable* because it serves to assure the person interviewed that his responses are being recorded accurately
   B. *undesirable* because it prevents the interviewer from clarifying uncertain points by asking additional questions
   C. *desirable* because it makes the time that the person interviewed must wait while the answer is written seem shorter
   D. *undesirable* because it destroys the confidentiality of the interview

25.____

26. Suppose that a stranger enters the office you are in charge of and asks for the address and telephone number of one of your employees.
   Of the following, it would be BEST for you to

   A. find out why he needs the information and release it if his reason is a good one
   B. explain that you are not permitted to release such information to unauthorized persons
   C. give him the information but tell him it must be kept confidential
   D. ask him to leave the office immediately

26.____

27. A member of the public approaches an employee who is at work at his desk. The employee cannot interrupt his work in order to take care of this person.
   Of the following, the BEST and MOST courteous way of handling this situation is for the employee to

   A. avoid looking up from his work until he is finished with what he is doing
   B. tell this person that he will not be able to take care of him for quite a while
   C. refer the individual to another employee who can take care of him right away
   D. chat with the individual while he continues with his work

27.____

28. You answer a phone call from a citizen who urgently needs certain information you do not have, but you think you know who may have it. He is angry because he has already been switched to two different offices.
   Of the following, it would be BEST for you to

   A. give him the phone number of the person you think may have the information he wants, but explain you are not sure
   B. tell him you regret you cannot help him because you are not sure who can give him the information
   C. advise him that the best way he can be sure of getting the information he wants is to write a letter to the agency
   D. get the phone number where he can be reached and tell him you will try to get the information he wants and will call him back later

28.____

29. Persons who have business with an agency often complain about the *red tape* which complicates or slows up what they are trying to accomplish.
   As a supervisor of a unit which deals with the public, the LEAST effective of the following actions which you could take to counteract this feeling on the part of a person who has business with your office is to

   A. assure him that your office will make every effort to take care of his matter as fast as possible
   B. tell him that because of the volume of work in your agency he must be patient with *red tape*

29.____

C. give him a reasonable date by which action on the matter he is concerned about will be completed and tell him to call you if he hasn't heard by then
D. give him an understanding of why the procedures he must comply with are necessary

30. If a receptionist is sorting letters at her desk and a caller appears to make an inquiry, the receptionist should

   A. ask the caller to have a seat and wait
   B. speak to the caller while continuing the sorting, looking up occasionally
   C. stop what she is doing and give undivided attention to the caller
   D. continue with the sorting until a logical break in the work is reached, then answer any inquiries

31. To avoid cutting off parts of letters when using an automatic letter opener, it is BEST to

   A. arrange all of the letters so that the addresses are right side up
   B. hold the envelopes up to the light to make sure their contents have not settled to the side that is to be opened
   C. strike the envelopes against a table or desk top several times so that the contents of all the envelopes settle to one side
   D. check the enclosures periodically to make sure that the machine has not been cutting into them

32. Requests to repair office equipment which appears to be unsafe should be given priority MAINLY because if repairs are delayed

   A. there may be injuries to staff
   B. there may be further deterioration of the equipment
   C. work flow may be interrupted
   D. the cost of repair may increase

33. Of the following types of documents, it is MOST important to retain and file

   A. working drafts of reports that have been submitted in final form
   B. copies of letters of good will which conveyed a message that could not be handled by phone
   C. interoffice orders for materials which have been received and verified
   D. interoffice memoranda regarding the routing of standard forms

34. Of the following, the BEST reason for discarding certain material from office files would be that the

   A. files are crowded
   B. material in the files is old
   C. material duplicates information obtainable from other sources in the files
   D. material is referred to most often by employees in an adjoining office

35. Of the following, the BEST reason for setting up a partitioned work area for the typists in your office is that

   A. an uninterrupted flow of work among the typists will be possible
   B. complaints about ventilation and lighting will be reduced
   C. the first-line supervisor will have more direct control over the typists
   D. the noise of the typewriters will be less disturbing to other workers

36. Of the following, the MAIN factor contributing to the expense of maintaining an office procedure manual would be the

   A. infrequent use of the manual
   B. need to revise it regularly
   C. cost of looseleaf binders
   D. high cost of printing

37. From the viewpoint of use of a typewriter to fill in a form, the MOST important design factor to consider is

   A. standard spacing
   B. box headings
   C. serial numbering
   D. vertical guide lines

38. Out-of-date and seldom used records should be removed PERIODICALLY from the files because

   A. overall responsibility for records will be transferred to the person in charge of the central storage files
   B. duplicate copies of every record are not needed
   C. valuable filing space will be regained and the time needed to find a current record will be cut down
   D. worthwhile suggestions on improving the filing system will result whenever this is done

39. In a certain office, file folders are constantly being removed from the files for use by administrators. At the same time, new material is coming in to be filed in some of these folders.
   Of the following, the BEST way to avoid delays in filing of the new material and to keep track of the removed folders is to

   A. keep a sheet listing all folders removed from the file, who has them, and a follow-up date to check on their return; attach to this list new material received for filing
   B. put an *out* slip in the place of any file folder removed, telling what folder is missing, date removed, and who has it; file new material received at front of files
   C. put a temporary *out* folder in place of the one removed, giving title or subject, date removed, and who has it; put into this temporary folder any new material received
   D. keep a list of all folders removed and who has them; forward any new material received for filing while a folder is out to the person who has it

40. Folders labeled *Miscellaneous* should be used in an alphabetic filing system MAINLY to

   A. provide quick access to recent material
   B. avoid setting up individual folders for all infrequent correspondents
   C. provide temporary storage for less important documents
   D. temporarily hold papers which will not fit into already crowded individual folders

41. Suppose that one of the office machines in your unit is badly in need of replacement.
   Of the following, the MOST important reason for postponing immediate purchase of a new machine would be that

   A. a later model of the machine is expected on the market in a few months
   B. the new machine is more expensive than the old machine
   C. the operator of the present machine will have to be instructed by the manufacturer in the operation of the new machine
   D. the employee operating the old machine is not complaining

42. If the four steps listed below for processing records were given in logical sequence, the one that would be the THIRD step is:

    A. Coding the records, using a chart or classification system
    B. Inspecting the records to make sure they have been released for filing
    C. Preparing cross-reference sheets or cards
    D. Skimming the records to determine filing captions

43. The suggestion that memos or directives which circulate among subordinates be initialed by each employee is a

    A. *poor* one because, with modern copying machines, it should be possible to supply every subordinate with a copy of each message for his personal use
    B. *good* one because it relieves the supervisor of blame for the action of subordinates who have read and initialed the messages
    C. *poor* one because initialing the memo or directive is no guarantee that the subordinate has read the material
    D. *good* one because it can be used as a record by the supervisor to show that his subordinates have received the message and were responsible for reading it

44. Of the following, the MOST important reason for microfilming office records is to

    A. save storage space needed to keep records
    B. make it easier to get records when needed
    C. speed up the classification of information
    D. shorten the time which records must be kept

45. Your office filing cabinets have become so overcrowded that it is difficult to use the files. Of the following, the MOST desirable step for you to take FIRST to relieve this situation would be to

    A. assign your assistant to spend some time each day reviewing the material in the files and to give you his recommendations as to what material may be discarded
    B. discard all material which has been in the files more than a given number of years
    C. submit a request for additional filing cabinets in your next budget request
    D. transfer enough material to the central storage room of your agency to give you the amount of additional filing space needed

46. Of the following, the USUAL order of the subdivisions in a standard published report is:

    A. Table of contents, body of report, index, appendix
    B. Index, table of contents, body of report, appendix
    C. Index, body of report, table of contents, appendix
    D. Table of contents, body of report, appendix, index

47. The BEST type of pictorial illustration to show the approximate percentage breakdown of the titles of employees in a department would be the

    A. flow chart             B. bar graph
    C. organization chart     D. line graph

48. You are reviewing a draft, written by one of your subordinates, of a report that is to be distributed to every bureau and division of your department.
Which one of the following would be the LEAST desirable characteristic of such a report?

    A. It gives information, explanations, conclusions, and recommendations for which purpose it was written.
    B. There is sufficient objective data presented to substantiate the conclusions reached and the recommendations made by the writer.
    C. The writing style and opinions of the writer are persuasive enough to win over to its conclusions those who read the report, although little data is given in support.
    D. It will be understood easily by the people to whom it will be distributed.

49. According to accepted practice, a business letter is addressed to an organization but marked for the attention of a specific individual whenever the sender wants

    A. only the person to whose attention the letter is sent to read the letter
    B. the letter to be opened and taken care of by someone else in the organization of the person for whose attention it is marked is away
    C. a reply only from the specific individual
    D. to improve the appearance and balance of the letter in cases where the company address is a long one

50. Which one of the following would be an ACCEPTABLE way to end a business letter?

    A. Hoping you will find this information useful, I remain
    B. Yours for continuing service
    C. I hope this letter gives you the information you need
    D. Trusting this gives you the information you desire, I am

# KEY (CORRECT ANSWERS)

| | | | | |
|---|---|---|---|---|
| 1. A | 11. B | 21. C | 31. C | 41. A |
| 2. D | 12. D | 22. D | 32. A | 42. A |
| 3. A | 13. C | 23. B | 33. D | 43. D |
| 4. B | 14. B | 24. D | 34. C | 44. A |
| 5. C | 15. B | 25. A | 35. D | 45. A |
| 6. B | 16. C | 26. B | 36. B | 46. D |
| 7. D | 17. D | 27. C | 37. A | 47. B |
| 8. C | 18. A | 28. D | 38. C | 48. C |
| 9. A | 19. C | 29. B | 39. C | 49. B |
| 10. A | 20. B | 30. C | 40. B | 50. C |

# TEST 2

DIRECTIONS: Each question or incomplete statement is followed by several suggested answers or completions. Select the one that BEST answers the question or completes the statement. *PRINT THE LETTER OF THE CORRECT ANSWER IN THE SPACE AT THE RIGHT.*

1. You are replying to a letter from an individual who asks for a pamphlet put out by your agency. The pamphlet is out of print. A new pamphlet with a different title, but dealing with the same subject, is available.
Of the following, it would be BEST that your reply indicate that

    A. you cannot send him the pamphlet he requested because it is out of print
    B. the pamphlet he requested is out of print, but he may be able to find it in the public library
    C. the pamphlet he requested is out of print, but you are sending him a copy of your agency's new pamphlet on the same subject
    D. since the pamphlet he requested is out of print, you would advise him to ask his friends or business acquaintances if they have a copy of it

2. An angry citizen sends a letter to your agency claiming that your office sent him the wrong form and complaining about the general inefficiency of city workers. Upon checking, you find that an incorrect form was indeed sent to this person.
In reply, you should

    A. admit the error, apologize briefly, and enclose the correct form
    B. send the citizen the correct form with a transmittal letter stating only that the form is enclosed
    C. send him the correct form without any comment
    D. advise the citizen that mistakes happen in every large organization and that you are enclosing the correct form

3. It has been suggested that the language level of a letter of reply written by a government employee be geared no higher than the probable educational level of the person to whom the letter is written.
This suggestion is a

    A. *good* one because it is easier for anyone to write letters simply, and this will make for a better reply
    B. *poor* one because it is not possible to judge, from one letter, the exact educational level of the writer
    C. *good* one because it will contribute to the recipient's comprehension of the contents of the letter
    D. *poor* one because the language should be at the simplest possible level so that anyone who reads the letter can understand it

4. Suppose that a large bureau has 187 employees. On a particular day, approximately 14% of these employees are not available for work because of absences due to vacation, illness, or other reasons. Of the remaining employees, 1/7 are assigned to a special project while the balance are assigned to the normal work of the bureau.
The number of employees assigned to the normal work of the bureau on that day is

    A. 112    B. 124    C. 138    D. 142

5. Suppose that you are in charge of a typing pool of 8 typists. Two typists type at the rate of 38 words per minute; three type at the rate of 40 words per minute; three type at the rate of 42 words per minute. The average typewritten page consists of 50 lines, 12 words per line. Each employee works from 9 to 5 with one hour off for lunch.
The total number of pages typed by this pool in one day is, on the average, CLOSEST to _____ pages.

   A. 205    B. 225    C. 250    D. 275

6. Suppose that part-time workers are paid $14.40 an hour, prorated to the nearest half hour, with pay guaranteed for a minimum of four hours if services are required for less than four hours. In one operation, part-time workers signed the time sheet as follows:

   | Worker | In | Out |
   |--------|----|----|
   | A | 8:00 A.M. | 11:35 A.M. |
   | B | 8:30 A.M. | 3:20 P.M. |
   | C | 7:55 A.M. | 11:00 A.M. |
   | D | 8:30 A.M. | 2:25 P.M. |

   How much would total payment to these part-time workers amount to for this operation, assuming that those who stayed after 12 Noon were not paid for one hour which they took off for lunch?

   A. $268.80    B. $273.60    C. $284.40    D. $297.60

7. He wanted to *ascertain* the facts before arriving at a conclusion.
   The word *ascertain* means MOST NEARLY

   A. disprove    B. determine    C. convert    D. provide

8. Did the supervisor *assent* to her request for annual leave? The word *assent* means MOST NEARLY

   A. allude    B. protest    C. agree    D. refer

9. The new worker was fearful that the others would *rebuff* her.
   The word *rebuff* means MOST NEARLY

   A. ignore    B. forget    C. copy    D. snub

10. The supervisor of that office does not *condone* lateness. The word *condone* means MOST NEARLY

    A. mind    B. excuse    C. punish    D. remember

11. Each employee was instructed to be as *concise* as possible when preparing a report.
    The word *concise* means MOST NEARLY

    A. exact    B. sincere    C. flexible    D. brief

Questions 12-21.

DIRECTIONS: Below are 10 sentences numbered 12 to 21. Some of the sentences contain an error in spelling, word usage, or sentence structure, or punctuation. Some sentences are correct as they stand, although there may be other correct ways of expressing the same thought. All incorrect sentences contain only one error. Mark your answer to each question as follows:

A. if the sentence has an error in spelling
B. if the sentence has an error in punctuation or capitalization
C. if the sentence has an error in word usage or sentence structure
D. if the sentence is correct

12. Because the chairman failed to keep the participants from wandering off into irrelevant discussions, it was impossible to reach a consensus before the meeting was adjourned.   12._____

13. Certain employers have an unwritten rule that any applicant, who is over 55 years of age, is automatically excluded from consideration for any position whatsoever.   13._____

14. If the proposal to build schools in some new apartment buildings were to be accepted by the builders, one of the advantages that could be expected to result would be better communication between teachers and parents of schoolchildren.   14._____

15. In this instance, the manufacturer's violation of the law against deseptive packaging was discernible only to an experienced inspector.   15._____

16. The tenants' anger stemmed from the president's going to Washington to testify without consulting them first.   16._____

17. Did the president of this eminent banking company say; "We intend to hire and train a number of these disad-vantaged youths?"   17._____

18. In addition, today's confidential secretary must be knowledgable in many different areas: for example, she must know modern techniques for making travel arrangements for the executive.   18._____

19. To avoid further disruption of work in the offices, the protesters were forbidden from entering the building unless they had special passes.   19._____

20. A valuable secondary result of our training conferences is the opportunities afforded for management to observe the reactions of the participants.   20._____

21. Of the two proposals submitted by the committee, the first one is the best.   21._____

Questions 22-26.

DIRECTIONS: In Questions 22 through 26, choose the sentence which is BEST from the point of view of English usage suitable for a business letter or report.

22.  A. It is the opinion of the Commissioners that programs which include the construction of cut-rate municipal garages in the central business district is inadvisable.   22._____
     B. Having reviewed the material submitted, the program for putting up cut-rate garages in the central business district seemed likely to cause traffic congestion.
     C. The Commissioners believe that putting up cut-rate municipal garages in the central business district is inadvisable.
     D. Making an effort to facilitate the cleaning of streets in the central business district, the building of cut-rate municipal garages presents the problem that it would encourage more motorists to come into the central city.

23.
  A. This letter, together with the reports, are to be sent to the principal.
  B. The reports, together with this letter, is to be sent to the principal.
  C. The reports and this letter is to be sent to the principal.
  D. This letter, together with the reports, is to be sent to the principal.

24.
  A. Each employee has to decide for themselves whether to take the examination.
  B. Each of the employees has to decide for himself whether to take the examination.
  C. Each of the employees has to decide for themselves whether to take the examination.
  D. Each of the employees have to decide for himself whether to take the examination.

25.
  A. The reason a new schedule is being prepared is that there has been a change in priorities.
  B. Because there has been a change in priorities is the reason why a new schedule is being made up.
  C. The reason why a new schedule is being made up is because there has been a change in priorities.
  D. Because of a change in priorities is the reason why a new schedule is being prepared.

26.
  A. The changes in procedure had an unfavorable affect upon the output of the unit.
  B. The increased output of the unit was largely due to the affect of the procedural changes.
  C. The changes in procedure had the effect of increasing the output of the unit.
  D. The increased output of the unit from the procedural changes were the effect.

Questions 27-33.

DIRECTIONS: Questions 27 through 33 are to be answered SOLELY on the basis of the information in the following extract, which is from a report prepared for Department X, which outlines the procedure to be followed in the case of transfers of employees.

*Every transfer, regardless of the reason therefor, requires completion of the record of transfer, Form DT 411. To denote consent to the transfer, DT 411 should contain the signatures of the transferee and the personnel officer(s) concerned, except that, in the case of an involuntary transfer, the signatures of the transferee's present and prospective supervisors shall be entered in Boxes 8A and 8B, respectively, since the transferee does not consent. Only a permanent employee may request a transfer; in such cases, the employee's attendance record shall be duly considered with regard to absences, latenesses, and accrued overtime balances. In the case of an inter-district transfer, the employee's attendance record must be included in Section 8A of the transfer request, Form DT 410, by the personnel officer of the district from which the transfer is requested. The personnel officer of the district to which the employee requested transfer may refuse to accept accrued overtime balances in excess of ten days.*

*An employee on probation shall be eligible for transfer. If such employee is involuntarily transferred, he shall be credited for the period of time already served on probation. However, if such transfer is voluntary, the employee shall be required to serve the entire period of his probation in the new position. An employee who has occurred a disability which prevents him from performing his normal duties may be transferred during the period of such disability to other appropriate duties. A disability transfer requires the completion of either Form DT414 if the disability is job-connected, or Form DT 415 if it is not a job-connected disability. In either case, the personnel officer of the district from which the transfer is made signs in Box 6A of the first two copies and the personnel officer of the district to which the transfer is made signs in Box 6B of the last two copies; or, in the case of an intra-district disability transfer, the personnel officer must sign in Box 6A of the first two copies and Box 6B of the last two copies*

27. When a personnel officer consents to an employee's request for transfer from his district, this procedure requires that the personnel officer sign Form(s)

    A. DT 411
    B. DT 410 and DT 411
    C. DT 411 and either Form DT 414 or DT 415
    D. DT 410 and DT 411, and either Form DT 414 or DT 415

28. With respect to the time record of an employee transferred against his wishes during his probationary period, this procedure requires that

    A. he serve the entire period of his probation in his present office
    B. he lose his accrued overtime balance
    C. his attendance record be considered with regard to absences and latenesses
    D. he be given credit for the period of time he has already served on probation

29. Assume you are a supervisor and an employee must be transferred into your office against his wishes.
    According to this procedure, the box you must sign on the record of transfer is

    A. 6A        B. 8A        C. 6B        D. 8B

30. Under this procedure, in the case of a disability transfer, when must Box 6A on Forms DT 414 and DT 415 be signed by the personnel officer of the district to which the transfer is being made?

    A. In all cases when either Form DT 414 or Form DT 415 is used
    B. In all cases when Form DT 414 is used and only under certain circumstances when Form DT 415 is used
    C. In all cases when Form DT 415 is used and only under certain circumstances when Form DT 414 is used
    D. Only under certain circumstances when either Form DT 414 or Form DT 415 is used

31. From the above passage, it may be inferred MOST correctly that the number of copies of Form DT 414 is

    A. no more than 2
    B. at least 3
    C. at least 5
    D. more than the number of copies of Form DT 415

32. A change in punctuation and capitalization only which would change one sentence into two and possibly contribute to somewhat greater ease of reading of this report extract would be MOST appropriate in the _____ sentence, _____ paragraph.

   A. 2nd; 1st
   B. 3rd; 1st
   C. next to the last; 2nd
   D. 2nd; 2nd

33. In the second paragraph, a word that is INCORRECTLY used is _____ in the _____ sentence.

   A. *shall;* 1st
   B. *voluntary;* 3rd
   C. *occurred;* 4th
   D. *intra-district;* last

Questions 34-38.

DIRECTIONS: Questions 34 through 38 are to be answered SOLELY on the basis of the information contained in the following passage.

*Positive discipline minimizes the amount of personal supervision required and aids in the maintenance of standards. When a new employee has been properly introduced and carefully instructed, when he has come to know the supervisor and has confidence in the supervisor's ability to take care of him, when he willingly cooperates with the supervisor, that employee has been under positive discipline and can be put on his own to produce the quantity and quality of work desired. Negative discipline, the fear of transfer to a less desirable location, for example, to a limited extent may restrain certain individuals from overt violation of rules and regulations governing attendance and conduct which in governmental agencies are usually on at least an agency-wide basis. Negative discipline may prompt employees to perform according to certain rules to avoid a penalty such as, for example, docking for tardiness.*

34. According to the above passage, it is reasonable to assume that in the area of discipline, the first-line supervisor in a governmental agency has GREATER scope for action in

   A. *positive* discipline because negative discipline is largely taken care of by agency rules and regulations
   B. *negative* discipline because rules and procedures are already fixed and the supervisor can rely on them
   C. *positive* discipline because the supervisor is in a position to recommend transfers
   D. *negative* discipline because positive discipline is reserved for people on a higher supervisory level

35. In order to maintain positive discipline of employees under his supervision, it is MOST important for a supervisor to

   A. assure each employee that he has nothing to worry about
   B. insist at the outset on complete cooperation from employees
   C. be sure that each employee is well trained in his job
   D. inform new employees of the penalties for not meeting standards

36. According to the above passage, a feature of negative discipline is that it

   A. may lower employee morale
   B. may restrain employees from disobeying the rules
   C. censures equal treatment of employees
   D. tends to create standards for quality of work

37. A REASONABLE conclusion based on the above passage is that positive discipline benefits a supervisor because

   A. he can turn over orientation and supervision of a new employee to one of his subordinates
   B. subordinates learn to cooperate with one another when working on an assignment
   C. it is easier to administer
   D. it cuts down, in the long run, on the amount of time the supervisor needs to spend on direct supervision

38. Based on the above passage, it is REASONABLE to assume that an important difference between positive discipline and negative discipline is that positive discipline

   A. is concerned with the quality of work and negative discipline with the quantity of work
   B. leads to a more desirable basis for motivation of the employee
   C. is more likely to be concerned with agency rules and regulations
   D. uses fear while negative discipline uses penalties to prod employees to adequate performance

Questions 39-50.

DIRECTIONS: Questions 39 through 50 are to be answered on the basis of the information given in the graph and chart below.

## ENROLLMENT IN POSTGRADUATE STUDIES

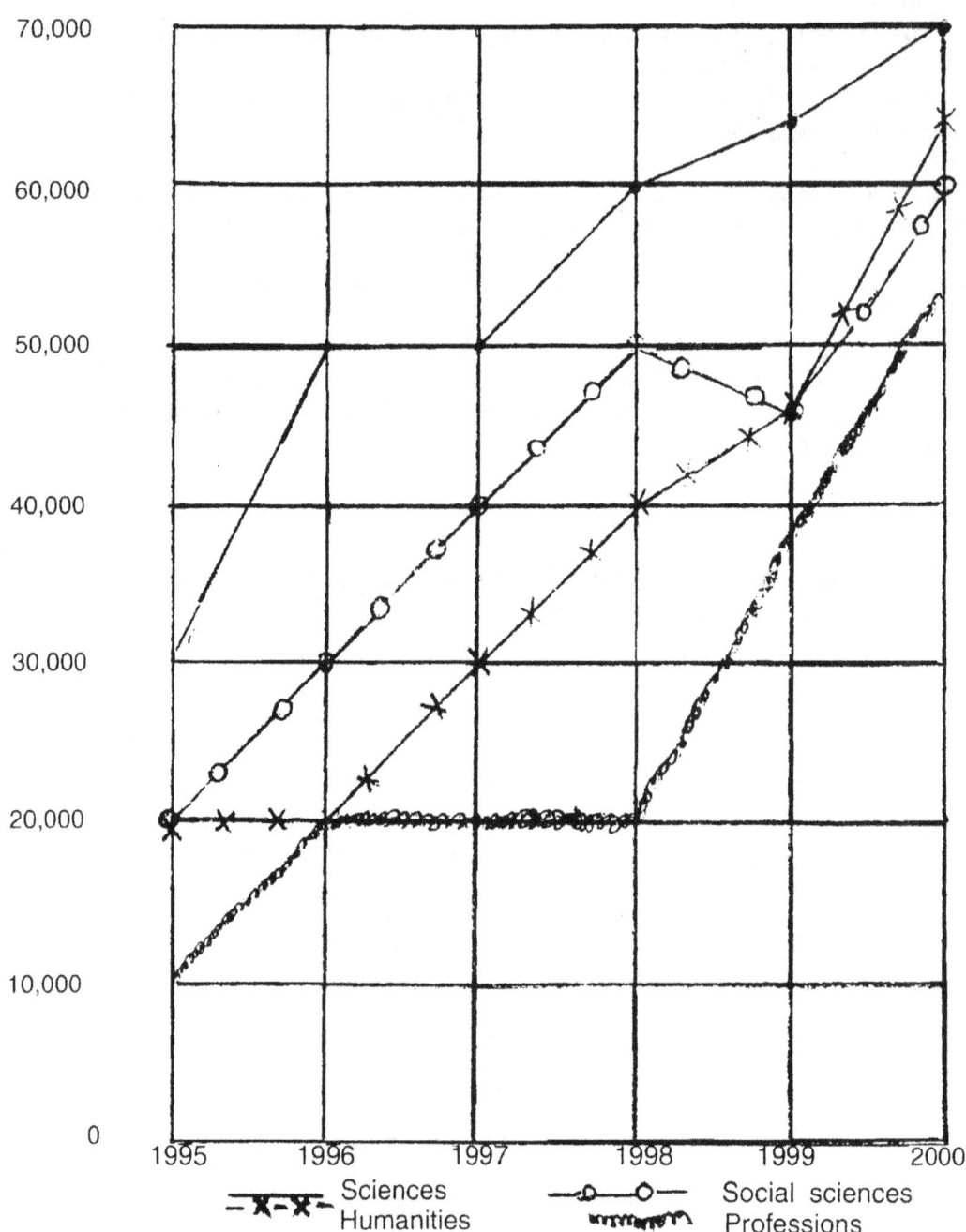

## ENROLLMENT IN POSTGRADUATE STUDIES

| Fields | Subdivisions | 1999 | 2000 |
|---|---|---|---|
| Sciences | Math | 10,000 | 12,000 |
| | Physical science | 22,000 | 24,000 |
| | Behavioral science | 32,000 | 35,000 |
| Humanities | Literature | 26,000 | 34,000 |
| | Philosophy | 6,000 | 8,000 |
| | Religion | 4,000 | 6,000 |
| | Arts | 10,000 | 16,000 |
| Social sciences | History | 36,000 | 46,000 |
| | Sociology | 8,000 | 14,000 |
| Professions | Law | 2,000 | 2,000 |
| | Medicine | 6,000 | 8,000 |
| | Business | 30,000 | 44,000 |

39. The number of students enrolled in the social sciences and in the humanities was the same in _____ and _____.

    A. 1997; 1999
    B. 1995; 1999
    C. 1999; 2000
    D. 1996; 1999

39.____

40. A comparison of the enrollment of students in the various postgraduate studies shows that in every year from 1995 through 2000, there were more students enrolled in the _____ than in the _____.

    A. professions; sciences
    B. humanities; professions
    C. social sciences; professions
    D. humanities; sciences

40.____

41. The number of students enrolled in the humanities was GREATER than the number of students enrolled in the professions by the same amount in _____ of the years.

    A. two    B. three    C. four    D. five

41.____

42. The one field of postgraduate study to show a decrease in enrollment in one year compared to the year immediately preceding is

    A. humanities
    B. sciences
    C. professions
    D. social sciences

42.____

43. If the proportion of arts students to all humanities students was the same in 1997 as in 2000, then the number of arts students in 1997 was

    A. 7,500    B. 13,000    C. 15,000    D. 5,000

43.____

44. In which field of postgraduate study did enrollment INCREASE by 20 percent from 1997 to 1998?

    A. Humanities
    B. Professions
    C. Sciences
    D. Social sciences

44.____

45. The GREATEST increase in overall enrollment took place between

    A. 1995 and 1996
    B. 1997 and 1998
    C. 1998 and 1999
    D. 1999 and 2000

45.____

46. Between 1997 and 2000, the combined enrollment of the sciences and social sciences increased by

    A. 40,000    B. 48,000    C. 50,000    D. 54,000

47. If the enrollment in the social sciences had decreased from 1999 to 2000 at the same rate as from 1998 to 1999, then the social science enrollment in 2000 would have differed from the humanities enrollment in 2000 MOST NEARLY by

    A. 6,000    B. 8,000    C. 12,000    D. 22,000

48. In the humanities, the GREATEST percentage increase in enrollment from 1999 to 2000 was in

    A. literature           B. philosophy
    C. religion             D. arts

49. If the proportion of behavioral science students to the total number of students in the sciences was the same in 1996 as in 1999, then the increase in behavioral science enrollment from 1996 to 2000 was

    A. 5,000    B. 7,000    C. 10,000    D. 14,000

50. If enrollment in the professions increased at the same rate from 2000 to 2001 as from 1999 to 2000, the enrollment in the professions in 2001 would be MOST NEARLY

    A. 85,000    B. 75,000    C. 60,000    D. 55,000

## KEY (CORRECT ANSWERS)

| | | | | |
|---|---|---|---|---|
| 1. C | 11. D | 21. C | 31. B | 41. B |
| 2. A | 12. C | 22. C | 32. B | 42. D |
| 3. C | 13. B | 23. D | 33. C | 43. A |
| 4. C | 14. D | 24. B | 34. A | 44. C |
| 5. B | 15. A | 25. A | 35. C | 45. D |
| 6. B | 16. D | 26. C | 36. B | 46. A |
| 7. B | 17. B | 27. A | 37. D | 47. D |
| 8. C | 18. A | 28. D | 38. B | 48. D |
| 9. D | 19. C | 29. D | 39. B | 49. C |
| 10. B | 20. D | 30. D | 40. C | 50. B |

# EXAMINATION SECTION
## TEST 1

DIRECTIONS: Each question or incomplete statement is followed by several suggested answers or completions. Select the one that BEST answers the question or completes the statement. *PRINT THE LETTER OF THE CORRECT ANSWER IN THE SPACE AT THE RIGHT.*

1. Assume that you have been placed in charge of a unit where the quality of the work performed is poor. You plan to discuss the matter of improving the quality of the work at a staff meeting of the unit.
   Of the following courses of action which you might take at this meeting, the BEST one is to

   A. describe a few cases of exceptionally poor work performance, then have the employees performing this work explain why their work was done poorly
   B. inform the staff that you will be criticized by your own superior if the quality of the unit's work does not improve, then discuss, in general terms, the problem of improving the quality of the work
   C. discuss the problem of improving the quality of the unit's work, then call upon each employee by name for his suggestions for improving the work he performs
   D. present the problem to the staff, then indicate and discuss specific methods for improving the quality of the work

   1.____

2. The competent supervisor realizes that procedures which have been followed for a considerable length of time can frequently be reconstructed and improved. He knows that charts, or diagrams, are often of inestimable value in bringing out forcibly and visibly the outstanding defects in a procedure.
   Of the following types of charts, the one which would ordinarily be of MOST value to a supervisor making a study of the clerical procedures in his unit is a(n) _____ chart.

   A. organization          B. circle or pie
   C. flow or process       D. bar or column

   2.____

3. Assume that you have received a letter requesting certain information. You know that the time required to obtain this information may extend from several days to several weeks. You may take either of two courses of action in replying to this letter. You may withhold your reply until the requested information has been obtained, or you may acknowledge immediately the receipt of the letter and send the information when it has been obtained.
   For you to take the FIRST rather than the second course of action would be

   A. *desirable;* you will thus reduce the amount of correspondence
   B. *undesirable;* a person requesting information should be informed as soon as possible that his request has been received and that it will be attended to
   C. *desirable;* if the information should be obtained within a few days, it would appear wasteful and ridiculous to have sent two letters in so short a period of time
   D. *undesirable;* some letters do not require any response at all

   3.____

4. In an office where applicants for employment are interviewed, it is MOST desirable that the office furniture be arranged so that the

   4.____

A. person being interviewed is seated where he can see the notes being recorded by the interviewer
B. person being interviewed cannot be seen by other interviewers
C. conversation between the interviewer and the person being interviewed cannot be overheard by others
D. interviewer faces the person being interviewed but has his back to others who are waiting to be interviewed

5. Of the following factors, the one which is of LEAST importance in determining the number of subordinates that an individual should be assigned to supervise is the    5.____

    A. nature of the work being supervised
    B. qualifications of the individual as a supervisor
    C. capabilities of the subordinates
    D. lines of promotion for the subordinates

6. Suppose that a large number of semi-literate residents of this city have been requesting the assistance of your department. You are asked to prepare a form which these applicants will be required to fill out before their requests will be considered.    6.____
In view of these facts, the one of the following factors to which you should give the GREATEST amount of consideration in preparing this form is the

    A. size of the form
    B. sequence of the information asked for on the form
    C. level of difficulty of the language used in the form
    D. number of times which the form will have to be reviewed

7. Suppose that the employees in your unit are required to perform a great deal of computation involving a large amount of addition and subtraction. Since accuracy is more important than speed in the work of your unit, employees are required to check all the figures used in the computations before turning in their work.    7.____
Of the following machines, the one which would be MOST practicable for the work of your unit is a

    A. listing adding machine
    B. comptometer
    C. punch card tabulating machine
    D. billing machine

8. A supervisor is frequently required to prepare various types of written reports.    8.____
The one of the following features which is LEAST desirable in a lengthy report is that

    A. the style of writing should be readable, interesting, and impersonal; it should not be too scholarly, nor make use of involved sentence structure
    B. recommendations and conclusions resulting from the facts incorporated in the body of the report must appear only at the end of the report so that readers can follow the writer's line of reasoning
    C. in determining the extent of technical detail and terminology to be used in the presentation of supporting data, such as charts, tables, graphs, case examples, etc., the technical knowledge of the prospective reader or readers should be kept in mind

D. the body of the report should mention all the pertinent facts and develop the writer's ideas in such a way that the recommendations will be a logical outgrowth of the arguments presented

9. Your department plans to install a suggestion box into which its employees may place their suggestions for improving departmental policies and procedures. As a reward for submitting a practical suggestion, additional vacation allowance will be granted to the author of each suggestion. The amount of additional vacation allowed will depend upon the value of the suggestion, as determined by a panel of judges.
To institute a procedure whereby the identity of the author will be concealed from the judges by the secretary of the department until the value of the suggestion has been determined would be

   A. *undesirable;* many employees will refrain from making suggestions if they know that the suggestion will be judged anonymously
   B. *desirable;* many employees will be encouraged to be frank and outspoken in their criticism; such a straightforward criticism is of more value to a department than suggestions for improvement
   C. *undesirable;* if a suggestion is not clearly presented, the judges will be unable to obtain clarifying information from the author
   D. *desirable;* it provides for strict impartiality in judging the worth of an idea and may thus encourage employee participation in the plan

10. The one of the following which should be considered the LEAST important objective of the city's service rating system is to

    A. rate the employees on the basis of their potential abilities
    B. establish a basis for assigning employees to special types of work
    C. provide a means for recognizing superior work performance
    D. reveal the need for training as well as the effectiveness of a training program

11. Instead of directing his attention solely toward devising new systems and procedures for performing established clerical operations, the alert office manager carefully studies these operations with a view to determining the value that accrues to the organization from their performance.
Of the following, the MOST valid implication of this statement is that

    A. established clerical operations may not be of sufficient benefit to the organization to justify their continuance
    B. devising new systems of performing clerical operations is no longer the function of the office manager
    C. the performance of established clerical operations usually brings little or no direct benefit to an organization
    D. devising better ways of performing a necessary clerical task may be of no value to an organization

12. A budget is a plan whereby a goal is set for future operations. It affords a medium for comparing actual expenditures with planned expenditures.
The one of the following which is the MOST accurate statement on the basis of this statement is that

    A. the budget serves as an accurate measure of past as well as future expenditures
    B. the budget presents an estimate of expenditures to be made in the future

C. budget estimates should be based upon past budget requirements
D. planned expenditures usually fall short of actual expenditures

13. Suppose that you are placed in charge of a unit in your department. You find that many of the employees have been disregarding the staff regulation requiring employees to be at their desks at 9:05 A.M.
Of the following, the LEAST desirable course of action for you to take would be to

   A. call a meeting of the staff and explain why it is essential that all employees be at their desks at 9:05 A.M.
   B. post conspicuously on the bulletin board a notice calling the employees' attention to the frequent violation of this regulation and requesting them to observe this regulation
   C. recommend an above-average service rating for all employees who consistently comply with this regulation
   D. summon the offenders and explain to them how their violation of this regulation results in decreasing the efficiency of the unit

14. Suppose that certain office responsibilities require you to be frequently absent from the unit you supervise. You have, therefore, decided to designate one of your staff members to act as unit head in your absence.
Of the following factors, the one which is MOST important in selecting the employee best fitted for this assignment is his

   A. manner and personal appearance
   B. estimated ability to perform work of a supervisory nature
   C. ability to perform his present duties
   D. relative seniority in the service

15. One of the assignments in the unit you supervise is the checking of a list of 500 unalphabetized names against an alphabetical 5x8 card index containing several thousand names. The clerk performing this task is to make sure that there is a card in the file for each name on the list.
The one of the following which you should suggest as the BEST procedure for the clerk to follow is for him to

   A. rewrite the names on the list in alphabetical order, look for the corresponding card in the file, and place a check mark next to each name on the list for which he finds a card
   B. take each name on the list in turn, look for the corresponding card in the file, and place a check mark in the corner of each card he finds
   C. go through all the cards in the file in consecutive order and place a check mark next to each name on the list for which he finds a card
   D. take each name on the list in turn, look for the corresponding card in the file, and place a check mark next to each name for which he finds a card

16. Suppose that you are in charge of a unit which maintains a rather intricate filing system. A new file clerk has been added to your staff.
Of the following assignments that may be given to this clerk, the one which requires the LEAST amount of knowledge of the filing system is

   A. placing material in the files
   B. removing papers from the files

C. classifying and coding material for filing
D. keeping a record of material taken from, and returned to, the files

17. In undertaking to improve the method of performing a certain job or operation, the new office manager should FIRST ascertain the

   A. present method of performing the job
   B. purpose of the job
   C. number and titles of employees assigned to the job
   D. methods used by other agencies to perform the same kind of job

18. The proofreading of a large number of reports has been assigned to two clerks. These clerks have been instructed to indicate all necessary corrections on a slip of paper, attach this correction slip to the reports, and send them to the typist for correction.
Of the following additional steps that might be taken before sending the reports to the typist, the BEST one is that the

   A. clerks should proofread each report in its entirety after the corrections have been made on it
   B. typist should make the necessary corrections and return the correction slip and the corrected reports to the clerks; the clerks should then examine the reports to see that all the requested corrections have been made properly
   C. typist should make the necessary corrections, placing a check mark opposite each correction noted on the correction slip; she should then review the correction slip to make sure that no correction has been omitted
   D. typist should make the necessary corrections, place a check mark opposite each correction noted on the correction slip, and return the reports and the correction slip to the clerks; the clerks should then review the correction slip to make sure that a check mark has been placed opposite each item on the correction slip

19. Suppose you are the supervisor of a unit in a city department. You notice that a clerk with long service in the department is arguing with a recently appointed clerk regarding the procedure to be followed in performing a certain task. Each is convinced he is right. The argument is disturbing the other employees.
Of the following, the BEST action for you to take in dealing with this problem is to

   A. call the clerks to your desk, discuss the matter with them, and then state which procedure is the correct one
   B. support the employee with the longer service, for to do otherwise will impair the morale of the office
   C. call the clerks to your desk and tell them to settle their differences without disturbing the others
   D. order the clerks to discontinue their argument immediately and to bring the matter up at the next staff conference, where the staff will determine which procedure is the correct one

20. Assume that you have devised a new procedure which you expected would result in a substantial reduction in the amount of paper used in performing the work of the unit you supervise. After trying out this new procedure in your unit for several weeks, you find that the quantity of paper saved is considerably less than you anticipated.
Of the following, the BEST action for you to take first is to

A. inform your staff that they are probably using paper unnecessarily and that in view of the current paper shortage, you expect them to conserve paper as much as possible
B. suspend the use of this new procedure until you can discover why it has not worked out as you anticipated
C. invite your subordinates to submit suggestions as to how the procedure may be improved
D. analyze the various processes involved in the new procedure to determine whether there are any factors which you may have overlooked

21. Assume that you are the head of the bureau of information in a city department. You are faced with the problem of replacing the clerk assigned to the information desk.
Of the following available employees, the one who should be given the assignment is

A. John Jones, a new clerk who specialized in English at college and recently received a Master of Arts degree; at present, he has no permanent assignment
B. Mary Smith, an excellent stenographer who has had much experience as secretary to one of the bureau heads; she is intelligent, pleasant in manner, and learns quickly
C. Richard Roe, a clerk who has been rated as *tactful, dependable,* and *resourceful* by the various bureau heads who have prepared his service rating reports during the four years that he has been in the department
D. Jane Doe, who is a diligent typist when she works alone but who disturbs the other typists by her constant stream of chatter when she works near them

22. The one of the following which is the MOST accurate statement regarding routine operations in an office is that

A. routine assignments should not last more than two or three days each week
B. methods for performing routine work should be standardized as much as is practicable
C. routine work performed by one employee should be checked by another employee
D. changes in the procedures of a unit should not affect the existing routine operations of the unit

23. Modern management realizes the importance of sound personnel practices in business administration. It has found that production is largely dependent upon the effective utilization of an employee's interests, capabilities, and skills.
Of the following, the MOST logical implication of the above statement is that

A. there should be one bureau in each business organization to take charge of both production and personnel administration
B. production cannot be increased without the utilization of a sound personnel policy
C. production will increase if the number of persons assigned to work in a business organization is increased
D. maximum efficiency in an organization cannot be achieved without proper placement of employees

24. In a city agency, 80 percent of the total number of employees are more than 25 years of age and 65 percent of the total number of employees are high school graduates.
The SMALLEST possible percent of employees who are both high school graduates and more than 25 years of age is

   A.  35%   B.  45%   C.  55%   D.  65%

25. Two clerical units, X and Y, each having a different number of clerks, are assigned to file registration cards. It takes Unit X, which contains 8 clerks, 21 days to file the same number of cards that Unit Y can file in 28 days. It is also a fact that Unit X can file 174,528 cards in 72 days.
Assuming that all the clerks in both units work at the same rate of speed, the number of cards which can be filed by Unit Y in 144 days, if 4 more clerks are added to the staff of Unit Y, is MOST NEARLY

   A.  349,000   B.  436,000   C.  523,000   D.  669,000

24.\_\_\_\_
25.\_\_\_\_

# KEY (CORRECT ANSWERS)

1. D
2. C
3. B
4. C
5. D

6. C
7. A
8. B
9. D
10. A

11. A
12. B
13. C
14. B
15. D

16. D
17. B
18. B
19. A
20. D

21. C
22. B
23. D
24. B
25. B

# TEST 2

DIRECTIONS: Each question or incomplete statement is followed by several suggested answers or completions. Select the one that BEST answers the question or completes the statement. *PRINT THE LETTER OF THE CORRECT ANSWER IN THE SPACE AT THE RIGHT.*

Questions 1-5.

DIRECTIONS: Each of Questions 1 through 5 consists of a statement containing five words in capital letters. One of these words in capital letters is not in keeping with the meaning which the statement is evidently intended to carry. The five words in capital letters in each statement are reprinted after the statement. In the space at the right, print the capital letter preceding the one of the five words which does MOST to spoil the true meaning of the statement.

1. Within each major DIVISION in a properly set up public or private organization, provision is made so that each NECESSARY activity is CARED for and lines of AUTHORITY and responsibility are clear-cut and INFINITE.

    A. Division  B. Necessary  C. Cared
    D. Authority  E. Infinite

    1._____

2. In public service, the scale of salaries paid must be INCIDENTAL to the services rendered, with due CONSIDERATION for the attraction of the desired MANPOWER and for the MAINTENANCE of a standard of living COMMENSURATE with the work to be performed.

    A. Incidental  B. Consideration  C. Manpower
    D. Maintenance  E. Commensurate

    2._____

3. An understanding of the AIMS of an organization by the staff will AID greatly in increasing the DEMAND of the correspondence work of the office, and will to a large extent DETERMINE the NATURE of the correspondence.

    A. Aims  B. Aid  C. Demand
    D. Determine  E. Nature

    3._____

4. BECAUSE the Civil Service Commission strongly feels that the MERIT system is a key factor in the MAINTENANCE of democratic government, it has adopted as one of its major DEFENSES the progressive democratization of its own PROCEDURES in dealing with candidates for positions in the public service.

    A. Because  B. Merit  C. Maintenance
    D. Defenses  E. Procedures

    4._____

5. Retirement and pensions systems are ESSENTIAL not only to provide employees with a means of support in the future, but also to prevent longevity and CHARITABLE considerations from UPSETTING the PROMOTIONAL opportunities for RETIRED members of the career service.

    A. Essential  B. Charitable  C. Upsetting
    D. Promotional  E. Retired

    5._____

90

6. Assume that two machines, each costing $5900, were purchased for your office. Each machine requires the services of an operator at a salary of $800 per month. These machines are to replace six clerks, two of whom earn $620 per month each, and four of whom earn $680 per month each.
   The number of months it will take for the cost of the machines to be made up from the savings in salaries is

   A. less than four months
   B. four months
   C. five months
   D. more than five months

7. Suppose that the amount of stationery used by your department in August decreased by 16% as compared with the amount used in July, and that the amount used in September increased by 25% as compared with the amount used in August.
   The amount of stationery used in September as compared with the amount used in July is

   A. greater by 5 percent
   B. less by 5 percent
   C. greater by 9 percent
   D. the same

8. This letter appears to have been written by some *indigent* person.
   The word *indigent,* as used in this sentence, means MOST NEARLY

   A. foreign-born
   B. needy
   C. uneducated
   D. angry

9. The conference began under *auspicious* circumstances.
   The word *auspicious,* as used in this sentence, means MOST NEARLY

   A. favorable
   B. chaotic
   C. questionable
   D. threatening

10. An *inordinate* amount of work was assigned to the newly appointed clerk.
    The word *inordinate,* as used in this sentence, means MOST NEARLY

    A. unanticipated
    B. adequate
    C. inexcusable
    D. excessive

11. The report which was obtained *surreptitiously* was very detailed and fully documented.
    The word *surreptitiously,* as used in this sentence, means MOST NEARLY

    A. stealthily
    B. a short time ago
    C. with great difficulty
    D. unexpectedly

12. We all knew him to be a man of *probity*.
    The word *probity,* as used in this sentence, means MOST NEARLY

    A. culture
    B. proven ability
    C. integrity
    D. dignity and poise

13. He made a *cursory* study of the problem before starting on the assignment.
    The word *cursory,* as used in this sentence, means MOST NEARLY

    A. detailed
    B. secret
    C. hasty
    D. methodical

14. The regulation had a *salutary* effect upon the members of the staff.
    The word *salutary,* as used in this sentence, means MOST NEARLY

| A. disturbing | B. beneficial |
| C. confusing | D. premature |

15. The *solicitous* supervisor discussed the employees' grievances with them.  15.____
    The word *solicitous*, as used in this sentence, means MOST NEARLY

    | A. concerned | B. impartial |
    | C. wise | D. experienced |

16. The employee *categorically* denied all responsibility for the error.  16.____
    The word *categorically*, as used in this sentence, means MOST NEARLY

    | A. repeatedly | B. loudly |
    | C. hesitantly | D. absolutely |

17. No *stipend* was specified in the agreement.  17.____
    The word *stipend*, as used in this sentence, means MOST NEARLY

    A. statement of working conditions
    B. receipt for payment
    C. compensation for services
    D. delivery date

18. A clerk who comes across the abbreviation *viz.* should know that it stands for  18.____

    | A. by way of | B. in the same place |
    | C. volume number | D. namely |

Questions 19-25.

DIRECTIONS:   Questions 19 through 25 are to be answered SOLELY on the basis of the following information.

Assume that the following regulations were established in your department to compute vacation allowances for services rendered by its employees during the period from June 1, 2014 through May 31, 2015. You are to determine the answer to each of the questions on the basis of these regulations.

VACATION REGULATIONS<br>(for the period June 1, 2014 - May 31, 2015)
The vacation allowance for this period is to be taken after May 31, 2015.

Standard Vacation Allowance
   Permanent per annum employees shall be granted 25 days vacation for a full year's service in such status. Employees who have served less than a full year in a permanent per annum status shall receive an allowance of 2 days for each month of such service.

   Per diem employees shall be granted 1 1/2 days vacation for each month of service in such status.

   Temporary employees shall be granted one day of vacation for each month of service in such status.

   No vacation credit shall accrue to employees for the time they are on leave of absence.

### Additional Allowance for Overtime
One day of vacation allowance shall be granted for each seven hours of accrued overtime. Where there is a balance of less than 7 hours of accrued overtime, one-half day of vacation shall be granted for each 3 1/2 hours of such overtime. In no case shall the additional vacation allowed for accrued overtime exceed 6 days.

### Deductions for Excessive Sick Leave
Sick leave allowance for all employees, regardless of length of service, shall be 12 days for the year. Sick leave taken in excess of 12 days shall be deducted from vacation allowance. Any unused sick leave balance will be canceled on May 31, 2015.

### Deductions for Excessive Lateness
Deductions for excessive lateness shall be made from vacation allowance in accordance with the following schedule:

| No. of Times Late | Deduction From Vacation Allowance |
|---|---|
| 0- 50 | no deduction |
| 51- 60 | 1/2 day |
| 61- 70 | 1 day |
| 71- 80 | 1 1/2 days |
| 81- 90 | 2 days |
| 91- 100 | 2 1/2 days |
| 101- 120 | 4 days |
| 121- 140 | 6 days |
| 141 or over | penalty to be determined by Secretary of Department |

### Unused Vacation
Unused vacation allowance earned during the previous year shall be added to the current vacation allowance, up to a maximum of twelve days.

19. Employee A served as a temporary employee from June 1, 2014 through January 31, 2015, and as a permanent per annum employee from February 1, 2015 through May 31, 2015. During the year, he accumulated 45 1/2 hours of overtime and was late 65 times. His vacation allowance should be _____ days.

    A. 16  B. 15  C. 21 1/2  D. 21

20. Employee B was newly appointed to the department as a per diem employee on September 1, 2014. During the year, he took 15 days of sick leave and was late 48 times. His vacation allowance should be _____ days.

    A. less than 10  B. 10 1/2
    C. 15           D. 12 1/2

21. Employee C has been a permanent per annum employee throughout the year. He had 15 days of vacation due him from the previous year. During the year, he was late 85 times, he took 10 days of sick leave, and he accumulated 38 1/2 hours of overtime. His vacation allowance should be _____ days.

    A. 38 1/2  B. 42 1/2
    C. 40 1/2  D. more than 43

22. Employee D was newly appointed to the department as a permanent per annum employee on July 1, 2014. He was on leave of absence from December 1, 2014 through February 28, 2015. During the year, he took 6 days of sick leave, he was late 70 times, and he accumulated 21 hours of overtime.
His vacation allowance should be _____ days.

    A.  24        B.  18        C.  17 1/2        D.  19 1/2

22._____

23. Employee E served as a per diem employee from June 1, 2014 through July 31, 2014, and as a permanent per annum employee from August 1, 2014 to May 31, 2015. He had 6 days of vacation due him from the previous year. During the year, he took 13 days of sick leave, he accumulated 70 days of overtime, and he was late 132 times.
His vacation allowance should be _____ days.

    A.  less than 29        B.  29
    C.  30               D.  more than 30

23._____

24. The MAXIMUM total vacation allowance which a permanent per annum employee can have due him by May 31, 2015 is _____ days.

    A.  43        B.  25        C.  31        D.  37

24._____

25. An employee who has served as a temporary employee for 6 months and as a permanent per annum employee for 6 months will earn exactly

    A.  two-thirds as much vacation as an employee who has been on a permanent per annum basis for the whole year
    B.  as much vacation as an employee who has been on a per diem basis for the whole year
    C.  as much vacation as an employee who has been on a per diem basis for 4 months and on a permanent per annum basis for 8 months
    D.  as much vacation as an employee who has been on a per diem basis for 8 months and on a permanent per annum basis for 4 months

25._____

# KEY (CORRECT ANSWERS)

1. E
2. A
3. C
4. D
5. E

6. C
7. A
8. B
9. A
10. D

11. A
12. C
13. C
14. B
15. A

16. D
17. C
18. D
19. D
20. B

21. C
22. B
23. A
24. A
25. B

# EXAMINATION SECTION
## TEST 1

DIRECTIONS: Each question or incomplete statement is followed by several suggested answers or completions. Select the one that BEST answers the question or completes the statement. *PRINT THE LETTER OF THE CORRECT ANSWER IN THE SPACE AT THE RIGHT.*

1. Miss Evans, secretary to a busy bureau chief, is authorized to answer those incoming letters which she feels competent to handle. One such letter is from a Mr. Brown who states that he is waiting for certain information requested by him three weeks ago. On looking through her files, Miss Evans finds a carbon copy of a two-page letter sent to Mr. Brown two weeks ago. This letter contains all the information requested.
   Of the following actions, the MOST appropriate one for Miss Evans to take is to

   A. make a duplicate copy of the original reply and send it together with an explanatory note to Mr. Brown
   B. inform Mr. Brown that the postal authorities are being requested to trace the original letter of reply which was sent to him two weeks ago
   C. send Mr. Brown the carbon copy of the original letter with a brief note calling his attention to the date on which the original letter had been sent
   D. retype the original letter, changing the date of the letter to the current date

2. *The secretary who is responsible for seeing that certain actions are taken by scheduled dates will find it desirable to maintain a follow-up system.*
   Of the following office tools, the one which is LEAST useful in maintaining such a follow-up system is a(n)

   A. tickler card file
   B. personal telephone number list
   C. standard desk calendar
   D. appointment book

3. Of the following, the chief objection to the establishment of a central transcribing unit is that where transcription work is centralized

   A. the training of new typists and stenographers is difficult and complicated
   B. distribution of work among the staff is generally unequal
   C. important work is likely to be delayed when a member of the staff is absent
   D. the possibility of leakage of information on confidential work is increased

4. A stenographer assigned as secretary to a bureau chief offers a suggestion for improving the working conditions in the bureau. This suggestion is rejected by the bureau chief because of several major defects.
   The MOST appropriate of the following actions for this stenographer to take is to

   A. continue to present this suggestion periodically until the bureau chief adopts it
   B. persuade other bureau employees to present the same suggestion so that the bureau chief may be led to believe that there is a very strong sentiment for the adoption of this suggestion
   C. acknowledge that there are objections to the adoption of the suggestion and continue making suggestions whenever such suggestions seem warranted
   D. revise the wording of the suggestion so that it appears to be a different one and present it later to the bureau chief as an entirely new suggestion

5. Of the following, the LEAST appropriate time to use onionskin paper is when

   A. several carbon copies must be typed at one time
   B. economy in using filing space is essential
   C. cost of postage is to be kept at a minimum
   D. paper possessing good writing, erasing, and creasing qualities is desired

6. A secretary should prepare cross-reference cards when a report which is to be filed in a subject file

   A. has outlived its usefulness
   B. contains inaccurate data
   C. deals with two or more topics
   D. includes information that will be consulted frequently

7. Of the following office practices, the one which would generally be found UNACCEPTABLE is

   A. inactive records that are to be stored for more than a year should be fastened with twine rather than with rubber bands
   B. if records are added to those previously stapled, the first staple must be removed before the second staple is used
   C. an incoming letter and the carbon copy of the reply should be attached together before being filed
   D. staples rather than paper clips should be used in attaching together records that are to be filed

8. The MAIN advantage of visible indexing over conventional nonvisible indexing is in

   A. lower cost of filing equipment
   B. locating records
   C. conserving filing space
   D. eliminating the need for guide cards

9. A new city employee will probably be MOST interested in his work if

   A. his supervisor permits him to work out his own methods of performing his assigned duties
   B. the rate of pay is equal to that paid in private industry
   C. he is both competent and temperamentally suited to do his work
   D. working conditions, such as hours of work, vacation allowances, and sick leave allowances are good

10. Of the following forms of letter arrangement, the one that is MOST helpful in saving typing time is the _____ form with _____ punctuation.

    A. block; open
    B. block; closed
    C. indented; open
    D. indented; closed

11. In reviewing her stenographic notes of a letter dictated by her bureau chief, the secretary noted that the bureau chief had dictated *Dear Joe* as his salutation but had neglected to indicate the form of complimentary close to be used. This letter is addressed to a former colleague of the bureau chief.
Of the following, the form that would be MOST appropriate for this letter is

   A. Very truly yours,
   B. Respectfully yours,
   C. Cordially yours,
   D. Yours truly,

12. The one of the following which is generally omitted from an inter-office memorandum is

   A. a statement of the subject of the memorandum
   B. a salutation and a complimentary close
   C. the name or title of the person issuing the memorandum
   D. the date of the memorandum

13. Eliminating the inside address on all business letters is, in general, considered

   A. *desirable;* it does away with an outmoded and unnecessary practice
   B. *undesirable;* the inside address is useful in identifying a letter after the envelope bearing the address has been discarded
   C. *desirable;* the appearance of the letter is improved and efficiency in typing letters is increased
   D. *undesirable;* many persons receiving such letters would not know where to address their replies

14. Assume that you are the head of the central stenographic unit of a city agency. A newly appointed member of your unit presents a suggestion for improving the procedures of your unit.
The MOST desirable of the following actions for you to take is to

   A. advise her to withhold her suggestion until she is fully acquainted with all the policies and procedures of the unit
   B. receive the suggestion without comment, since praise may give the employee false hopes and criticism may discourage her from offering other suggestions in the future
   C. thank her for her suggestion but do not adopt it since it presents the ideas of one who is inadequately acquainted with all the phases of the unit's problems
   D. discuss the suggestion with this new employee since she may have applied a new and fresh viewpoint to the unit's procedures

15. Assume that you are in charge of a unit in which employees are frequently required to work in pairs on common tasks. Two of your subordinates frequently engage in heated disputes when they are assigned to work together on such tasks.
Of the following actions you may take in handling this problem, the MOST desirable one for you to take FIRST is to

   A. inform the staff, at a staff conference, that quarreling during office hours will not be tolerated
   B. find out why they quarrel and take the necessary steps to settle the differences
   C. recommend that one of the employees be transferred to another unit
   D. warn them that both will be subject to immediate dismissal if further disputes arise between them

16. Of the following factors, the one to which the supervisor should give the GREATEST consideration in planning the training of a new employee is

    A. the extent to which the new employee already possesses the skills and knowledge needed for satisfactory job performance
    B. whether the supervisor is to do the training or delegate the task to a qualified assistant
    C. the desirability of arranging a tour of the various units in the agency to reveal their interrelationships
    D. the usefulness of visual aids, such as charts, film slides, and pictures, as an aid in training

17. The head of a central transcribing unit is responsible for the quality and accuracy of the work performed by her staff.
    In handling errors made by members of her staff, the unit head should be concerned CHIEFLY with

    A. determining how best to reprimand the persons responsible for the errors
    B. finding out who is ultimately responsible for the errors
    C. recording each error made by a staff member in that staff member's personal record
    D. preventing such errors from being made again

18. Of the following, the LEAST acceptable procedure to follow in training a new employee is to

    A. reduce the job to be taught to its simpler units and start with the simple elements and gradually work up to the more complex elements
    B. depart from the natural order in which a job is performed if the training process is facilitated by following a different order
    C. impress upon the new employee that correctness in method of performing an operation must precede development of speed of performance
    D. devote the same amount of time to the training of all new employees when preparing them for the same job assignments

19. The experienced supervisor knows that the MOST acceptable of the following statements regarding the instruction and training of subordinates is that

    A. if left alone, each employee develops a method of working which is best for his own individual ability and temperament
    B. instruction manuals should describe both the correct and the incorrect methods of performing an operation
    C. written instructions are particularly valuable for operations which are not performed frequently
    D. the instructor should have the trainee perform an operation before showing the trainee the proper method of performing the operation

20. The staff of a central transcribing unit has been wasteful in the use of stationery, paper, and other office supplies.
    Of the following, the MOST desirable action for the unit supervisor to take to reduce this waste is to

A. determine the average quantity of supplies used daily by each staff member and then allot that quantity daily to each staff member
B. find out which employees have been most wasteful of supplies and reprimand these employees
C. discuss this matter at a conference with the staff, pointing out the necessity for, and methods of, eliminating waste
D. issue supplies for an assignment at the time the assignment is made and limit the quantity to the amount needed for that assignment only

21. The decision of a secretary to set up and maintain a subject filing system is MOST justified if 21.____

    A. speed in placing material in the files is of primary importance
    B. she is generally asked to obtain all the filed material dealing with a particular transaction or topic
    C. the system must be simple enough to permit its use by practically any employee with a little knowledge of filing
    D. there is to be no need to classify material before filing it

22. Several filing operations are performed by a secretary in operating and maintaining a subject filing system. Of these filing operations, the two which the secretary can MOST practicably perform at the same time are 22.____

    A. coding and placing material in the files
    B. classifying and placing material in the files
    C. placing material in the files and charging out borrowed material
    D. classifying and coding material for the files

23. The one of the following that is NOT generally considered to be an advantage of the use of printed form letters in replying to inquiries is that they 23.____

    A. are flexible and may be easily changed to meet varying situations
    B. save the time of the stenographer or typist by reducing the amount of typing required
    C. relieve the dictator of the task of dictating letters containing identical wording
    D. make possible prompter replies to inquiries

24. A secretary to a division chief is required to take care of all the details relating to a conference of unit heads over which the division chief is to preside. 24.____
    Of the following, the LEAST appropriate action for the secretary to take before the scheduled time of the conference is to

    A. collect all material that will be needed at the conference
    B. see that the conference room is in readiness for the conference
    C. inform each unit head of the division chief's views on the matters to be discussed
    D. make sure that each unit head has received notice of this meeting in advance

25. The use of well-designed office forms in an agency contributes MOST directly to the 25.____

    A. gradual increase in the number of forms used
    B. improvement of public relations because of public appreciation of efficient management
    C. uniform interpretation of agency policies
    D. simplification of clerical procedures and increased speed office processes

26. Impartiality is considered to be one of the MOST important qualifications of a supervisor. This is so MAINLY because

   A. the supervisor should rotate responsible assignments among the members of his staff
   B. a supervisor should be able to train his subordinates to be impartial
   C. impartiality and intellectual honesty are closely related
   D. staff cooperation tends to deteriorate when a supervisor shows favoritism

27. Of the following systems of filing, the one that is considered the BEST for safeguarding confidential records is the

   A. alphabetical
   B. numerical
   C. geographical
   D. subject

28. Business letters sometimes contain trite words or expressions which merely *pad* a sentence without contributing to the meaning of the sentence.
    Of the following sentences, the one which does NOT contain such a word or expression is:

   A. In answer to your inquiry of March 27, we beg to state that your application has been approved.
   B. I have before me your request of March 27 and will give it due consideration.
   C. Enclosed please find the permit which you requested in your letter of March 27.
   D. If you do not receive the permit by April 20, please wire us collect.

29. In an address to his supervisory staff, the administrative official stated: *Not everyone who declares that man is a rational being treats living men as rational.*
    Of the following, the MOST direct implication of this quotation is that

   A. although professing otherwise, some individuals do not have an honest respect for the points of view of other individuals
   B. individuals differ not only with respect to their intellectual capacities but also with respect to emotional stability
   C. although not everyone concedes man's ability to think rationally, those who do acknowledge this ability also concede that it varies with the individual
   D. not all individuals who are treated as rational men react rationally to this treatment, but react in a manner dictated by their individual experiences

30. On the basis of his experience, the personnel director came to the conclusion that monotony is dependent upon the traits of the individual rather than the characteristics of the task.
    Of the following, the statement that gives this conclusion MOST support is that

   A. the breaking down of former trades into many repetitive tasks has tended to increase the number of monotonous tasks
   B. some workers desire to perform certain tasks which other workers find dull and uninteresting
   C. the amount of satisfaction derived from work performance is dependent upon the amount of creative effort required to perform the assigned task
   D. monotonous tasks contain common characteristics

Questions 31-40.

DIRECTIONS: Each of Questions 31 through 40 consists of four words. In each question, one of the words may be spelled incorrectly or all four words may be spelled correctly. If one of the words in a question is spelled incorrectly, print in the space at the right the letter preceding the word which is spelled incorrectly. If all four words are spelled correctly, print the letter E.

| | | | | |
|---|---|---|---|---|
| 31. | A. vehicular<br>C. manageable | B. gesticulate<br>D. fullfil | | 31._____ |
| 32. | A. inovation<br>C. chastise | B. onerous<br>D. irresistible | | 32._____ |
| 33. | A. A. familiarize<br>C. oscillate | B. dissolution<br>D. superflous | | 33._____ |
| 34. | A. census<br>C. adherence | B. defender<br>D. inconceivable | | 34._____ |
| 35. | A. voluminous<br>C. bankrupcy | B. liberalize<br>D. conversion | | 35._____ |
| 36. | A. justifiable<br>C. perpatrate | B. executor<br>D. dispelled | | 36._____ |
| 37. | A. boycott<br>C. enterprise | B. abeyence<br>D. circular | | 37._____ |
| 38. | A. spontaineous<br>C. analyze | B. dubious<br>D. premonition | | 38._____ |
| 39. | A. intelligible<br>C. genuine | B. apparently<br>D. crucial | | 39._____ |
| 40. | A. plentiful<br>C. carreer | B. ascertain<br>D. preliminary | | 40._____ |

Questions 41-55.

DIRECTIONS: Each of sentences 41 through 55 may be classified under one of the following four categories:
    A. faulty because of incorrect grammar
    B. faulty because of incorrect punctuation
    C. faulty because of incorrect capitalization
    D. correct

Examine each sentence carefully to determine under which of the above four options it is best classified. Then, in the space at the right, print the letter preceding the option which is the BEST of the four suggested above. Each faulty sentence contains but one type of error. Consider a sentence correct if it contains none of the types of faults mentioned, even though there may be other correct ways of expressing the same thought.

41. The experiments conducted by professor Alford were described at a recent meeting of our organization. 41.___

42. I shall be glad to discuss these matters with whoever represents the Municipal Credit Union. 42.___

43. In my opinion, neither Mr. Price nor Mr. Roth knows how to operate this office appliance. 43.___

44. The supervisor, as well as the other stenographers, were unable to transcribe Miss Johnson's shorthand notes. 44.___

45. Important functions such as, recruiting and training, are performed by our unit. 45.___

46. Realizing that many students are interested in this position, we sent announcements to all the High Schools. 46.___

47. After pointing out certain incorrect conclusions, the report was revised by Mr. Clark and submitted to Mr. Batson. 47.___

48. The employer contributed two hundred dollars; the employees, one hundred dollars. 48.___

49. He realized that the time, when a supervisor could hire and fire, was over. 49.___

50. The complaints received by Commissioner Regan was the cause of the change in policy. 50.___

51. Any report, that is to be sent to the Federal Security Administration, must be approved and signed by Mr. Yound. 51.___

52. Of the two stenographers, Miss Rand is the more accurate. 52.___

53. Since the golf courses are crowded during the Summer, more men are needed to maintain the courses in good playing condition. 53.___

54. Although he invited Mr. Frankel and I to attend a meeting of the Civil Service Assembly, we were unable to accept his invitation. 54.___

55. The delay in preparing the report was caused, in his opinion, by the lack of proper supervision and coordination. 55.___

56. *This assignment was handled EXPEDITIOUSLY.* The word *expeditiously* means MOST NEARLY 56.___

    A. clumsily     B. without preparation
    C. speedily     D. on a trial basis

57. *Miss Lind is SCRUPULOUS in performing her secretarial duties.* The word *scrupulous* means MOST NEARLY 57.___

    A. slow     B. conscientious
    C. careless     D. gracious

58. To *APPRISE* means MOST NEARLY to 58.___

    A. award     B. inform
    C. dispossess     D. discover

59. *His work on this matter is OPPORTUNE.* The word *opportune* means MOST NEARLY

   A. timely   B. biased   C. hostile   D. hopeful

60. *His actions had a DELETERIOUS effect on the other employees.*
   The word *deleterious* means MOST NEARLY

   A. restraining   B. highly pleasing
   C. harmful   D. misleading

61. *The size of the staff was increased and the gain in output was COMMENSURATE.*
   The word *commensurate* means MOST NEARLY

   A. praiseworthy   B. enormous
   C. of equal extent   D. trivial in proportion

62. *Miss Hunter is ASSIDUOUS in keeping these records.* The word *assiduous* means MOST NEARLY

   A. negligent   B. untrained
   C. unrestricted   D. diligent

63. *His bookkeeper said that our account was DORMANT.*
   The word *dormant* means MOST NEARLY

   A. inadequate   B. transferred
   C. inactive   D. overdrawn

64. *The supervisor's criticisms were CAUSTIC.*
   The word *caustic* means MOST NEARLY

   A. sarcastic and severe   B. unfair and undeserved
   C. ominous but justified   D. fitful and unsteady

65. The word *impediment* means MOST NEARLY

   A. hindrance   B. trick or deception
   C. insinuation   D. urgent matter

66. *This procedure did not PRECLUDE errors in judgment.*
   The word *preclude* means MOST NEARLY

   A. arise from   B. prevent
   C. account for   D. define

67. *The statements made at the initial conference were RETRACTED at a subsequent meeting.*
   The word *retracted* means MOST NEARLY

   A. developed   B. criticized
   C. endorsed   D. withdrawn

68. *He was unwilling to SUPPLANT his immediate superior.*
   The word *supplant* means MOST NEARLY

   A. fill the needs of   B. request aid from
   C. take the place of   D. withhold support for

69. *Miss Olin has a PREPOSSESSING manner.*
    The word *prepossessing* means MOST NEARLY

    A. authoritative    B. likable
    C. apologetic       D. deceiving

70. *The methods used to solve these critical problems were ANALOGOUS.*
    The word *analogous* means MOST NEARLY

    A. similar    B. unconventional
    C. clever     D. unsound

71. Three grades of bond paper are used in a central transcribing unit. The cost per ream of paper is 95 cents for Grade A, 85 cents for Grade B, and 80 cents for Grade C.
    If the central transcribing unit used 6 reams of Grade A paper, 14 reams of Grade B paper, and 20 reams of Grade C paper, the average cost per ream of the bond paper used by this unit is between _____ and _____ cents.

    A. 81; 83    B. 83; 85    C. 85; 87    D. 87; 90

72. The Complaint Bureau of a city agency is composed of an investigation unit, a clerical unit, and a central transcribing unit. The sum of $132,000 has been appropriated for the operation of this bureau. Of this sum, $85,000 is to be allotted to the clerical unit.
    Of this bureau's total appropriation, the percentage that is left for the central transcribing unit is MOST NEARLY

    A. 20%    B. 30%    C. 40%    D. 50%

73. Three typists were assigned to address a total of 2,655 postcards. Typist A addressed the postcards at the rate of 170 per hour. Typist B addressed the postcards at the rate of 150 per hour. Typist C's rate is not known. After the three typists had addressed postcards for three and a half hours, Typist C was taken off this assignment. It was necessary for Typist A and Typist B to work two and a half hours more to complete this assignment. The rate per hour at which Typist C addressed the postcards was

    A. less than 150
    B. between 150 and 170
    C. more than 170 but less than 200
    D. more than 200

Questions 74-80.

DIRECTIONS: Each of Questions 74 through 80 consists of a set of four topics proposed for inclusion in a manual of procedure for Stenographers, Grade 2, employed in a city agency. This manual is designed to guide the Stenographers, Grade 2, in properly performing secretarial duties and such tasks as are generally assigned to members of a central stenographic and typing unit.

From each set of four topics, select the one topic which you consider LEAST pertinent for inclusion in the manual of procedure. For each question, indicate as your answer the capital letter preceding the topic which you consider the LEAST pertinent for the manual.

74.   A. Care of the typewriter
      B. Uses of the typewriter tabulator
      C. How to make repairs on the typewriter
      D. Techniques in typing statistical tables

75.   A. Style and format of memoranda
      B. Courtesy titles and forms of address, salutations, and complimentary close
      C. How to proofread material typed from copy
      D. Rules for editing technical reports

76.   A. Techniques in designing forms
      B. Cautions in cutting mimeograph stencils
      C. How to correct typographical errors
      D. Suggested methods of handling carbon paper

77.   A. Protecting confidential matters
      B. When to use window envelopes
      C. Basic symbols used in operating the stenotype machine
      D. How to answer and screen incoming telephone calls

78.   A. Receiving callers
      B. Follow-up file
      C. Specimen forms and form letters
      D. Opportunities for promotion and transfer

79.   A. Procedure in sending telegrams
      B. Definitions of technical terms frequently used in agency's correspondence and reports
      C. How to supervise typists and stenographers
      D. Preparing records for filing

80.   A. How to make long-distance telephone calls
      B. Use of abbreviations
      C. Regulations on absences and lateness
      D. Proper heading for second page of letter

# KEY (CORRECT ANSWERS)

| | | | | | | | |
|---|---|---|---|---|---|---|---|
| 1. | A | 21. | B | 41. | C | 61. | C |
| 2. | B | 22. | D | 42. | D | 62. | D |
| 3. | D | 23. | A | 43. | D | 63. | C |
| 4. | C | 24. | C | 44. | A | 64. | A |
| 5. | D | 25. | D | 45. | B | 65. | A |
| 6. | C | 26. | D | 46. | C | 66. | B |
| 7. | B | 27. | B | 47. | A | 67. | D |
| 8. | B | 28. | D | 48. | D | 68. | C |
| 9. | C | 29. | A | 49. | B | 69. | B |
| 10. | A | 30. | B | 50. | A | 70. | A |
| 11. | C | 31. | D | 51. | B | 71. | B |
| 12. | B | 32. | A | 52. | D | 72. | A |
| 13. | B | 33. | D | 53. | C | 73. | D |
| 14. | D | 34. | E | 54. | A | 74. | C |
| 15. | B | 35. | C | 55. | D | 75. | D |
| 16. | A | 36. | C | 56. | C | 76. | A |
| 17. | D | 37. | B | 57. | B | 77. | C |
| 18. | D | 38. | A | 58. | B | 78. | D |
| 19. | C | 39. | E | 59. | A | 79. | C |
| 20. | C | 40. | C | 60. | C | 80. | C |

# RECORD KEEPING
# EXAMINATION SECTION
## TEST 1

DIRECTIONS: Each question or incomplete statement is followed by several suggested answers or completions. Select the one that BEST answers the question or completes the statement. *PRINT THE LETTER OF THE CORRECT ANSWER IN THE SPACE AT THE RIGHT.*

Questions 1-15.

DIRECTIONS: Questions 1 through 15 are to be answered on the basis of the following list of company names below. Arrange a file alphabetically, word-by-word, disregarding punctuation, conjunctions, and apostrophes. Then answer the questions.

    A Bee C Reading Materials
    ABCO Parts
    A Better Course for Test Preparation
    AAA Auto Parts Co.
    A-Z Auto Parts, Inc.
    Aabar Books
    Abbey, Joanne
    Boman-Sylvan Law Firm
    BMW Autowerks
    C Q Service Company
    Chappell-Murray, Inc.
    E&E Life Insurance
    Emcrisco
    Gigi Arts
    Gordon, Jon & Associates
    SOS Plumbing
    Schmidt, J.B. Co.

1. Which of these files should appear FIRST?
    A. ABCO Parts
    B. A Bee C Reading Materials
    C. A Better Course for Test Preparation
    D. AAA Auto Parts Co.

2. Which of these files should appear SECOND?
    A. A-Z Auto Parts, Inc.
    B. A Bee C Reading Materials
    C. A Better Course for Test Preparation
    D. AAA Auto Parts Co.

3. Which of these files should appear THIRD?
   A. ABCO Parts
   B. A Bee C Reading Materials
   C. Aabar Books
   D. AAA Auto Parts Co.

4. Which of these files should appear FOURTH?
   A. Aabar Books
   B. ABCO Parts
   C. Abbey, Joanne
   D. AAA Auto Parts Co.

5. Which of these files should appear LAST?
   A. Gordon, Jon & Associates
   B. Gigi Arts
   C. Schmidt, J.B. Co.
   D. SOS Plumbing

6. Which of these files should appear between A-Z Auto Parts, Inc. and Abbey, Joanne?
   A. A Bee C Reading Materials
   B. AAA Auto Parts Co.
   C. ABCO Parts
   D. A Better Course for Test Preparation

7. Which of these files should appear between ABCO Parts and Aabar Books?
   A. A Bee C Reading Materials
   B. Abbey, Joanne
   C. Aabar Books
   D. A-Z Auto Parts

8. Which of these files should appear between Abbey, Joanne and Boman-Sylvan Law Firm?
   A. A Better Course for Test Preparation
   B. BMW Autowerks
   C. Chappell-Murray, Inc.
   D. Aabar Books

9. Which of these files should appear between Abbey, Joanne and C Q Service?
   A. A-Z Auto Parts, Inc.
   B. BMW Autowerks
   C. Choices A and B
   D. Chappell-Murray, Inc.

10. Which of these files should appear between C Q Service Company and Emcrisco?
    A. Chappell-Murray, Inc.
    B. E&E Life Insurance
    C. Gigi Arts
    D. Choices A and B

11. Which of these files should NOT appear between C Q Service Company and E&E Life Insurance?
    A. Gordon, Jon & Associates
    B. Emcrisco
    C. Gigi Arts
    D. All of the above

12. Which of these files should appear between Chappell-Murray, Inc. and      12.____
    Gigi Arts?
    A. C Q Service Inc., E&E Life Insurance, and Emcrisco
    B. Emcrisco, E&E Life Insurance, and Gordon, Jon & Associates
    C. E&E Life Insurance, and Emcrisco
    D. Emcrisco and Gordon, Jon & Associates

13. Which of these files should appear between Gordon, Jon & Associates and    13.____
    SOS Plumbing?
    A. Gigi Arts              B. Schmidt,J.B. Co.
    C. Choices A and B        D. None of the above

14. Each of the choices lists the four files in their proper alphabetical order    14.____
    EXCEPT
    A. E&E Life Insurance; Gigi Arts; Gordon, Jon & Associates; SOS Plumbing
    B. E&E Life Insurance; Emcrisco; Gigi Arts; SOS Plumbing
    C. Emcrisco; Gordon, Jon & Associates; SOS Plumbing; Schmidt, J.B. Co.
    D. Emcrisco; Gigi Arts; Gordon, Jon & Associates; SOS Plumbing

15. Which of the choices lists the four files in their proper alphabetical order?   15.____
    A. Gigi Arts; Gordon, Jon & Associates; SOS Plumbing; Schmidt, J.B. Co.
    B. Gordon, Jon & Associates; Gigi Arts; Schmidt, J.B. Co.; SOS Plumbing
    C. Gordon, Jon & Associates; Gigi Arts; SOS Plumbing; Schmidt, J.B. Co.
    D. Gigi Arts; Gordon, Jon & Associates; Schmidt, J.B. Co.; SOS Plumbing

16. The alphabetical filing order of two businesses with identical names is     16.____
    determined by the
    A. length of time each business has been operating
    B. addresses of the businesses
    C. last name of the company president
    D. no one of the above

17. In an alphabetical filing system, if a business name includes a number, it should   17.____
    be
    A. disregarded
    B. considered a number and placed at the end of an alphabetical section
    C. treated as though it were written in words and alphabetized accordingly
    D. considered a number and placed at the beginning of an alphabetical
       section

18. If a business name includes a contraction (such as *don't* or *it's*), how should   18.____
    that word be treated in an alphabetical system?
    A. Divide the word into its separate parts and treat it as two words
    B. Ignore the letters that come after the apostrophe
    C. Ignore the word that contains the contraction
    D. Ignore the apostrophe and consider all letters in the contraction

19. In what order should the parts of an address be considered when using an alphabetical filing system?
    A. City or town; state; street name; house or building number
    B. State; city or town; street name; house or building number
    C. House or building number; street name; city or town; state
    D. Street name; city or town; state

    19._____

20. A business record should be cross-referenced when a(n)
    A. organization is known by an abbreviated name
    B. business has a name change because of a sale, incorporation, or other reason
    C. business is known by a *coined* or common name which differs from a dictionary spelling
    D. all of the above

    20._____

21. A geographical filing system is MOST effective when
    A. location is more important than name
    B. many names or titles sound alike
    C. dealing with companies who have offices all over the world
    D. filing personal and business files

    21._____

Questions 22-25.

DIRECTIONS: Questions 22 through 25 are to be answered on the basis of the list of items below, which are to be filed geographically. Organize the items geographically and then answer the questions.

   I. University Press at Berkeley, U.S.
   II. Maria Sanchez, Mexico City, Mexico
   III. Great Expectations Ltd. in London, England
   IV. Justice League, Cape Town, South Africa, Africa
   V. Crown Pearls Ltd. in London, England
   VI. Joseph Prasad in London, England

22. Which of the following arrangements of the items is composed according to the policy of: *Continent, Country, City, Firm or Individual Name*?
    A. V, III, IV, VI, II, I          B. IV, V, III, VI, II, I
    C. I, IV, V, III, VI, II          D. IV, V, III, VI, I, II

    22._____

23. Which of the following files is arranged according to the policy of: *Continent, Country, City, Firm or Individual Name*?
    A. South Africa; Africa; Cape Town; Justice League
    B. Mexico; Mexico City; Maria Sanchez
    C. North America; United States; Berkeley; University Press
    D. England; Europe; London; Prasad, Joseph

    23._____

24. Which of the following arrangements of the items is composed according to the policy of: *Country, City, Firm or Individual Name*?
    A. V, VI, III, II, IV, I
    B. I, V, VI, III, II, IV
    C. VI, V, III, II, IV, I
    D. V, III, VI, II, IV, I

25. Which of the following files is arranged according to a policy of: *Country, City, Firm or Individual Name*?
    A. England; London; Crown Pearls Ltd.
    B. North America; United States; Berkeley; University Press
    C. Africa; Cape Town; Justice League
    D. Mexico City; Mexico; Maria Sanchez

26. Under which of the following circumstances would a phonetic filing system be MOST effective?
    A. When the person in charge of filing can't spell very well
    B. With large files with names that sound alike
    C. With large files with names that are spelled alike
    D. All of the above

Questions 27-29.

DIRECTIONS: Questions 27 through 29 are to be answered on the basis of the following list of numerical files.

   I.   391-023-100
   II.  361-132-170
   III. 385-732-200
   IV.  381-432-150
   V.   391-632-387
   VI.  361-423-303
   VII. 391-123-271

27. Which of the following arrangements of the files follows a consecutive-digit system?
    A. II, III, IV, I    B. I, V, VII, III    C. II, IV, III, I    D. III, I, V, VII

28. Which of the following arrangements follows a terminal-digit system?
    A. I, VII, II, IV, III
    B. II, I, IV, V, VII
    C. VII, VI, V, IV, III
    D. I, IV, II, III, VII

29. Which of the following lists follows a middle-digit system?
    A. I, VII, II, VI, IV, V, III
    B. I, II, VII, IV, VI, V, III
    C. VII, II, I, III, V, VI, IV
    D. VII, I, II, IV, VI, V, III

Questions 30-31.

DIRECTIONS: Questions 30 and 31 are to be answered on the basis of the following information.

    I. Reconfirm Laura Bates appointment with James Caldecort on December 12 at 9:30 A.M.
    II. Laurence Kinder contact Julia Lucas on August 3 and set up a meeting for week of September 23 at 4 P.M.
    III. John Lutz contact Larry Waverly on August 3 and set up appointment for September 23 at 9:30 A.M.
    IV. Call for tickets for Gerry Stanton August 21 for New Jersey on September 23, flight 143 at 4:43 P.M.

30. A chronological file for the above information would be
    A. IV, III, II, I    B. III, II, IV, I    C. IV, II, III, I    D. III, I, II, IV

31. Using the above information, a chronological file for the date September 23 would be
    A. II, III, IV    B. III, I, IV    C. III, II, IV    D. IV, III, II

Questions 32-34.

DIRECTIONS: Questions 32 through 34 are to be answered on the basis of the following information.

    I. Call Roger Epstein, Ashoke Naipaul, Jon Anderson, and Sara Washingon on April 19 at 1:00 P.M. to set up meeting with Alika D'Ornay for June 6 in New York.
    II. Call Martin Ames before noon on April 19 to confirm afternoon meeting with Bob Greenwood on April 20th.
    III. Set up meeting room at noon for 2:30 P.M. meeting on April 19th.
    IV. Ashley Stanton contact Bob Greenwood at 9:00 A.M. on April 20 and set up meeting for June 6 at 8:30 A.M.
    V. Carol Guiland contact Shelby Van Ness during afternoon of April 20 and set up meeting for June 6 at 10:00 A.M.
    VI. Call airline and reserve tickets on June 6 for Roger Epstein trip to Denver on July 8.
    VII. Meeting at 2:30 P.M. on April 19th.

32. A chronological file for all of the above information would be
    A. II, I, III, VII, V, IV, VI    B. III, VII, II, I, IV, V, VI
    C. III, VII, I, II, V, IV, VI    D. II, III, I, VII, IV, V, VI

33. A chronological file for the date of April 19th would be
    A. II, III, VII, I    B. II, III, I, VII    C. VII, I, III, II    D. III, VII, I, II

34. Add the following information to the file, and then create a chronological file for April 20th: VIII. April 20: 3:00 P.M. meeting between Bob Greenwood and Martin Ames.  34.____
    A. IV, V, VIII   B. IV, VIII, V   C. VIII, V, IV   D. V, IV, VIII

35. The PRIMARY advantage of computer records over a manual system is  35.____
    A. speed of retrieval   B. accuracy
    C. cost   D. potential file loss

## KEY (CORRECT ANSWERS)

| | | | | | | | |
|---|---|---|---|---|---|---|---|
| 1. | B | 11. | D | 21. | A | 31. | C |
| 2. | C | 12. | C | 22. | B | 32. | D |
| 3. | D | 13. | B | 23. | C | 33. | B |
| 4. | A | 14. | C | 24. | D | 34. | A |
| 5. | D | 15. | D | 25. | A | 35. | A |
| 6. | C | 16. | B | 26. | B | | |
| 7. | B | 17. | C | 27. | C | | |
| 8. | B | 18. | D | 28. | D | | |
| 9. | C | 19. | A | 29. | A | | |
| 10. | D | 20. | D | 30. | B | | |

# EXAMINATION SECTION

## TEST 1

DIRECTIONS: Each question or incomplete statement is followed by several suggested answers or completions. Select the one that BEST answers the question or completes the statement. *PRINT THE LETTER OF THE CORRECT ANSWER IN THE SPACE AT THE RIGHT.*

Questions 1-22.

DIRECTIONS: Read through each group of words. Indicate in the space at the right the letter of the misspelled word.

1. A. miniature     B. recession       1.____
   C. accommodate  D. supress

2. A. mortgage      B. illogical       2.____
   C. fasinate      D. pronounce

3. A. calendar      B. heros           3.____
   C. ecstasy       D. librarian

4. A. initiative    B. extraordinary   4.____
   C. villian       D. exaggerate

5. A. absence       B. sense           5.____
   C. dosn't        D. height

6. A. curiosity     B. ninety          6.____
   C. truely        D. grammar

7. A. amateur       B. definate        7.____
   C. meant         D. changeable

8. A. excellent     B. studioes        8.____
   C. achievement   D. weird

9. A. goverment     B. description     9.____
   C. sergeant      D. desirable

10. A. proceed      B. anxious        10.____
    C. neice        D. precede

11. A. environment  B. omitted        11.____
    C. apparant     D. misconstrue

12. A. comparative  B. hindrance      12.____
    C. benefited    D. unamimous

13.  A. embarrass  B. recommend  13._____
    C. desciple  D. argument

14.  A. sophomore  B. suprintendent  14._____
    C. concievable  D. disastrous

15.  A. agressive  B. questionnaire  15._____
    C. occurred  D. rhythm

16.  A. peaceable  B. conscientious  16._____
    C. redicule  D. deterrent

17.  A. mischievious  B. writing  17._____
    C. competition  D. athletics

18.  A. auxiliary  B. synonymous  18._____
    C. maneuver  D. repitition

19.  A. existence  B. optimistic  19._____
    C. acquitted  D. tragedy

20.  A. hypocrisy  B. parrallel  20._____
    C. exhilaration  D. prevalent

21.  A. convalesence  B. infallible  21._____
    C. destitute  D. grotesque

22.  A. magnanimity  B. asassination  22._____
    C. incorrigible  D. pestilence

Questions 23-40.

DIRECTIONS: In Questions 23 through 40, one sentence fragment contains an error in punctuation or capitalization. Indicate the letter of the INCORRECT sentence fragment and place it in the space at the right.

23.  A. Despite a year's work  23._____
    B. in a well-equipped laboratory
    C. my Uncle failed to complete his research
    D. now he will never graduate.

24.  A. Gene, if you are going to sleep  24._____
    B. all afternoon I will enter
    C. that ladies' golf tournament
    D. sponsored by the Chamber of Commerce.

25. A. Seeing the cat slink toward the barn,
    B. the farmer's wife jumped off the
    C. ladder picked up a broom, and began
    D. shouting at the top of her voice.

    25.____

26. A. Extending over southeast Idaho and
    B. northwest Wyoming, the Tetons
    C. are noted for their height; however the
    D. highest peak is actually under 14,000 feet.

    26.____

27. A. "Sarah, can you recall the name
    B. of the English queen
    C. who supposedly said, 'We are not
    D. amused?"

    27.____

28. A. My aunt's graduation present to me
    B. cost, I imagine more than she could
    C. actually afford.  It's a
    D. Swiss watch with numerous features.

    28.____

29. A. On the left are examples of buildings
    B. from the Classical Period; two temples
    C. one of which was dedicated to Zeus; the
    D. Agora, a marketplace; and a large arch.

    29.____

30. A. Tired of sonic booms, the people who
    B. live near Springfield's Municipal Airport
    C. formed an anti noise organization
    D. with the amusing name of Sound Off.

    30.____

31. A. "Joe, Mrs. Sweeney said, "your family
    B. arrives Sunday.  Since you'll be in
    C. the Labor Day parade, we could ask Mr.
    D. Krohn, who has a big car, to meet them."

    31.____

32. A. The plumber emerged from the basement and
    B. said, "Mr. Cohen I found the trouble in
    C. your water heater.  Could you move those
    D. Schwinn bikes out of my way?"

    32.____

33. A. The President walked slowly to the
    B. podium, bowed to Edward Everett Hale
    C. the other speaker, and began his formal address:
    D. "Fourscore and seven years ago...."

    33.____

34. A. Mr. Fontana, I hope, will arrive before
    B. the beginning of the ceremonies; however,
    C. if his plane is delayed, I have a substitute
    D. speaker who can be here at a moments' notice.

    34.____

35. A. Gladys wedding dress, a satin creation,
    B. lay crumpled on the floor; her veil,
    C. torn and streaked, lay nearby. "Jilted!"
    D. shrieked Gladys. She was clearly annoyed.

35.____

36. A. Although it is poor grammar, the word
    B. hopefully has become television's newest
    C. pet expression; I hope (to use the correct
    D. form) that it will soon pass from favor.

36.____

37. A.          Plaza Apartment Hotel
    B.          103 Tower road
    C.          Hampstead, Iowa 52025
    D.          March 13, 2021

37.____

38. A. Circulation Department
    B. British History Illustrated
    C. 3000 Walnut Street
    D. Boulder Colorado 80302

38.____

39. A. Dear Sirs:
    B.    Last spring I ordered a subscription to your
    C. magazine. I had read and enjoyed the May
    D. issue containing the article titled "kings."

39.____

40. A.    I have not however, received a
    B. single issue. Will you check this?
    C.    Sincerely,
    D. Maria Herrera

40.____

Questions 41-70.

DIRECTIONS: Questions 41 through 70 represent common grammatical concerns: subject-verb agreement, appropriate use of pronouns, and appropriate use of verbs. Read each sentence and indicate the letter of the grammatically CORRECT answer in the space at the right.

41. THE REIVERS, one of William Faulkner's last works, _____ made into a movie starring Steve McQueen.
    A. has been    B. have been    C. are being    D. were

41.____

42. He _____ on the ground, his eyes fastened on an ant slowly pushing a morsel of food toward the ant hill.
    A. layed       B. laid         C. had laid     D. lay

42.____

43. Nobody in the tri-cities _____ to admit that a flood could be disastrous.
    A. are willing              B. have been willing
    C. is willing               D. were willing

43.____

44. "_____," the senator asked, "have you convinced to run against the incumbent?"      44._____
    A. Who      B. Whom      C. Whomever      D. Womsoever

45. Of all the psychology courses that I took, Statistics 101 _____ the most demanding.      45._____
    A. was      B. are      C. is      D. were

46. Neither the conductor nor the orchestra members _____ the music to be applauded so enthusiastically.      46._____
    A. were expecting      B. was expecting
    C. is expected      D. has been expecting

47. The requirements for admission to the Lettermen's Club _____ posted outside the athletic director's office for months.      47._____
    A. was      B. was being      C. has been      D. have been

48. Please give me a list of the people _____ to compete in the kayak race.      48._____
    A. whom you think have planned      B. who you think has planned
    C. who you think is planning      D. who you think are planning

49. I saw Eloise and Abelard earlier today; _____ were riding around in a fancy 1956 MG.      49._____
    A. she and him      B. her and him      C. she and he      D. her and he

50. If you _____ the trunk in the attic, I'll unpack it later today.      50._____
    A. can sit      B. are able to sit
    C. can set      D. have sat

51. _____ all of the flour been used, or may I borrow three cups?      51._____
    A. Have      B. Has      C. Is      D. Could

52. In exasperation, the cycle shop's owner suggested that _____ there too long.      52._____
    A. us boys were      B. we boys were
    C. us boys had been      D. we boys had been

53. Idleness as well as money _____ the root of all evil.      53._____
    A. have been      B. were to have been
    C. is      D. are

54. Only the string players from the quartet—Gregory, Isaac, _____—remained after the concert to answer questions.      54._____
    A. him, and I      B. he, and I
    C. him, and me      D. he, and me

55. Of all the antiques that _____ for sale, Gertrude chose to buy a stupid glass thimble.      55._____
    A. was      B. is
    C. would have      D. were

56. The detective snapped, "Don't confuse me with theories about _____ you believe committed the crime!"
    A. who  B. whom  C. whomever  D. which

57. _____ when we first called, we might have avoided our present predicament.
    A. The plumber's coming
    B. If the plumber would have come
    C. If the plumber had come
    D. If the plumber was to have come

58. We thought the sun _____ in the north until we discovered that our compass was defective.
    A. had rose
    B. had risen
    C. had rised
    D. had raised

59. Each play of Shakespeare's _____ more than _____ share of memorable characters.
    A. contain its
    B. contains; its
    C. contains; it's
    D. contain; their

60. Our English teacher suggested to _____ seniors that either Tolstoy or Dickens _____ the outstanding novelist of the nineteenth century.
    A. we; was considered
    B. we; were considered
    C. us; was considered
    D. us; were considered

61. Sherlock Holmes, together with his great friend and companion Dr. Watson, _____ to aid the woman _____ had stumbled into the room.
    A. has agreed; who
    B. have agreed; whom
    C. has agreed; whom
    D. have agreed; who

62. Several of the deer _____ when they spotted my backpack _____ open in the meadow.
    A. was frightened; laying
    B. were frightened; lying
    C. were frightened; laying
    D. was frightened; lying

63. After the Scholarship Committee announces _____ selection, hysterics often _____.
    A. it's; occur
    B. its; occur
    C. their; occur
    D. their; occurs

64. I _____ the key on the table last night so you and _____ could find it.
    A. layed; her
    B. lay; she
    C. laid; she
    D. laid; her

65. Some of the antelope _____ wandered away from the meadow where the rancher _____ the block of salt.
    A. has; sat
    B. has; set
    C. have; had set
    D. has; sets

66. Macaroni and cheese _____ best to us (that is, to Andy and _____) when Mother adds extra cheddar cheese.
    A. tastes; I
    B. tastes; me
    C. taste; me
    D. taste; I

66._____

67. Frank said, "It must have been _____ called the phone company."
    A. she who
    B. she whom
    C. her who
    D. her whom

67._____

68. The herd _____ moving restlessly at every bolt of lightning; it was either Ted or _____ who saw the beginning of the stampede.
    A. was; me
    B. were; I
    C. was; I
    D. have been; me

68._____

69. The foreman _____ his lateness by saying that his alarm clock _____ until six minutes before eight.
    A. explains; had not rang
    B. explained; has not rung
    C. has explained; rung
    D. explained; hadn't rung

69._____

70. Of all the coaches, Ms. Cox is the only one who _____ that Sherry dives more gracefully than _____.
    A. is always saying; I
    B. is always saying; me
    C. are always saying; I
    D. were always saying; me

70._____

Questions 71-90.

DIRECTIONS: Choose the word in Questions 71 through 90 that is MOST opposite in meaning to the italicized word.

71. *fact*
    A. statistic
    B. statement
    C. incredible
    D. conjecture

71._____

72. *stiff*
    A. fastidious
    B. babble
    C. supple
    D. apprehensive

72._____

73. *blunt*
    A. concise
    B. tactful
    C. artistic
    D. humble

73._____

74. *foreign*
    A. pertinent
    B. comely
    C. strange
    D. scrupulous

74._____

75. *anger*
    A. infer
    B. pacify
    C. taint
    D. revile

75._____

76. *frank*
    A. earnest
    B. reticent
    C. post
    D. expensive

76._____

77. *secure*
   A. precarious   B. acquire   C. moderate   D. frenzied                            77.____

78. *petty*
   A. harmonious           B. careful
   C. forthright           D. momentous                                              78.____

79. *concede*
   A. dispute             B. reciprocate
   C. subvert             D. propagate                                               79.____

80. *benefit*
   A. liquidation         B. bazaar
   C. detriment           D. profit                                                  80.____

81. *capricious*
   A. preposterous        B. constant
   C. diabolical          D. careless                                                81.____

82. *boisterous*
   A. devious   B. valiant   C. girlish   D. taciturn                                82.____

83. *harmony*
   A. congruence   B. discord   C. chagrin   D. melody                               83.____

84. *laudable*
   A. auspicious          B. despicable
   C. acclaimed           D. doubtful                                                84.____

85. *adherent*
   A. partisan   B. stoic   C. renegade   D. recluse                                 85.____

86. *exuberant*
   A. frail   B. corpulent   C. austere   D. bigot                                   86.____

87. *spurn*
   A. accede   B. flail   C. efface   D. annihilate                                  87.____

88. *spontaneous*
   A. hapless             B. corrosive
   C. intentional         D. willful                                                 88.____

89. *disparage*
   A. abolish   B. exude   C. incriminate   D. extol                                 89.____

90. *timorous*
   A. succinct   B. chaste   C. audacious   D. insouciant                            90.____

## KEY (CORRECT ANSWERS)

| | | | | |
|---|---|---|---|---|
| 1. D | 21. A | 41. A | 61. A | 81. B |
| 2. C | 22. B | 42. D | 62. | 82. D |
| 3. B | 23. C | 43. C | 63. B | 83. B |
| 4. C | 24. B | 44. B | 64. C | 84. B |
| 5. C | 25. C | 45. A | 65. C | 85. C |
| 6. C | 26. C | 46. A | 66. B | 86. C |
| 7. B | 27. D | 47. D | 67. A | 87. A |
| 8. B | 28. B | 48. A | 68. C | 88. C |
| 9. A | 29. B | 49. C | 69. D | 89. D |
| 10. C | 30. C | 50. C | 70. A | 90. C |
| 11. C | 31. A | 51. B | 71. D | |
| 12. D | 32. B | 52. D | 72. C | |
| 13. C | 33. B | 53. C | 73. B | |
| 14. C | 34. D | 54. B | 74. A | |
| 15. A | 35. A | 55. D | 75. B | |
| 16. C | 36. B | 56. B | 76. B | |
| 17. A | 37. B | 57. C | 77. A | |
| 18. D | 38. D | 58. B | 78. D | |
| 19. B | 39. D | 59. B | 79. A | |
| 20. B | 40. A | 60. C | 80. C | |

# PREPARING WRITTEN MATERIAL
# EXAMINATION SECTION
# TEST 1

DIRECTIONS: Each of the sentences in this test may be classified under one of the following four categories:
- A. Faulty because of incorrect grammar or word usage
- B. Faulty because of incorrect punctuation
- C. Faulty because of incorrect capitalization or incorrect spelling
- D. Correct

Examine each sentence carefully to determine under which of the above four options it is best classified. Then, in the space to the right, print the capital letter preceding the option which is the BEST of the four suggested above. (Note that each faulty sentence contains but one type of error. Consider a sentence to be correct if it contains none of the types of errors mentioned, even though there may be other correct ways of expressing the same thought.)

1. He sent the notice to the clerk who you hired yesterday.     1.____

2. It must be admitted, however that you were not informed of this change.     2.____

3. Only the employee who have served in this grade for at least two years are eligible for promotion.     3.____

4. The work was divided equally between she and Mary.     4.____

5. He thought that you were not available at that time.     5.____

6. When the messenger returns; please give him this package.     6.____

7. The new secretary prepared, typed, addressed, and delivered, the notices.     7.____

8. Walking into the room, his desk can be seen at the rear.     8.____

9. Although John has worked here longer than She, he produces a smaller amount of work.     9.____

10. She said she could of typed this report yesterday.     10.____

11. Neither one of these procedures are adequate for the efficient performance of this task.     11.____

12. The typewriter is the tool of the typist; the cash register, the tool of the cashier.     12.____

13. "The assignment must be completed as soon as possible" said the supervisor.    13._____

14. As you know, office handbooks are issued to all new Employees.    14._____

15. Writing a speech is sometimes easier than to deliver it before an audience.    15._____

16. Mr. Brown our accountant, will audit the accounts next week.    16._____

17. Give the assignment to whomever is able to do it most efficiently.    17._____

18. The supervisor expected either your or I to file these reports.    18._____

## KEY (CORRECT ANSWERS)

| | | | |
|---|---|---|---|
| 1. | A | 11. | A |
| 2. | B | 12. | C |
| 3. | D | 13. | B |
| 4. | A | 14. | C |
| 5. | D | 15. | A |
| 6. | B | 16. | B |
| 7. | B | 17. | A |
| 8. | A | 18. | A |
| 9. | C | | |
| 10. | A | | |

# TEST 2

DIRECTIONS: Each of the sentences in this test may be classified under one of the following four categories:
- A. Faulty because of incorrect grammar or word usage
- B. Faulty because of incorrect punctuation
- C. Faulty because of incorrect capitalization or incorrect spelling
- D. Correct

Examine each sentence carefully to determine under which of the above four options it is best classified. Then, in the space to the right, print the capital letter preceding the option which is the BEST of the four suggested above. (Note that each faulty sentence contains but one type of error. Consider a sentence to be correct if it contains none of the types of errors mentioned, even though there may be other correct ways of expressing the same thought.)

1. The fire apparently started in the storeroom, which is usually locked.   1.____
2. On approaching the victim, two bruises were noticed by this officer.   2.____
3. The officer, who was there examined the report with great care.   3.____
4. Each employee in the office had a seperate desk.   4.____
5. All employees including members of the clerical staff, were invited to the lecture.   5.____
6. The suggested Procedure is similar to the one now in use.   6.____
7. No one was more pleased with the new procedure than the chauffeur.   7.____
8. He tried to persaude her to change the procedure.   8.____
9. The total of the expenses charged to petty cash were high.   9.____
10. An understanding between him and I was finally reached.   10.____

## KEY (CORRECT ANSWERS)

| | | | | |
|---|---|---|---|---|
| 1. | D | | 6. | C |
| 2. | A | | 7. | D |
| 3. | B | | 8. | C |
| 4. | C | | 9. | A |
| 5. | B | | 10. | A |

# TEST 3

DIRECTIONS: Each of the sentences in this test may be classified under one of the following four categories:
  A. Faulty because of incorrect grammar or word usage
  B. Faulty because of incorrect punctuation
  C. Faulty because of incorrect capitalization or incorrect spelling
  D. Correct

Examine each sentence carefully to determine under which of the above four options it is best classified. Then, in the space to the right, print the capital letter preceding the option which is the BEST of the four suggested above. (Note that each faulty sentence contains but one type of error. Consider a sentence to be correct if it contains none of the types of errors mentioned, even though there may be other correct ways of expressing the same thought.)

1. They told both he and I that the prisoner had escaped.  1._____

2. Any superior officer, who, disregards the just complaint of his subordinates, is remiss in the performance of his duty.  2._____

3. Only those members of the national organization who resided in the Middle West attended the conference in Chicago.  3._____

4. We told him to give the national organization assignment to whoever was available.  4._____

5. Please do not disappoint and embarass us by not appearing in court.  5._____

6. Although the office's speech proved to be entertaining, the topic was not relevent to the main theme of the conference.  6._____

7. In February all new officers attended a training course in which they were learned in their principal duties and the fundamental operating procedure of the department.  7._____

8. I personally seen inmate Jones threaten inmates Smith and Green with bodily harm if they refused to participate in the plot.  8._____

9. To the layman, who on a chance visit to the prison observes everything functioning smoothly, the maintenance of prison discipline may seem to be a relatively easily realizable objective.  9._____

10. The prisoners in cell block fourty were forbidden to sit on the cell cots during the recreation hour.  10._____

## KEY (CORRECT ANSWERS)

1. A
2. B
3. C
4. D
5. C
6. C
7. A
8. A
9. D
10. C

# TEST 4

DIRECTIONS: Each of the sentences in this test may be classified under one of the following four categories:
  A. Faulty because of incorrect grammar or word usage
  B. Faulty because of incorrect punctuation
  C. Faulty because of incorrect capitalization or incorrect spelling
  D. Correct

Examine each sentence carefully to determine under which of the above four options it is best classified. Then, in the space to the right, print the capital letter preceding the option which is the BEST of the four suggested above. (Note that each faulty sentence contains but one type of error. Consider a sentence to be correct if it contains none of the types of errors mentioned, even though there may be other correct ways of expressing the same thought.)

1. I cannot encourage you any.                                    1.____
2. You always look well in those sort of clothes.                 2.____
3. Shall we go to the park?                                       3.____
4. The man whome he introduced was Mr. Carey.                     4.____
5. She saw the letter laying here this morning.                   5.____
6. It should rain before the Afternoon is over.                   6.____
7. They have already went home.                                   7.____
8. That Jackson will be elected is evident.                       8.____
9. He does not hardly approve of us.                              9.____
10. It was he, who won the prize.                                 10.____

## KEY (CORRECT ANSWERS)

1. A    6. C
2. A    7. A
3. D    8. D
4. C    9. A
5. A    10. B

# TEST 5

DIRECTIONS: Each of the sentences in this test may be classified under one of the following four categories:
  A. Faulty because of incorrect grammar or word usage
  B. Faulty because of incorrect punctuation
  C. Faulty because of incorrect capitalization or incorrect spelling
  D. Correct

Examine each sentence carefully to determine under which of the above four options it is best classified. Then, in the space to the right, print the capital letter preceding the option which is the BEST of the four suggested above. (Note that each faulty sentence contains but one type of error. Consider a sentence to be correct if it contains none of the types of errors mentioned, even though there may be other correct ways of expressing the same thought.)

1. Shall we go to the park. 1.____
2. They are, alike, in this particular way. 2.____
3. They gave the poor man sume food when he knocked on the door. 3.____
4. I regret the loss caused by the error. 4.____
5. The students' will have a new teacher. 5.____
6. They sweared to bring out all the facts. 6.____
7. He decided to open a branch store on 33rd street. 7.____
8. His speed is equal and more than that of a racehorse. 8.____
9. He felt very warm on that Summer day. 9.____
10. He was assisted by his friend, who lives in the next house. 10.____

## KEY (CORRECT ANSWERS)

| | | | |
|---|---|---|---|
| 1. | B | 6. | A |
| 2. | B | 7. | C |
| 3. | C | 8. | A |
| 4. | D | 9. | C |
| 5. | B | 10. | D |

# TEST 6

DIRECTIONS: Each of the sentences in this test may be classified under one of the following four categories:
- A. Faulty because of incorrect grammar or word usage
- B. Faulty because of incorrect punctuation
- C. Faulty because of incorrect capitalization or incorrect spelling
- D. Correct

Examine each sentence carefully to determine under which of the above four options it is best classified. Then, in the space to the right, print the capital letter preceding the option which is the BEST of the four suggested above. (Note that each faulty sentence contains but one type of error. Consider a sentence to be correct if it contains none of the types of errors mentioned, even though there may be other correct ways of expressing the same thought.)

1. The climate of New York is colder than California.  1.____
2. I shall wait for you on the corner.  2.____
3. Did we see the boy who, we think, is the leader.  3.____
4. Being a modest person, John seldom talks about his invention.  4.____
5. The gang is called the smith street bos.  5.____
6. He seen the man break into the store.  6.____
7. We expected to lay still there for quite a while.  7.____
8. He is considered to be the Leader of his organization.  8.____
9. Although I recieved an invitation, I won't go.  9.____
10. The letter must be here some place.  10.____

## KEY (CORRECT ANSWERS)

1. A     6. A
2. D     7. A
3. B     8. C
4. D     9. C
5. C     10. A

# TEST 7

DIRECTIONS: Each of the sentences in this test may be classified under one of the following four categories:
- A. Faulty because of incorrect grammar or word usage
- B. Faulty because of incorrect punctuation
- C. Faulty because of incorrect capitalization or incorrect spelling
- D. Correct

Examine each sentence carefully to determine under which of the above four options it is best classified. Then, in the space to the right, print the capital letter preceding the option which is the BEST of the four suggested above. (Note that each faulty sentence contains but one type of error. Consider a sentence to be correct if it contains none of the types of errors mentioned, even though there may be other correct ways of expressing the same thought.)

1. I though it to be he.                                                1._____
2. We expect to remain here for a long time.                            2._____
3. The committee was agreed.                                            3._____
4. Two-thirds of the building are finished.                             4._____
5. The water was froze.                                                 5._____
6. Everyone of the salesmen must supply their own car.                  6._____
7. Who is the author of Gone With the Wind?                             7._____
8. He marched on and declaring that he would never surrender.           8._____
9. Who shall I say called?                                              9._____
10. Everyone has left but they.                                         10._____

## KEY (CORRECT ANSWERS)

| | | | |
|---|---|---|---|
| 1. | A | 6. | A |
| 2. | D | 7. | B |
| 3. | D | 8. | A |
| 4. | A | 9. | D |
| 5. | A | 10. | D |

# TEST 8

DIRECTIONS: Each of the sentences in this test may be classified under one of the following four categories:
- A. Faulty because of incorrect grammar or word usage
- B. Faulty because of incorrect punctuation
- C. Faulty because of incorrect capitalization or incorrect spelling
- D. Correct

Examine each sentence carefully to determine under which of the above four options it is best classified. Then, in the space to the right, print the capital letter preceding the option which is the BEST of the four suggested above. (Note that each faulty sentence contains but one type of error. Consider a sentence to be correct if it contains none of the types of errors mentioned, even though there may be other correct ways of expressing the same thought.)

1. Who did we give the order to?
2. Send your order in immediately.
3. I believe I paid the Bill.
4. I have not met but one person.
5. Why aren't Tom, and Fred, going to the dance?
6. What reason is there for him not going?
7. The seige of Malta was a tremendous event.
8. I was there yesterday I assure you
9. Your ukulele is better than mine.
10. No one was there only Mary.

## KEY (CORRECT ANSWERS)

1. A     6. A
2. D     7. C
3. C     8. B
4. A     9. C
5. B     10. A

# TEST 9

DIRECTIONS: In each of the following groups of sentences, one of the four sentences is faulty in grammar, punctuation, or capitalization. Select the INCORRECT sentence in each case.

1. A. If you had stood at home and done your homework, you would not have failed in arithmetic.
   B. Her affected manner annoyed every member of the audience.
   C. How will the new law affect our income taxes?
   D. The plants were not affected by the long, cold winter, but they succumbed to the drought of summer.

   1.____

2. A. He is one of the most able men who have been in the Senate.
   B. It is he who is to blame for the lamentable mistake.
   C. Haven't you a helpful suggestion to make at this time?
   D. The money was robbed from the blind man's cup.

   2.____

3. A. The amount of children in this school is steadily increasing.
   B. After taking an apple from the table, she went out to play.
   C. He borrowed a dollar from me.
   D. I had hoped my brother would arrive before me.

   3.____

4. A. Whom do you think I hear from every week?
   B. Who do you think is the right man for the job?
   C. Who do you think I found in the room?
   D. He is the man whom we considered a good candidate for the presidency.

   4.____

5. A. Quietly the puppy laid down before the fireplace.
   B. You have made your bed; now lie in it.
   C. I was badly sunburned because I had lain too long in the sun.
   D. I laid the doll on the bed and left the room.

   5.____

## KEY (CORRECT ANSWERS)

1. A
2. D
3. A
4. C
5. A

# PREPARING WRITTEN MATERIAL

# PARAGRAPH REARRANGEMENT
# COMMENTARY

The sentences that follow are in scrambled order. You are to rearrange them in proper order and indicate the letter choice containing the correct answer at the space at the right.

Each group of sentences in this section is actually a paragraph presented in scrambled order. Each sentence in the group has a place in that paragraph; no sentence is to be left out. You are to read each group of sentences and decide upon the best order in which to put the sentences so as to form a well-organized paragraph.

The questions in this section measure the ability to solve a problem when all the facts relevant to its solution are not given.

More specifically, certain positions of responsibility and authority require the employee to discover connection between events sometimes, apparently, unrelated. In order to do this, the employee will find it necessary to correctly infer that unspecified events have probably occurred or are likely to occur. This ability becomes especially important when action must be taken on incomplete information.

Accordingly, these questions require competitors to choose among several suggested alternatives, each of which presents a different sequential arrangement of the events. Competitors must choose the MOST logical of the suggested sequences.

In order to do so, they may be required to draw on general knowledge to infer missing concepts or events that are essential to sequencing the given events. Competitors should be careful to infer only what is essential to the sequence. The plausibility of the wrong alternatives will always require the inclusion of unlikely events or of additional chains of events which are NOT essential to sequencing the given events.

It's very important to remember that you are looking for the best of the four possible choices, and that the best choice of all may not even be one of the answers you're given to choose from.

There is no one right way to solve these problems. Many people have found it helpful to first write out the order of the sentences, as they would have arranged them, on their scrap paper before looking at the possible answers. If their optimum answer is there, this can save them some time. If it isn't, this method can still give insight into solving the problem. Others find it most helpful to just go through each of the possible choices, contrasting each as they go along. You should use whatever method feels comfortable and works for you.

While most of these types of questions are not that difficult, we've added a higher percentage of the difficult type, just to give you more practice. Usually there are only one or two questions on this section that contain such subtle distinctions that you're unable to answer confidently. And you then may find yourself stuck deciding between two possible choices, neither of which you're sure about.

# EXAMINATION SECTION

## TEST 1

DIRECTIONS: The following groups of sentences need to be arranged in an order that makes sense. Select the letter preceding the sequence that represents the BEST sentence order. *PRINT THE LETTER OF THE CORRECT ANSWER IN THE SPACE AT THE RIGHT.*

1. 
   I. The keyboard was purposely designed to be a little awkward to slow typists down.
   II. The arrangement of letters on the keyboard of a typewriter was not designed for the convenience of the typist.
   III. Fortunately, no one is suggesting that a new keyboard be designed right away.
   IV. If one were, we would have to learn to type all over again.
   V. The reason was that the early machines were slower than the typists and would jam easily.
   The CORRECT answer is:
   A. I, III, IV, II, V
   B. II, V, I, IV, III
   C. V, I, II, III, IV
   D. II, I, V, III, IV

2. 
   I. The majority of the new service jobs are part-time or low-paying.
   II. According to the U.S. Bureau of Labor Statistics, jobs in the service sector constitute 72% of all jobs in this country.
   III. If more and more workers receive less and less money, who will buy the goods and services needed to keep the economy going?
   IV. The service sector is by far the fastest growing part of the United States economy.
   V. Some economists look upon this trend with great concern.
   The CORRECT answer is:
   A. II, IV, I, V, III
   B. II, III, IV, I, V
   C. V, IV, II, III, I
   D. III, I, II, IV, V

3. 
   I. They can also affect one's endurance.
   II. This can stabilize blood sugar levels, and ensure that the brain is receiving a steady, constant, supply of glucose, so that one is *hitting on all cylinders* while taking the test.
   III. By food, we mean real food, not junk food or unhealthy snacks.
   IV. For this reason, it is important not to skip a meal, and to bring food with you to the exam.
   V. One's blood sugar levels can affect how clearly one is able to think and concentrate during an exam.
   The CORRECT answer is:
   A. V, IV, II, III, I
   B. V, II, I, IV, III
   C. V, I, IV, III, II
   D. V, IV, I, III, II

1.____

2.____

3.____

141

4.  I. Those who are the embodiment of desire are absorbed in material quests, and those who are the embodiment of feeling are warriors who value power more than possession.
    II. These qualities are in everyone, but in different degrees.
    III. But those who value understanding yearn not for goods or victory, but for knowledge.
    IV. According to Plato, human behavior flows from three main sources: desire, emotion, and knowledge.
    V. In the perfect state, the industrial forces would produce but not rule, the military would protect but not rule, and the forces of knowledge, the philosopher kings, would reign.
    The CORRECT answer is:
    A. IV, V, I, II, III
    B. V, I, II, III, IV
    C. IV, III, II, I, V
    D. IV, II, I, III, V

5.  I. Of the more than 26,000 tons of garbage produced daily in New York City, 12,000 tons arrive daily at Fresh Kills.
    II. In a month, enough garbage accumulates there to fill the Empire State Building.
    III. In 1937, the Supreme Court halted the practice of dumping the trash of New York City into the sea.
    IV. Although the garbage is compacted, in a few years the mounds of garbage at Fresh Kills will be the highest points south of Maine's Mount Desert Island on the Eastern Seaboard.
    V. Instead, tugboats now pull barges of much of the trash to Staten Island and the largest landfill in the world, Fresh Kills.
    The CORRECT answer is:
    A. III, V, IV, I, II
    B. III, V, II, IV, I
    C. III, V, I, II, IV
    D. III, II, V, IV, I

6.  I. Communists rank equality very high, but freedom very low.
    II. Unlike communists, conservatives place a high value on freedom and a very low value on equality.
    III. A recent study demonstrated that one way to classify people's political beliefs is to look at the importance placed on two words: freedom and equality.
    IV. Thus, by demonstrating how members of these groups feel about the two words, the study has proved to be useful for political analysts in several European countries.
    V. According to the study, socialists and liberals rank both freedom and equality very high, while fascists rate both very low.
    The CORRECT answer is:
    A. III, V, I, II, IV
    B. V, IV, III, I, II
    C. III, V, IV, II, I
    D. III, I, II, IV, V

7.
   I. "Can there be anything more amazing than this?"
   II. If the riddle is successfully answered, his dead brothers will be brought back to life.
   III. "Even though man sees those around him dying every day," says Dharmaraj, "he still believes and acts as if he were immortal."
   IV. "What is the cause of ceaseless wonder?" asks the Lord of the Lake.
   V. In the ancient epic, The Mahabharata, a riddle is asked of one of the Pandava brothers.
   The CORRECT answer is:
   A. V, II, I, IV, III
   B. V, IV, III, I, II
   C. V, II, IV, III, I
   D. V, II, IV, I, III

8.
   I. On the contrary, the two main theories—the cooperative (neoclassical) theory and the radical (labor theory)—clearly rest on very different assumptions, which have very different ethical overtones.
   II. The distribution of income is the primary factor in determining the relative levels of material well-being that different groups or individuals attain.
   III. Of all issues in economics, the distribution of income is one of the most controversial.
   IV. The neoclassical theory tends to support the existing income distribution (or minor changes), while the labor theory ends to support substantial changes in the way income is distributed.
   V. The intensity of the controversy reflects the fact that different economic theories are not purely neutral, *detached* theories with no ethical or moral implications.
   The CORRECT answer is:
   A. II, I, V, IV, III
   B. III, II, V, I, IV
   C. III, V, II, I, IV
   D. III, V, IV, I, II

9.
   I. The pool acts as a broker and ensures that the cheapest power gets used first.
   II. Every six seconds, the pool's computer monitors all of the generating stations in the state and decides which to ask for more power and which to cut back.
   III. The buying and selling of electrical power is handled by the New York Power Pool in Guilderland, New York.
   IV. This is to the advantage of both the buying and selling utilities.
   V. The pool began operation in 1970, and consists of the state's eight electric utilities.
   The CORRECT answer is:
   A. V, I, II, III, IV
   B. IV, II, I, III, V
   C. III, V, I, IV, II
   D. V, III, IV, II, I

10. 
I. Modern English is much simpler grammatically than Old English.
II. Finnish grammar is very complicated; there are some fifteen cases, for example.
III. Chinese, a very old language, may seem to be the exception, but it is the great number of characters/words that must be mastered that makes it so difficult to learn, not its grammar.
IV. The newest literary language—that is, written as well as spoken—is Finish, whose literary roots go back only to about the middle of the nineteenth century.
V. Contrary to popular belief, the longer a language is been in use the simpler its grammar—not the reverse.

The CORRECT answer is:
A. IV, I, II, III, V
B. V, I, IV, II, III
C. I, II, IV, III, V
D. IV, II, III, I, V

10.____

## KEY (CORRECT ANSWERS)

1. D     6. A
2. A     7. C
3. C     8. B
4. D     9. C
5. C     10. B

# TEST 2

DIRECTIONS: This type of question tests your ability to recognize accurate paraphrasing, well-constructed paragraphs, and appropriate style and tone. It is important that the answer you select contains only the facts or concepts given in the original sentences. It is also important that you be aware of incomplete sentences, inappropriate transitions, unsupported opinions, incorrect usage, and illogical sentence order. Paragraphs that do not include all the necessary facts and concepts, that distort them, or that add new ones are not considered correct.

The format for this section may vary. Sometimes, long paragraphs are given, and emphasis is placed on style and organization. Our first five questions are of this type. Other times, the paragraphs are shorter, and there is less emphasis on style and more emphasis on accurate representation of information. Our second group of five questions are of this nature.

For each of Questions 1 through 10, select the paragraph that BEST expresses the ideas contained in the sentences above it. *PRINT THE LETTER OF THE CORRECT ANSWER IN THE SPACE AT THE RIGHT.*

1. 
   I. Listening skills are very important for managers.
   II. Listening skills are not usually emphasized.
   III. Whenever managers are depicted in books, manuals or the media, they are always talking, never listening.
   IV. We'd like you to read the enclosed handout on listening skills and to try to consciously apply them this week.
   V. We guarantee they will improve the quality of your interactions.

   1.____

   A. Unfortunately, listening skills are not usually emphasized for managers. Managers are always depicted as talking, never listening. We'd like you to read the enclosed handout on listening skills. Please try to apply these principles this week. If you do, we guarantee they will improve the quality of your interactions.
   B. The enclosed handout on listening skills will be important improving the quality of your interactions. We guarantee it. All you have to do is take sometime this week to read and to consciously try to apply the principles. Listening skills are very important for manages, but they are not usually emphasized. Whenever managers are depicted in books, manuals or the media, they are always talking, never listening.
   C. Listening well is one of the most important skills a manager can have, yet it's not usually given much attention. Think about any representation of managers in books, manuals, or in the media that you may have seen. They're always talking, never listening. We'd like you to read the enclosed handout on listening skills and consciously try to apply them the rest of the week. We guarantee you will see a difference in the quality of your interactions.

D. Effective listening, one very important tool in the effective manager's arsenal, is usually not emphasized enough. The usual depiction of managers in books, manuals or the media is one in which they are always talking, never listening. We'd like you to read the enclosed handout and consciously try to apply the information contained therein throughout the rest of the week. We feel sure that you will see a marked difference in the quality of your interactions.

2. 
I. Chekhov wrote three dramatic masterpieces which share certain themes and formats: <u>Uncle Vanya</u>, <u>The Cherry Orchard</u>, and <u>The Three Sisters</u>.
II. They are primarily concerned with the passage of time and how this erodes human aspirations.
III. The plays are haunted by the ghosts of the wasted life.
IV. The characters are concerned with life's lesser problems; however, such as the inability to make decisions, loyalty to the wrong cause, and the inability to be clear.
V. This results in sweet, almost aching, type of a sadness referred to as Chekhovian.

2.____

    A. Chekhov wrote three dramatic masterpieces: <u>Uncle Vanya</u>, <u>The Cherry Orchard</u>, and <u>The Three Sisters</u>. These masterpieces share certain themes and formats: the passage of time, how time erodes human aspirations, and the ghosts of wasted life. Each masterpiece is characterized by a sweet, almost aching, type of sadness that has become known as Chekhovian. The sweetness of this sadness hinges on the fact that it is not the great tragedies of life which are destroying these characters, but their minor flaws: indecisiveness, misplaced loyalty, unclarity.
    B. <u>The Cherry Orchard</u>, <u>Uncle Vanya</u>, and <u>The Three Sisters</u> are three dramatic masterpieces written by Chekhov that use similar formats to explore a common theme. Each is primarily concerned with the way that passing time wears down human aspirations, and each is haunted by the ghosts of the wasted life. The characters are shown struggling futilely with the lesser problems of life: indecisiveness, loyalty to the wrong cause, and the inability to be clear. These struggles create a mood of sweet, almost aching, sadness that has become known as Chekhovian.
    C. Chekhov's dramatic masterpieces are, along with <u>The Cherry Orchard</u>, <u>Uncle Vanya</u>, and <u>The Three Sisters</u>. These plays share certain thematic and formal similarities. They are concerned most of all with the passage of time and the way in which time erodes human aspirations. Each play is haunted by the specter of the wasted life. Chekhov's characters are caught, however, by life's lesser snares: indecisiveness, loyalty to the wrong cause, and unclarity. The characteristic mood is a sweet, almost aching type of sadness that has come to be known as Chekhovian.
    D. A Chekhovian mood is characterized by sweet, almost aching, sadness. The term comes from three dramatic tragedies by Chekhov which revolve around the sadness of a wasted life. The three masterpieces (<u>Uncle Vanya</u>, <u>The Three Sisters</u>, and <u>The Cherry Orchard</u>) share the same

theme and format. The plays are concerned with how the passage of time erodes human aspirations. They are peopled with characters who are struggling with life's lesser problems. These are people who are indecisive, loyal to the wrong causes, or are unable to make themselves clear.

3.
   I. Movie previews have often helped producers decide which parts of movies they should take out or leave in.
   II. The first 1933 preview of <u>King Kong</u> was very helpful to the producers because many people ran screaming from the theater and would not return when four men first attacked by Kong were eaten by giant spiders.
   III. The 1950 premiere of <u>Sunset Boulevard</u> resulted in the filming of an entirely new beginning, and a delay of six months in the film's release.
   IV. In the original opening scene, William Holden was in a morgue talking with thirty-six other "corpses" about the ways some of them had died.
   V. When he began to tell them of his life with Gloria Swanson, the audience found this hilarious, instead of taking the scene seriously.

3. _____

   A. Movie previews have often helped producers decide what parts of movies they should leave in or take out. For example, the first preview of <u>King Kong</u> in 1933 was very helpful. In one scene, four men were first attacked by Kong and then eaten by giant spiders. Many members of the audience ran screaming from the theater and would not return. The premiere of the 1950 film <u>Sunset Boulevard</u> was also very helpful. In the original opening scene, William Holden was in a morgue with thirty-six other "corpses," discussing the ways some of them had died. When he began to tell them of his life with Gloria Swanson, the audience found this hilarious. They were supposed to take the scene seriously. The result was a delay of six months in the release of the film while a new beginning was added.
   B. Movie previews have often helped producers decide whether they should change various parts of a movie. After the 1933 preview of <u>King Kong</u>, a scene in which four men who had been attacked by Kong were eaten by giant spiders was taken out as many people ran screaming from the theater and would not return. The 1950 premiere of <u>Sunset Boulevard</u> also led to some changes. In the original opening scene, William Holden was in a morgue talking with thirty-six other "corpses" about the ways some of them had died. When he began to tell them of his life with Gloria Swanson, the audience found this hilarious, instead of taking the scene seriously.
   C. What do <u>Sunset Boulevard</u> and <u>King Kong</u> have in common? Both show the value of using movie previews to test audience reaction. The first 1933 preview of <u>King Kong</u> showed that a scene showing four men being eaten by giant spiders after having been attacked by Kong was too frightening for many people. They ran screaming from the theater and couldn't be coaxed back. The 1950 premiere of <u>Sunset Boulevard</u> was also a scream, but not the kind the producers intended. The movie opens

with William Holden lying in a morgue discussing the ways they had died with thirty-six other "corpses." When he began to tell them of his life with Gloria Swanson, the audience couldn't take him seriously. Their laughter caused a six-month delay while the beginning was rewritten.
D. Producers very often use movie previews to decide if changes are needed. The premiere of Sunset Boulevard in 1950 led to a new beginning and a six-month delay in film release. At the beginning, William Holden and thirty-six other "corpses" discuss the ways some of them died. Rather than taking this seriously, the audience thought it was hilarious when he began to tell them of his life with Gloria Swanson. The first 1933 preview of King Kong was very helpful for its producers because one scene so terrified the audience that many of them ran screaming from the theater and would not return. In this particular scene, four men who had first been attacked by Kong were eaten by giant spiders.

4.   I.  It is common for supervisors to view employees as "things" to be manipulated.    4.____
    II.  This approach does not motivate employees, nor does the carrot-and-stick approach because employees often recognize these behaviors and resent them.
    III. Supervisors can change these behaviors by using self-inquiry and persistence.
    IV.  The best managers genuinely respect those they work with, are supportive and helpful, and are interested in working as a team with those they supervise.
    V.   They disagree with the Golden Rule that says "he or she who has the gold makes the rules."

   A. Some managers act as if they think the Golden Rule means "he or she who has the gold makes the rules." They show disrespect to employees by seeing them as "things" to be manipulated. Obviously, this approach does not motivate employees any more than the carrot-and-stick approach motivates them. The employees are smart enough to spot these behaviors and resent them. On the other hand, the managers genuinely respect those they work with, are supportive and helpful, and are interested in working as a team. Self-inquiry and persistence can change even the former type of supervisor into the latter.
   B. Many supervisors all into the trap of viewing employees as "things" to be manipulated, or try to motivate them by using a carrot-and-stick approach. These methods do not motivate employees, who often recognize the behaviors and resent them. Supervisors can change these behaviors, however, by using self-inquiry and persistence. The best managers are supportive and helpful, and have genuine respect for those with whom they work. They are interested in working as a team with those they supervise. To them, the Golden Rule is not "he or she who has the gold makes the rules."
   C. Some supervisors see employees as "things" to be used or manipulated using a carrot-and-stick technique. These methods don't work. Employees often see through them and resent them. A supervisor who

wants to change may do so. The techniques of self-inquiry and persistence can be used to turn him or her into the type of supervisor who doesn't think the Golden Rule is "he or she who has the gold makes the rules." They may become like the best managers who treat those with whom they work with respect and give them help and support. These are the manager who know how to build a team.

D. Unfortunately, many supervisors act as if their employees are objects whose movements they can position at will. This mistaken belief has the same result as another popular motivational technique—the carrot-and-stick approach. Both attitudes can lead to the same result—resentment from those employees who recognize the behaviors for what they are. Supervisors who recognize these behaviors can change through the use of persistence and the use of self-inquiry. It's important to remember that the best managers respect their employees. They readily give necessary help and support and are interested in working as a team with those they supervise. To these managers, the Golden Rule is not "he or she who has the gold makes the rules."

5.  I. The first half of the nineteenth century produced a group of pessimistic poets—Byron, De Musset, Heine, Pushkin, and Leopardi.
    II. It also produced a group of pessimistic composers—Schubert, Chopin, Schumann, and even the later Beethoven.
    III. Above all, in philosophy, there was the profoundly pessimistic philosopher, Schopenhauer.
    IV. The Revolution was dead, the Bourbons were restored, the feudal barons were reclaiming their land, and progress everywhere was being suppressed, as the great age was over.
    V. "I thank God," said Goethe, "that I am not young in so thoroughly finished a world."

    5.____

    A. "I thank God," said Goethe, "that I am not young in so thoroughly finished a world." The Revolution was dead, the Bourbons were restored, the feudal barons were reclaiming their land, and progress everywhere was being suppressed. The first half of the nineteenth century produced a group of pessimistic poets: Byron, De Musset, Heine, Pushkin, and Leopardi. It also produced pessimistic composers: Schubert, Chopin, Schumann. Although Beethoven came later, he fits into this group, too. Finally and above all, it also produced a profoundly pessimistic philosopher, Schopenhauer. The great age was over.
    B. The first half of the nineteenth century produced a group of pessimistic poets: Byron, De Musset, Heine, Pushkin, and Leopardi. It produced a group of pessimistic composers: Schubert, Chopin, Schumann, and even the later Beethoven. Above all, it produced a profoundly pessimistic philosopher, Schopenhauer. For each of these men, the great age was over. The Revolution was dead, and the Bourbons were restored. The feudal barons were reclaiming their land, and progress everywhere was being suppressed.

C. The great age was over. The Revolution was dead—the Bourbons were restored, and the feudal barons were reclaiming their land. Progress everywhere was being suppressed. Out of this climate came a profound pessimism. Poets, like Byron, De Musset, Heine, Pushkin, and Leopardi; composers, like Schubert, Chopin, Schumann, and even the later Beethoven; and above all, a profoundly pessimistic philosopher, Schopenauer. This pessimism which arose in the first half of the nineteenth century is illustrated by these words of Goethe, "I thank God that I am not young in so thoroughly finished a world."

D. The first half of the nineteenth century produced a group of pessimistic poets, Byron, De Musset, Heine, Pushkin, and Leopardi—and a group of pessimistic composers, Schubert, Chopin, Schumann, and the later Beethoven. Above it all, it produced a profoundly pessimistic philosopher, Schopenhauer. The great age was over. The Revolution was dead, the Bourbons were restored, the feudal barons were reclaiming their land, and progress everywhere was being suppressed. "I thank God," said Goethe, "that I am not young in so thoroughly finished a world."

6.  I. A new manager sometimes may feel insecure about his or her competence in the new position.
    II. The new manager may then exhibit defensive or arrogant behavior towards those one supervises, or the new manager may direct overly flattering behavior toward one's new supervisor.

    A. Sometimes, a new manager may feel insecure about his or her ability to perform well in this new position. The insecurity may lead him or her to treat others differently. He or she may display arrogant or defensive behavior towards those he or she supervises, or be overly flattering to his or her new supervisor.
    B. A new manager may sometimes feel insecure about his or her ability to perform well in the new position. He or she may then become arrogant, defensive, or overly flattering towards those he or she works with.
    C. There are times when a new manager may be insecure about how well he or she can perform in the new job. The new manager may also behave defensive or act in an arrogant way towards those he or she supervises, or overly flatter his or her boss.
    D. Sometimes a new manager may feel insecure about his or her ability to perform well in the new position. He or she may then display arrogant or defensive behavior towards those they supervise, or become overly flattering towards their supervisors.

6.____

7.  I. It is possible to eliminate unwanted behavior by bringing it under stimulus control—tying the behavior to a cue, and then never, or rarely, giving the cue.
    II. One trainer successfully used this method to keep an energetic young porpoise from coming out of her tank whenever she felt like it, which was potentially dangerous.
    III. Her trainer taught her to do it for a reward, in response to a hand signal, and then rarely gave the signal.

7.____

A. Unwanted behavior can be eliminated by tying the behavior to a cue, and then never, or rarely, giving the cue. This is called stimulus control. One trainer was able to use this method to keep an energetic young porpoise from coming out of her tank by teaching her to come out for a reward in response to a hand signal, and then rarely giving the signal.
B. Stimulus control can be used to eliminate unwanted behavior. In this method, behavior is tied to a cue, and then the cue is rarely, if ever, given. One trainer was able to successfully use stimulus control to keep an energetic young porpoise from coming out of her tank whenever she felt like it—a potentially dangerous practice. She taught the porpoise to come out for a reward when she gave a hand signal, and then rarely gave the signal.
C. It is possible to eliminate behavior that is undesirable by bringing it under stimulus control by tying behavior to a signal, and then rarely giving the signal. One trainer successfully used this method to keep an energetic porpoise from coming out of her tank, a potentially dangerous situation. Her trainer taught the porpoise to do it for a reward, in response to a hand signal, and then would rarely give the signal.
D. By using stimulus control, it is possible to eliminate unwanted behavior by tying the behavior to a cue, and then rarely or never give the cue. One trainer was able to use this method to successfully stop a young porpoise from coming out of her tank whenever she felt like it. To curb this potentially dangerous practice, the porpoise was taught by the trainer to come out of the tank for a reward, in response to a hand signal, and then rarely given the signal.

8. 
I. There is a great deal of concern over the safety of commercial trucks, caused by their greatly increased role in serious accidents since federal deregulation in 1981.
II. Recently, 60 percent of trucks in New York and Connecticut and 70 percent of trucks in Maryland randomly stopped by state troopers failed safety inspections.
III. Sixteen states in the United States require no training at all for truck drivers.

8.____

A. Since federal deregulation in 1981, there has been a great deal of concern over the safety of commercial trucks, and their greatly increased role in serious accidents. Recently, 60 percent of trucks in New York and Connecticut, and 70 percent of trucks in Maryland failed safety inspections. Sixteen states in the United States require no training at all for truck drivers.
B. There is a great deal of concern over the safety of commercial trucks since federal deregulation in 1981. Their role in serious accidents has greatly increased. Recently, 60 percent of trucks randomly stopped in Connecticut and New York and 70 percent in Maryland failed safety inspections conducted by state troopers. Sixteen states in the United States provide no training at all for truck drivers.
C. Commercial trucks have a greatly increased role in serious accidents since federal deregulation in 1981. This has led to a great deal of concern.

Recently, 70 percent of trucks in Maryland and 60 percent of trucks in New York and Connecticut failed inspection of those that were randomly stopped by state troopers. Sixteen states in the United States require no training for all truck drivers.

D. Since federal deregulation in 1981, the role that commercial trucks have played in serious accidents has greatly increased, and this has led to a great deal of concern. Recently, 60 percent of trucks in New York and Connecticut, and 70 percent of trucks in Maryland randomly stopped by state troopers failed safety inspections. Sixteen states in the U.S. don't require any training for truck drivers.

9.  I. No matter how much some people have, they still feel unsatisfied and want more, or want to keep what they have forever.
    II. One recent television documentary showed several people flying from New York to Paris for a one-day shopping spree to buy platinum earrings, because they were bored.
    III. In Brazil, some people were ordering coffins that cost a minimum of $45,000 and are equipping them with deluxe stereos, televisions, and other graveyard necessities.

    9.____

    A. Some people, despite having a great deal, still feel unsatisfied and want more, or think they can keep what they have forever. One recent documentary on television showed several people enroute from Paris to New York for a one day shopping spree to buy platinum earrings, because they were bored. Some people in Brazil are even ordering coffins equipped with such graveyard necessities as deluxe stereos and televisions. The price of the coffins start at $45,000.
    B. No matter how much some people have, they may feel unsatisfied. This leads them to want more, or to want to keep what they have forever. Recently, a television documentary depicting several people flying from New York to Paris for a one day shopping spree to buy platinum earrings. They were bored. Some people in Brazil are ordering coffins that cost at least $45,000 and come equipped with deluxe televisions, stereos and other necessary graveyard items.
    C. Some people will be dissatisfied no matter how much they have. They may want more, or they may want to keep what they have forever. One recent television documentary showed several people, motivated by boredom, jetting from New York to Paris for a one-day shopping spree to buy platinum earrings. In Brazil, some people are ordering coffins equipped with deluxe stereos, televisions and other graveyard necessities. The minimum price for these coffins—$45,000.
    D. Some people are never satisfied. No matter how much they have they still want more, or think they can keep what they have forever. One television documentary recently showed several people flying from New York to Paris for the day to buy platinum earrings because they were bored. In Brazil, some people are ordering coffins that cost $45,000 and are equipped with deluxe stereos, televisions and other graveyard necessities.

9 (#2)

10. 
I. A television signal or video signal has three parts.
II. Its parts are the black-and-white portion, the color portion, and the synchronizing (sync) pulses, which keep the picture stable.
III. Each video source, whether it's a camera or a video-cassette recorder contains its own generator of these synchronizing pulses to accompany the picture that it's sending in order to keep it steady and straight.
IV. In order to produce a clean recording, a video-cassette recorder must "lock-up" to the sync pulses that are part of the video it is trying to record, and this effort may be very noticeable if the device does not have gunlock.

10.____

A. There are three parts to a television or video signal: the black-and-white part, the color part, and the synchronizing (sync) pulses, which keep the picture stable. Whether it's a video-cassette recorder or a camera, each video source contains its own pulse that synchronizes and generates the picture it's sending in order to keep it straight and steady. A video-cassette recorder must "lock up" to the sync pulses that are part of the video it's trying to record. If the device doesn't have gunlock, this effort must be very noticeable.

B. A video signal or television is comprised of three parts: the black-and-white portion, the color portion, and the sync (synchronizing) pulses, which keep the picture stable. Whether it's a camera or a video-cassette recorder, each video source contains its own generator of these synchronizing pulses. These accompany the picture that it's sending in order to keep it straight and steady. A video-cassette recorder must "lock up" to the sync pulses that are part of the video it is trying to record in order to produce a clean recording. This effort may be very noticeable if the device does not have gunlock.

C. There are three parts to a television or video signal: the color portion, the black-and-white portion, and the sync (synchronizing pulses). These keep the picture stable. Each video source, whether it's a video-cassette recorder or a camera, generates these synchronizing pulses accompanying the picture it's sending in order to keep it straight and steady. If a clean recording is to be produced, a video-cassette recorder must store the sync pulses that are part of the video it is trying to record. This effort may not be noticeable if the device does not have gunlock.

D. A television signal or video signal has three parts: the black-and-white portion, the color portion, and the synchronizing (sync) pulses. It's the sync pulses which keep the picture stable, which accompany it and keep it steady and straight. Whether it's a camera or a video-cassette recorder, each video source contains its own generator of these synchronizing pulses. To produce a clean recording, a video-cassette recorder must "lock up" to the sync pulses that are part of the video it is trying to record. If the device does not have gunlock, this effort may be very noticeable.

## KEY (CORRECT ANSWERS)

1. C
2. B
3. A
4. B
5. D

6. A
7. B
8. D
9. C
10. D

# READING COMPREHENSION
# UNDERSTANDING AND INTERPRETING WRITTEN MATERIAL
# EXAMINATION SECTION

This exam section includes some passages and questions related to functions of the first computerized offices, which consisted of typewriters and other such manual office equipment.

## TEST 1

DIRECTIONS: Each question or incomplete statement is followed by several suggested answers or completions. Select the one that BEST answers the question or completes the statement. *PRINT THE LETTER OF THE CORRECT ANSWER IN THE SPACE AT THE RIGHT.*

Questions 1-2.

DIRECTIONS: Questions 1 and 2 are to be answered SOLELY on the basis of the following passage.

The employees in a unit or division of a government agency may be referred to as a work group. Within a government agency which has existed for some time, the work groups will have evolved traditions of their own. The persons in these work groups acquire these traditions as part of the process of work adjustment within their groups. Usually, a work group in a large organization will contain *oldtimers*, *newcomers*, and *in-betweeners*. Like the supervisor of a group, who is not necessarily an oldtimer or the oldest member, oldtimers usually have great influence. They can recall events unknown to others and are a storehouse of information and advice about current problems in the light of past experience. They pass along the traditions of the group to the others who, in turn, become oldtimers themselves. Thus, the traditions of the group which have been honored and revered by long acceptance are continued.

1. According to the above passage, the traditions of a work group within a government agency are developed
    A. at the time the group is established
    B. over a considerable period of time
    C. in order to give recognition to oldtimers
    D. for the group before it is established

2. According to the above passage, the oldtimers within a work group
    A. are the means by which long accepted practices and customs are perpetuated
    B. would best be able to settle current problems that arise
    C. are honored because of the changes they have made in the traditions
    D. have demonstrated that they have learned to do their work well

Questions 3-4.

DIRECTIONS: Questions 3 and 4 are to be answered SOLELY on the following passage.

In public agencies, the success of a person assigned to perform first-line supervisory duties depends in large part upon the personal relations between him and his subordinate employees. The goal of supervising effort is something more than to obtain compliance with procedures established by some central office. The major objective is work accomplishment. In order for this goal to be attained, employees must want to attain it and must exercise initiative in their work. Only if employees are generally satisfied with the type of supervision which exists in an organization will they put forth their best efforts.

3. According to the above passage, in order for employees to try to do their work as well as they can, it is essential that
    A. they participate in determining their working conditions and rates of pay
    B. their supervisors support the employees' viewpoints in meetings with higher management
    C. they are content with the supervisory practices which are being used
    D. their supervisors make the changes in working procedures that the employees request

4. It can be inferred from the above passage that the goals of a unit in a public agency will not be reached unless the employees in the unit
    A. wish to reach them and are given the opportunity to make individual contributions to the work
    B. understand the relationship between the goals of the unit and goals of the agency
    C. have satisfactory personal relationships with employees of other units in the agency
    D. carefully follow the directions issued by higher authorities

Questions 5-9.

DIRECTIONS: Questions 5 through 9 are to be answered SOLELY on the basis of the following passage.

In an employee thinks he can save money, time, or material for the city or has an idea about how to do something better than it is being done, he shouldn't keep it to himself. He should send his ideas to the Employees' Suggestion Program, using the special form which is kept on hand in all departments. An employee may send in as many ideas as he wishes. To make sure that each idea is judged fairly, the name of the suggester is not made known until an award is made. The awards are certificate of merit or cash prizes ranging from $10 to $500.

5. According to the above passage, an employee who knows how to do a job in a better way should
    A. be sure it saves enough time to be worthwhile
    B. get paid the money he saves for the city
    C. keep it to himself to avoid being accused of causing a speed-up
    D. send his idea to the Employees' Suggestion Program

6. In order to send his idea to the Employees' Suggestion Program, an employee should
   A. ask the Department of Personnel for a special form
   B. get the special form in his own department
   C. mail the idea using Special Delivery
   D. send it on plain, white letter-size paper

7. An employee may send to the Employees' Suggestion Program
   A. as many ideas as he can think of
   B. no more than one idea each week
   C. no more than ten ideas in a month
   D. only one idea on each part of the job

8. The reason the name of an employee who makes a suggestion is not made known at first is to
   A. give the employee a larger award
   B. help the judges give more awards
   C. insure fairness in judging
   D. only one idea on each part of the job

9. An employee whose suggestion receives an award may be given a
   A. bonus once a year
   B. certificate for $10
   C. cash prize of up to $500
   D. salary increase of $500

Questions 10-12.

DIRECTIONS: Questions 10 through 12 are to be answered SOLELY on the basis of the following passage.

According to the rules of the Department of Personnel, the work of every permanent city employee is reviewed and rated by his supervisor at least once a year. The civil service rating system gives the employee and his supervisor a chance to talk about the progress made during the past year as well as about those parts of the job in which the employee needs to do better. In order to receive a pay increase each year, the employee must have a satisfactory service rating. Service ratings also count toward an employee's final mark on a promotion examination.

10. According to the above passage, a permanent city employee is rated AT LEAST once
    A. before his work is reviewed
    B. every six months
    C. yearly by his supervisor
    D. yearly by the Department of Personnel

11. According to the above passage, under the rating system the supervisor and the employee can discuss how
    A. much more work needs to be done next year
    B. the employee did his work last year
    C. the work can be made easier next year
    D. the work of the Department can be increased

12. According to the above passage, a permanent city employee will NOT receive a yearly pay increase
    A. if he received a pay increase the year before
    B. if he used his service rating for his mark on a promotion examination
    C. if his service rating is unsatisfactory
    D. unless he got some kind of a service rating

Questions 13-16.

DIRECTIONS: Questions 13 through 16 are to be answered SOLELY on the basis of the following passage.

It is an accepted fact that the rank and file employee can frequently advance worthwhile suggestions toward increasing efficiency. For this reason, an Employees' Suggestion System has been developed and put into operation. Suitable means have been provided at each departmental location for the confidential submission of suggestions. Numerous suggestions have been received thus far and, after study, about five percent of the ideas submitted are being translated into action. It is planned to set up, eventually, monetary awards for all worthwhile suggestions.

13. According to the above passage, a MAJOR reason why an Employees' Suggestion System was established is that
    A. an organized program of improvement is better than a haphazard one
    B. employees can often give good suggestions to increase efficiency
    C. once a fact is accepted, it is better to act on it than to do nothing
    D. the suggestions of rank and file employees were being neglected

14. According to the above passage, under the Employees' Suggestion System,
    A. a file of worthwhile suggestions will eventually be set up at each departmental location
    B. it is possible for employees to turn in suggestions without fellow employees knowing of it
    C. means have been provided for the regular and frequent collection of suggestions submitted
    D. provision has been made for the judging of worthwhile suggestions by an Employees' Suggestion Committee

15. According to the above passage, it is reasonable to assume that
    A. all suggestions must be turned in at a central office
    B. employees who make worthwhile suggestions will be promoted
    C. not all the prizes offered will be monetary ones
    D. prizes of money will be given for the best suggestions

16. According to the above passage, of the many suggestions made,
    A. all are first tested
    B. a small part are put into use
    C. most are very worthwhile
    D. samples are studied

Questions 17-20.

DIRECTIONS: Questions 17 through 20 are to be answered SOLELY on the basis of the following passage.

Employees may be granted leaves of absence without pay at the discretion of the Personnel Officer. Such a leave without pay shall begin on the first working day on which the employee does not report for duty and shall continue to the first day on which the employee returns to duty. The Personnel Division may vary the dates of the leave for the record so as to conform with payroll periods, but in no case shall an employee be off the payroll for a different number of calendar days than would have been the case if the actual dates mentioned above had been used. An employee who has vacation or overtime to his credit, which is available for normal use, may take time off immediately prior to beginning a leave of absence without pay, chargeable against all or part of such vacation or overtime.

17. According to the above passage, the Personnel Officer must
    A. decide if a leave of absence without pay should be granted
    B. require that a leave end on the last working day of a payroll period
    C. see to it that a leave of absence to conform with a payroll period
    D. vary the dates of a leave of absence to conform with a payroll period

17.____

18. According to the above passage, the exact dates of a leave of absence without pay may be varied provided that the
    A. calendar days an employee is off the payroll equal the actual leave granted
    B. leave conforms to an even number of payroll periods
    C. leave when granted made provision for variance to simplify payroll records
    D. Personnel Officer approves the variation

18.____

19. According to the above passage, a leave of absence without pay must extend from the
    A. first day of a calendar period to the first day the employee resumes work
    B. first day of a payroll period to the last calendar day of the leave
    C. first working day missed to the first day on which the employee resumes work
    D. last day on which an employee works through the first day he returns to work

19.____

20. According to the above passage, an employee may take extra time off just before the start of a leave of absence without pay if
    A. he charges this extra time against his leave
    B. he has a favorable balance of vacation or overtime which has been frozen
    C. the vacation or overtime that he would normally use for a leave without pay has not been charged in this way before
    D. there is time to his credit which he may use

20.____

Question 21.

DIRECTIONS: Question 21 is to be answered SOLELY on the basis of the following passage.

In considering those things which are motivators and incentives to work, it might be just as erroneous not to give sufficient weight to money as an incentive as it is to give too much weight. It is not a problem of establishing a rank-order of importance, but one of knowing that motivation is a blend or mixture rather than a pure element. It is simple to say that cultural factors count more than financial considerations, but this leads only to the conclusion that our society is financial-oriented.

21. Based on the above passage, in our society, cultural and social motivations to work are
    A. things which cannot be avoided
    B. melded to financial incentives
    C. of less consideration than high pay
    D. not balanced equally with economic or financial considerations

21._____

Question 22.

DIRECTIONS: Question 22 is to be answered SOLELY on the basis of the following passage.

A general principle of training and learning with respect to people is that they learn more readily if they receive *feedback*. Essential to maintaining proper motivational levels is knowledge of results which indicate level of progress. Feedback also assists the learning process by identifying mistakes. If this kind of information were not given to the learner, then improper or inappropriate job performance may be instilled.

22. Based on the above passage, which of the following is MOST accurate?
    A. Learning will not take place without feedback.
    B. In the absence of feedback, improper or inappropriate job performance will be learned.
    C. To properly motivate a learner, the learner must have his progress made known to him.
    D. Trainees should be told exactly what to do if they are to learn properly

22._____

Questions 23.

DIRECTIONS: Question 23 is to be answered SOLELY on the basis of the following passage.

In a democracy, the obligation of public officials is twofold. They must not only do an efficient and satisfactory job of administration, but also they must persuade the public that it is an efficient and satisfactory job. It is a burden which, if properly assumed, will make democracy work and perpetuate reform government.

23. The above passage means that
    A. public officials should try to please everybody

23._____

B. public opinion is instrumental if determining the policy of public officials
C. satisfactory performance of the job of administration will eliminate opposition to its work
D. frank and open procedure in a public agency will aid in maintaining progressive government

Question 24.

DIRECTIONS: Question 24 is to be answered SOLELY on the basis of the following passage.

Upon retirement for service, a member shall receive a retirement allowance which shall consist of an annuity which shall be the actuarial equivalent of his accumulated deductions at the time of his retirement and a pension, in addition to his annuity, which shall be equal to one service-fraction of his final compensation, multiplied by the number of years of service since he last became a member credited to him, and a pension which is the actuarial equivalent of the reserve-for-increased-take-home-pay to which he may then be entitled, if any.

24. According to the above passage, a retirement allowance shall consist of a(n)  24.____
    A. annuity, plus a pension, plus an actuarial equivalent
    B. annuity, plus a pension, plus reserve-for-increased-take-home-pay, if any
    C. annuity, plus reserve-for-increased-take-home-pay, if any, plus final compensation
    D. pension, plus reserve-for-increased-take-home-pay, if any, plus accumulated deductions

Question 25.

DIRECTIONS: Question 25 is to be answered SOLELY on the basis of the following passage.

Membership in the retirement system shall cease upon the occurrence of any one of the following conditions: when the time out of service of any member who has total service of less than 25 years, shall aggregate more than 5 years; when the time out of service of any member who has total service of 25 years or more, shall aggregate more than 10 years; when any member shall have withdrawn more than 50% of his accumulated deductions; or when any member shall have withdrawn the cash benefit provided by Section B3.35.0 of the Administrative Code.

25. According to the information in the above passage, membership in the  25.____
    retirement system shall cease when an employee
    A. with 17 years of service has been on a leave of absence for 3 years
    B. withdraws 50% of his accumulated deductions
    C. with 28 years of service has been out of service for 10 years
    D. withdraws his cash benefits

## KEY (CORRECT ANSWERS)

| | | | |
|---|---|---|---|
| 1. | B | 11. | B |
| 2. | A | 12. | C |
| 3. | C | 13. | B |
| 4. | A | 14. | B |
| 5. | D | 15. | D |
| 6. | B | 16. | B |
| 7. | A | 17. | A |
| 8. | C | 18. | A |
| 9. | B | 19. | C |
| 10. | C | 20. | D |

21. B
22. C
23. D
24. B
25. D

# TEST 2

DIRECTIONS: Each question or incomplete statement is followed by several suggested answers or completions. Select the one that BEST answers the question or completes the statement. *PRINT THE LETTER OF THE CORRECT ANSWER IN THE SPACE AT THE RIGHT.*

Questions 1-6.

DIRECTIONS: Questions 1 through 6 are to be answered SOLELY on the basis of the following passage.

Since almost every office has some contact with data-processed records, a stenographer should have some understanding of the basic operations of data processing. Data processing systems now handle a vast majority of all office paperwork. On coded forms and other specialized media, data are recorded before being fed into the computer for processing. The data written on the source document is converted in highly advanced ways in order to make the information accessible to the user. After data has been converted, it must be verified to guarantee absolute accuracy. In this manner, data becomes a permanent record which can be read by computers that compare, store, compute, and otherwise process data at high speeds.

One key person in a computer installation is a programmer, the man or woman who puts business and scientific problems into special symbolic languages that can be read by the computer. Jobs done by the computer range all the way from payroll operations to chemical process control, but most computer applications are directed toward management data. Most programmers employed by business come to their positions with college degrees; the rest are promoted to their positions from within the organization on the basis of demonstrated ability without regard to education.

1. Of the following, the BEST title for the above passage is  1.____
   A. The Stenographer As Data Processor
   B. The Relation of Data Input to Stenography
   C. Understanding Data Processing
   D. Permanent Office Records

2. According to the above passage, a stenographer should understand the basic  2.____
   operations of data processing because
   A. almost every office today has contact with data processed by computer
   B. any office worker may be asked to verify the accuracy of data
   C. most offices are involved in the production of permanent records
   D. data may be converted into computer language by specialized media

3. According to the above passage, data accuracy is reviewed during the _____  3.____
   stage.
   A. processing
   B. verification
   C. programming
   D. stenographic

163

4. According to the above passage, computers are used MOST often to handle
   A. management data
   B. problems of higher education
   C. the control of chemical processes
   D. payroll operations

5. Computer programming is taught in many colleges and business schools. The above passage implies that programmers in industry
   A. must have professional training
   B. need professional training to advance
   C. must have at least a college education to do adequate programming tasks
   D. do not necessarily need college education to do programming work

6. According to the above passage, data to be processed by computer should be
   A. recent    B. basic    C. complete    D. verified

Questions 7-10.

DIRECTIONS: Questions 7 through 10 are to be answered SOLELY on the basis of the following passage.

There is nothing that will take the place of good sense on the part of the stenographer. You may be perfect in transcribing exactly what the dictator says and your speed may be adequate, but without an understanding of the dictator's intent as well as his words, you are likely to be a mediocre secretary.

A serious error that is made when taking dictation is putting down something that does not make sense. Most people who dictate material would rather be asked to repeat and explain than to receive transcribed material which has errors due to inattention or doubt. Many dictators request that their grammar be corrected by their secretaries, but unless specifically asked to do so, secretaries should not do it without first checking with the dictator. Secretaries should be aware that, in some cases, dictators may use incorrect grammar or slang expressions to create a particular effect.

Some people dictate commas, periods, and paragraphs, while others expect the stenographer to know when, where, and how to punctuate. A well-trained secretary should be able to indicate the proper punctuation by listening to the pauses and tones of the dictator's voice.

A stenographer who has taken dictation from the same person for a period of time should be able to understand him under most conditions. By increasing her tack, alertness, and efficiency, a secretary can become more competent.

7. According to the above passage, which of the following statements concerning the dictation of punctuation is CORRECT?
   A. Dictator may use incorrect punctuation to create a desired style.
   B. Dictator should indicate all punctuation.

C. Stenographer should know how to punctuate based on the pauses and tones of the dictator.
D. Stenographer should not type any punctuation if it has not been dictated to her.

8. According to the above passage, how should secretaries handle grammatical errors in a dictation?  8.____
Secretaries should
   A. *not correct* grammatical errors unless the dictator is aware that this is being done
   B. *correct* grammatical errors by having the dictator repeat the line with proper pauses
   C. *correct* grammatical errors if they have checked the correctness in a grammar book
   D. *correct* grammatical errors based on their own good sense

9. If a stenographer is confused about the method of spacing and indenting of a report which has just been dictated to her, she GENERALLY should  9.____
   A. do the best she can
   B. ask the dictator to explain what she should do
   C. try to improve her ability to understand dictated material
   D. accept the fact that her stenographic ability is not adequate

10. In the last line of the first paragraph, the word *mediocre* means MOST NEARLY  10.____
    A. superior    B. respected    C. disregarded    D. second-rate

Questions 11-12.

DIRECTIONS: Questions 11 and 12 are to be answered SOLELY on the basis of the following passage.

The number of legible carbon copies required to be produced determines the weight of the carbon paper to be used. When only one copy is made, heavy carbon paper is satisfactory. Most typists, however, use medium-weight carbon paper and find it serviceable for up to three or four copies. If five or more copies are to be made, it is wise to use light carbon paper. On the other hand, the finish of carbon paper to be used depends largely on the stroke of the typist and, in lesser degree, on the number of copies to be made and on whether the typewriter has pica or elite type. A soft-finish carbon paper should be used if the typist's touch is light or if a noiseless machine is used. It is desirable for the average typist to use medium-finish carbon paper for ordinary work, when only a few carbon copies are required. Elite type requires a harder carbon finish than pica type for the same number of copies.

11. According to the above passage, the lighter the carbon paper used, the  11.____
    A. softer the finish of the carbon paper will be
    B. greater the number of legible carbon copies that can be made
    C. greater the number of times the carbon paper can be used
    D. lighter the typist's touch should be

12. According to the above passage, the MOST important factor which determines whether the finish of carbon paper to be used in typing should be hard, medium, or soft is
    A. the touch of the typist
    B. the number of carbon copies required
    C. whether the type in the typewriter is pica or elite
    D. whether a machine with pica type will produce the same number of carbon copies as a machine with elite type

12.____

Questions 13-16.

DIRECTIONS: Questions 13 through 16 are to be answered SOLELY on the basis of the following passage.

Looking back at past developments in office work, advances were made at higher speeds and at greater efficiency thanks largely to the typewriter. The typewriter was a substitute for handwriting and, in the hands of a skilled typist, not only turned out letters and other documents at least three times faster than a penman, but turned out the greater volume more uniformly and legibly. With the use of carbon paper and onionskin paper, identical copies could be made at the same time.

The typewriter, besides its effect on the conduct of business and government, had a very important effect on the position of women. The typewriter did much to bring women into business and government, and in a short time span, women far outnumbered men as typists. Many women used the keys of the typewriter to climb the ladder to professional managerial positions.

The typewriter, as its name implies, employs type to make an ink impression on paper. For many years, the manual typewriter was the standard machine used. Eventually, the electric typewriter became dominant, leading to innovations in and widespread use of completely automatic electronic typewriters.

The mechanism of the office manual typewriter includes a set of keys arranged systematically in rows; a semicircular frame of type, connected to the keys by levers; the carriage, or paper carrier; a rubber roller, called a platen, against which the type strikes; and an inked ribbon which makes the impression of the type character when the key strikes it.

13. The above passage mentions a number of good features of the combination of a skilled typist and a typewriter.
    Of the following the feature which is NOT mentioned in the passage is
    A. speed   B. reliability   C. uniformity   D. legibility

13.____

14. According to the above passage, a skilled typist can
    A. turn out at least five carbon copies of typed matter
    B. type at least three times faster than a penman can write
    C. type more than 80 words in a minute
    D. readily move into a managerial position

14.____

15. According to the above passage, which of the following is NOT part of the mechanism of a manual typewriter?  15.____
    A. Carbon paper
    B. Platen
    C. Paper carrier
    D. Inked ribbon

16. According to the above passage, the typewriter helped  16.____
    A. men more than women in business
    B. women in career advancement into management
    C. men and women equally, but women have taken better advantage of it
    D. more women than men, because men generally dislike routine typing work

Questions 17-21.

DIRECTIONS: Questions 17 through 21 are to be answered SOLELY on the basis of the following passage.

The recipient gains an impression of a typewritten letter before he begins to read the message. Factors which provide for a good first impression include margins and spacing that are visually pleasing, formal parts of the letter which are correctly placed according to the style of the letter, copy which is free of obvious erasures and over-strikes, and transcript that is even and clear. The problem for the typist is that of how to produce that first, positive impression of her work.

There are several general rules which a typist can follow when she wishes to prepare a properly spaced letter on a sheet of letterhead. Ordinarily, the width of a letter should not be less than four inches nor more than six inches. The side margins should also have a desirable relation to the bottom margin and the space between the letterhead and the body of the letter. Usually the most appealing arrangement is when the side margins are even and the bottom margin is slightly wider than the side margins. In some offices, however, standard line length is used for all business letter, and the secretary then varies the spacing between the date line and the inside address according to the length of the letter.

17. The BEST title for the above passage would be  17.____
    A. Writing Office Letters
    B. Making Good First Impressions
    C. Judging Well-Typed Letters
    D. Good Placing and Spacing for Office Letters

18. According to the above passage, which of the following might be considered the way in which people very quickly judge the quality of work which has been typed? By  18.____
    A. measuring the margins to see if they are correct
    B. looking at the spacing and cleanliness of the typescript
    C. scanning the body of the letter for meaning
    D. reading the date line and address for errors

19. What, according to the above passage, would be definitely UNDESIRABLE as the average line length of a typed letter?  19.____
    A. 4"   B. 6"   C. 5"   D. 7"

20. According to the above passage, when the line length is kept standard, the secretary  20.____
    A. does not have to vary the spacing at all since this also is standard
    B. adjusts the spacing between the date line and inside address for different lengths of letters
    C. uses the longest line as a guidance for spacing between the date line and inside address
    D. varies the number of spaces between the lines

21. According to the above passage, side margins are MOST pleasing when they  21.____
    A. are even and somewhat smaller than the bottom margin
    B. are slightly wider than the bottom margin
    C. vary with the length of the letter
    D. are figured independently from the letterhead and the body of the letter

Questions 22-25.

DIRECTIONS: Questions 22 through 25 are to be answered SOLELY on the basis of the following passage.

Typed pages can reflect the simplicity of modern art in a machine age. Lightness and evenness can be achieved by proper layout and balance of typed lines and white space. Instead of solid, cramped masses of uneven, crowded typing, there should be a pleasing balance up and down as well as horizontal.

To have real balance, your page must have a center. The eyes see the center of the sheet slightly above the real center. This is the way both you and the reader see it. Try imagining a line down the center of the page that divides the paper in equal halves. On either side of your paper, white space and blocks of typing need to be similar in size and shape. Although left and right margins should be equal, top and bottom margins need not be as exact. It looks better to hold a bottom border wider than a top margin, so that your typing rests upon a cushion of white space. To add interest to the appearance of the page, try making one paragraph between one-half and two-thirds the size of an adjacent paragraph.

Thus, by taking full advantage of your typewriter, the pages that you type will not only be accurate but will also be attractive.

22. It can be inferred from the above passage that the basic importance of proper balancing on a typed page is that proper balancing  22.____
    A. makes a typed page a work of modern art
    B. provides exercise in proper positioning of a typewriter
    C. increases the amount of typed copy on the paper
    D. draws greater attention and interest to the page

23. A reader will tend to see the center of a typed page  23.____
    A. somewhat higher than the true center
    B. somewhat lower than the true center
    C. on either side of the true center
    D. about two-thirds of an inch above the true center

24. Which of the following suggestions is NOT given by the above passage?  24.____
    A. Bottom margins may be wider than top borders.
    B. Keep all paragraphs approximately the same size.
    C. Divide your page with an imaginary line down the middle.
    D. Side margins should be equalized.

25. Of the following, the BEST title for the above passage is  25.____
    A. Increasing the Accuracy of the Typed Page
    B. Determination of Margins for Typed Copy
    C. Layout and Balance of the Typed Page
    D. How to Take Full Advantage of the Typewriter

## KEY (CORRECT ANSWERS)

| | | | | |
|---|---|---|---|---|
| 1. | C | | 11. | B |
| 2. | A | | 12. | A |
| 3. | B | | 13. | B |
| 4. | A | | 14. | B |
| 5. | D | | 15. | A |
| 6. | D | | 16. | B |
| 7. | C | | 17. | D |
| 8. | A | | 18. | B |
| 9. | B | | 19. | D |
| 10. | D | | 20. | B |

| | |
|---|---|
| 21. | A |
| 22. | D |
| 23. | A |
| 24. | B |
| 25. | C |

# TEST 3

DIRECTIONS: Each question or incomplete statement is followed by several suggested answers or completions. Select the one that BEST answers the question or completes the statement. *PRINT THE LETTER OF THE CORRECT ANSWER IN THE SPACE AT THE RIGHT.*

Questions 1-5.

DIRECTIONS: Questions 1 through 5 are to be answered SOLELY on the basis of the following passage.

A written report is a communication of information from one person to another. It is an account of some matter especially investigated, however routine that matter may be. The ultimate basis of any good written report is facts, which become known through observation and verification. Good written reports may seem to be no more than general ideas and opinions. However, in such cases, the facts leading too these opinions were gathered, verified, and reported earlier, and the opinions are dependent upon these facts. Good style, proper form, and emphasis cannot make a good written report out of unreliable information and bad judgment; but on the other hand, solid investigation and brilliant thinking are not likely to become very useful until they are effectively communicated to others. If a person's work calls for written reports, then his work is often no better than his written reports.

1. Based on the information in the above passage, it can be concluded that opinions expressed in a report should be
   A. based on facts which are gathered and reported
   B. emphasized repeatedly when they result from a special investigation
   C. kept to a minimum
   D. separated from the body of the report

   1.____

2. In the above passage, the one of the following which is mentioned as a way of establishing facts is
   A. authority            B. reporting
   C. communication        D. verification

   2.____

3. According to the above passage, the characteristic shared by ALL written reports is that they are
   A. accounts of routine matters       B. transmissions of information
   C. reliable and logical              D. written in proper form

   3.____

4. Which of the following conclusions can logically be drawn from the information given in the above passage?
   A. Brilliant thinking can make up for unreliable information in a report.
   B. One method of judging an individual's work is the quality of the written reports he is required to submit.
   C. Proper form and emphasis can make a good report out of unreliable information.
   D. Good written reports that seem to be no more than general ideas should be rewritten.

   4.____

2 (#3)

5. Which of the following suggested titles would be MOST appropriate for the above passage?
   A. Gathering and Organizing Facts
   B. Techniques of Observation
   C. Nature and Purpose of Reports
   D. Reports and Opinions: Differences and Similarities

5.____

Questions 6-8.

DIRECTIONS: Questions 6 through 8 are to be answered SOLELY on the basis of the following passage.

The most important unit of the mimeograph machine is a perforated metal drum over which is stretched a cloth ink pad. A reservoir inside the drum contains the ink which flows through the perforations and saturates the ink pad. To operate the machine, the operator first removes from the machine the protective sheet, which keeps the ink from drying while the machine is not in use. He then hooks the stencil face down on the drum, draws the stencil smoothly over the drum, and fastens the stencil at the bottom. The speed with which the drum turns determines the blackness of the copies printed. Slow turning gives heavy, black copies; fast turning gives light, clear-cut reproductions. If reproductions are run on other than porous paper, slip-sheeting is necessary to prevent smearing. Often, the printed copy fails to drop readily as it comes from the machine. This may be due to static electricity. To remedy this difficulty, the operator fastens a strip of tinsel from side to side near the impression roller so that the printed copy just touches the soft stems of the tinsel as it is ejected from the machine, thus grounding the static electricity to the frame of the machine.

6. According to the above passage,
   A. turning the drum fast produces light copies
   B. stencils should be placed face up on the drum
   C. ink pads should be changed daily
   D. slip-sheeting is necessary when porous paper is being used

6.____

7. According to the above passage, when a mimeograph machine is not in use, the
   A. ink should be drained from the drum
   B. ink pad should be removed
   C. machine should be covered with a protective sheet
   D. counter should be set at zero

7.____

8. According to the above passage, static electricity is grounded to the frame of the mimeograph machine by means of
   A. a slip-sheeting device
   B. a strip of tinsel
   C. an impression roller
   D. hooks located at the top of the drum

8.____

Questions 9-10.

DIRECTIONS: Questions 9 and 10 are to be answered SOLELY on the basis of the following passage.

The proofreading of material typed from copy is performed more accurately and more speedily when two persons perform this work as a team. The person who did not do the typing should read aloud the original copy while the person who did the typing should check the reading against the typed copy. The reader should speak very slowly and repeat the figures, using a different grouping of number when repeating the figures. For example, in reading 1967, the reader may say *one-nine-six-seven* on first reading the figure and *nineteen-sixty-seven* on repeating the figure. The reader should read all punctuation marks, taking nothing for granted. Since mistakes can occur anywhere, everything typed should be proofread. To avoid confusion, the proofreading team should use the standard proofreading marks, which are given in most dictionaries.

9. According to the above passage, the  9.____
    A. person who holds the typed copy is called the reader
    B. two members of a proofreading team should take turns in reading the typed copy aloud
    C. typed copy should be checked by the person who did the typing
    D. person who did not do the typing should read aloud from the typed copy

10. According to the above passage,  10.____
    A. it is unnecessary to read the period at the end of a sentence
    B. typographical errors should be noted on the original copy
    C. each person should develop his own set of proofreading marks
    D. figures should be read twice

Questions 11-16.

DIRECTIONS: Questions 11 through 16 are to be answered SOLELY on the basis of the following passage.

Basic to every office is the need for proper lighting. Inadequate lighting is a familiar cause of fatigue and serves to create a somewhat dismal atmosphere in the office. One requirement of proper lighting is that it be of an appropriate intensity. Intensity is measured in foot-candles. According to the Illuminating Engineering Society of New York, for casual seeing tasks such as in reception rooms, inactive file rooms, and other service areas, it is recommending that the amount of light be 30 foot-candle. For ordinary seeing tasks such as reading, work in active file rooms, and in mailrooms, the recommended lighting is 100 foot-candles. For very difficult seeing tasks such as accounting, transcribing, and business machine use, the recommended lighting is 150 foot-candles.

Lighting intensity is only one requirement. Shadows and glare are to be avoided. For example, the larger the proportion of a ceiling filled with lighting units, the more glare-free and comfortable the lighting will be. Natural lighting from window is not too dependable because on dark wintry days, windows yield little usable light, and on sunny afternoons, the glare from windows may be very distracting. Desks should not face the windows. Finally, the main lighting source ought to be overhead and to the left of the user.

11. According to the above passage, insufficient light in the office may cause  11.____
    A. glare   B. tiredness   C. shadows   D. distraction

12. Based on the above passage, which of the following must be considered when planning lighting arrangements? The  12.____
    A. amount of natural light present
    B. amount of work to be done
    C. level of difficulty of work to be done
    D. type of activity to be carried out

13. It can be inferred from the above passage that a well-coordinated lighting scheme is LIKELY to result in  13.____
    A. greater employee productivity   B. elimination of light reflection
    C. lower lighting cost   D. more use of natural light

14. Of the following, the BEST title for the above passage is  14.____
    A. Characteristics of Light
    B. Light Measurement Devices
    C. Factors to Consider When Planning Lighting Systems
    D. comfort vs. Cost When Devising Lighting Arrangements

15. According to the above passage, a foot-candle is a measurement of the  15.____
    A. number of bulbs used
    B. strength of the light
    C. contrast between glare and shadow
    D. proportion of the ceiling filled with lighting units

16. According to the above passage, the number of foot-candles of light that would be needed to copy figures onto a payroll is _____ foot-candles.  16.____
    A. less than 30   B. 100   C. 30   D. 140

Questions 17-23.

DIRECTIONS:  Questions 17 through 23 are to be answered SOLELY on the basis of the following passage.

## FEE SCHEDULE

1. A candidate for any baccalaureate degree is not required to pay tuition fees for undergraduate courses until he exceeds 128 credits. Candidates exceeding 128 credits in undergraduate courses are charged at the rate of $100 a credit for each credit of undergraduate course work in excess of 128. Candidates for a baccalaureate degree who are taking graduate courses must pay the same fee as any other student taking graduate courses.

5 (#3)

B. Non-degree students and college graduates are charged tuition fees for courses, whether undergraduate or graduate, at the rate of $180 a credit. For such students, there is an additional charge of $150 for each class hour per week in excess of the number of course credits. For example, if a three-credit course meets five hours a week, there is an additional charge for the extra two hours. Graduate courses are shown with a (G) before the course number.

C. All students are required to pay the laboratory fees indicated after the number of credits given for that course.

D. All students must pay a $250 general fee each semester.

E. Candidates for a baccalaureate degree are charged a $150 medical insurance fee for each semester. All other students are charged a $100 medical insurance fee each semester.

17. Miss Burton is not a candidate for a degree. She registers for the following courses in the spring semester: Economics 12, 4 hours a week, 3 credits; History (G 23, 4 hours a week, 3 credits; English 1, 2 hours a week, 2 credits. The TOTAL amount in fees that Miss Burton must pay is  
    A. less than $2,000  
    B. at least $2,000 but less than $2,100  
    C. at least $2,100 but less than $2,200  
    D. $2,200 or over

17.____

18. Miss Gray is not a candidate for a degree. She registers for the following courses in the fall semester: History 3, 3 hours a week, 3 credits; English 5, 3 hours a week, 2 credits; Physics 5, 6 hours a week, 3 credits, laboratory fee $60; Mathematics 7, 4 hours a week, 3 credits. The TOTAL amount in fees that Miss Gray must pay is  
    A. less than $3,150  
    B. at least $3,150 but less than $3,250  
    C. at least $3,250 but less than $3,350  
    D. $3,350 or over

18.____

19. Mr. Wall is a candidate for the Bachelor of Arts degree and has completed 126 credits. He registers for the following courses in the spring semester, his final semester at college; French 4, 3 hours a week, 3 credits; Physics (G) 15, 6 hours a week, 3 credits, laboratory fee $80; History (G) 33, 4 hours a week, 3 credits. The TOTAL amount in fees that this candidate must pay is  
    A. less than $2,100  
    B. at least $2,100 but less than $2,300  
    C. at least $2,300 but less than $2,500  
    D. $2,500

19.____

6 (#3)

20. Mr. Tindall, a candidate for the B.A. degree, has completed 122 credits of undergraduate courses. He registers for the following courses in his final semester: English 31, 3 hours a week, 3 credits; Philosophy 12, 4 hours a week, 4 credits; Anthropology 15, 3 hours a week, 3 credits; Economics (G) 68, 3 hours a week, 3 credits.
The TOTAL amount in fees that Mr. Tindall must pay in his final semester is
    A. less than $1,200
    B. at least $1,200 but less than $1,400
    C. at least $1,400 but less than $1,600
    D. $1,600

20.____

21. Mr. Cantrell, who was graduated from the college a year ago, registers for graduate courses in the fall semester. Each course for which he register carries the same number of credits as the number of hours a week it meets. If he pays a total of $1,530, including a $100 laboratory fee, the number of credits for which he is registered is
    A. 4    B. 5    C. 6    D. 7

21.____

22. Miss Jayson, who is not a candidate for a degree, has registered for several courses including a lecture course in History. She withdraws from the course in History for which she had paid the required course fee of $690.
The number of hours that this course is scheduled to meet is
    A. 4    B. 5    C. 2    D. 3

22.____

23. Mr. Van Arsdale, a graduate of a college in Iowa, registers for the following courses in one semester: Chemistry 35, 5 hours a week, 3 credits; Biology 14, 4 hours a week, 3 credits, laboratory fee $150; Mathematics (G) 179, 3 hours a week, 3 credits.
The TOTAL amount in fees that Mr. Van Arsdale must pay is
    A. less than $2,400
    B. at least $2,400 but less than $2,500
    C. at least $2,500 but less than $2,600
    D. at least $2,600 or over

23.____

Questions 24-25.

DIRECTIONS:  Questions 24 and 25 are to be answered SOLELY on the basis of the following passage.

   A duplex envelope is an envelope composed of two sections securely fastened together so that they become one mailing piece. This type of envelope makes it possible for a first class letter to be delivered simultaneously with third or fourth class matter and yet not require payment of the much higher first class postage rate on the entire mailing. First class postage is paid only on the letter which goes in the small compartment, third or fourth class postage being paid on the contents of the larger compartment. The larger compartment generally has an ungummed flap or clasp for sealing. The first class or smaller compartment has a gummed flap for sealing. Postal regulations require that the exact amount of postage applicable to each compartment be separately attached to it.

24. On the basis of the above passage, it is MOST accurate to state that
    A. the smaller compartment is placed inside the larger compartment before mailing
    B. the two compartments may be detached and mailed separately
    C. two classes of mailing matter may be mailed as a unit at two different postage rates
    D. the more expensive postage rate is paid on the matter in the larger compartment

25. When a duplex envelope is used, the
    A. first class compartment may be sealed with a clasp
    B. correct amount of postage must be placed on each compartment
    C. compartment containing third or fourth class mail requires a gummed flap for sealing
    D. full amount of postage for both compartments may be placed on the larger compartment

## KEY (CORRECT ANSWERS)

| | | | |
|---|---|---|---|
| 1. | A | 11. | C |
| 2. | D | 12. | D |
| 3. | B | 13. | A |
| 4. | B | 14. | C |
| 5. | C | 15. | B |
| 6. | A | 16. | D |
| 7. | C | 17. | B |
| 8. | B | 18. | A |
| 9. | C | 19. | B |
| 10. | D | 20. | B |

21. C
22. A
23. C
24. C
25. B

# PHILOSOPHY, PRINCIPLES, PRACTICES, AND TECHNICS
# OF
# SUPERVISION, ADMINISTRATION, MANAGEMENT, AND ORGANIZATION

## TABLE OF CONTENTS

| | Page |
|---|---|
| MEANING OF SUPERVISION | 1 |
| THE OLD AND THE NEW SUPERVISION | 1 |
| THE EIGHT (8) BASIC PRINCIPLES OF THE NEW SUPERVISION | 1 |
|     I.   Principle of Responsibility | 1 |
|     II.   Principle of Authority | 2 |
|     III.   Principle of Self-Growth | 2 |
|     IV.   Principle of Individual Worth | 2 |
|     V.   Principle of Creative Leadership | 2 |
|     VI.   Principle of Success and Failure | 2 |
|     VII.   Principle of Science | 3 |
|     VIII.   Principle of Cooperation | 3 |
| WHAT IS ADMINISTRATION? | 3 |
|     I.   Practices Commonly Classed as "Supervisory" | 3 |
|     II.   Practices Commonly Classed as "Administrative" | 3 |
|     III.   Practices Commonly Classed as Both "Supervisory" and "Administrative" | 4 |
| RESPONSIBILITIES OF THE SUPERVISOR | 4 |
| COMPETENCIES OF THE SUPERVISOR | 4 |
| THE PROFESSIONAL SUPERVISOR-EMPLOYEE RELATIONSHIP | 4 |
| MINI-TEXT IN SUPERVISION, ADMINISTRATION, MANAGEMENT, AND ORGANIZATION | 5 |
|     I.   Brief Highlights | 5 |
|         A.   Levels of Management | 6 |
|         B.   What the Supervisor Must Learn | 6 |
|         C.   A Definition of Supervision | 6 |
|         D.   Elements of the Team Concept | 6 |
|         E.   Principles of Organization | 6 |
|         F.   The Four Important Parts of Every Job | 7 |
|         G.   Principles of Delegation | 7 |
|         H.   Principles of Effective Communications | 7 |
|         I.   Principles of Work Improvement | 7 |
|         J.   Areas of Job Improvement | 7 |
|         K.   Seven Key Points in Making Improvements | 8 |

| | | | |
|---|---|---|---|
| | L. | Corrective Techniques for Job Improvement | 8 |
| | M. | A Planning Checklist | 8 |
| | N. | Five Characteristics of Good Directions | 9 |
| | O. | Types of Directions | 9 |
| | P. | Controls | 9 |
| | Q. | Orienting the New Employee | 9 |
| | R. | Checklist for Orienting New Employees | 9 |
| | S. | Principles of Learning | 10 |
| | T. | Causes of Poor Performance | 10 |
| | U. | Four Major Steps in On-the-Job Instructions | 10 |
| | V. | Employees Want Five Things | 10 |
| | W. | Some Don'ts in Regard to Praise | 11 |
| | X. | How to Gain Your Workers' Confidence | 11 |
| | Y. | Sources of Employee Problems | 11 |
| | Z. | The Supervisor's Key to Discipline | 11 |
| | AA. | Five Important Processes of Management | 12 |
| | BB. | When the Supervisor Fails to Plan | 12 |
| | CC. | Fourteen General Principles of Management | 12 |
| | DD. | Change | 12 |
| II. | Brief Topical Summaries | | 13 |
| | A. | Who/What is the Supervisor? | 13 |
| | B. | The Sociology of Work | 13 |
| | C. | Principles and Practices of Supervision | 14 |
| | D. | Dynamic Leadership | 14 |
| | E. | Processes for Solving Problems | 15 |
| | F. | Training for Results | 15 |
| | G. | Health, Safety, and Accident Prevention | 16 |
| | H. | Equal Employment Opportunity | 16 |
| | I. | Improving Communications | 16 |
| | J. | Self-Development | 17 |
| | K. | Teaching and Training | 17 |
| | | 1. The Teaching Process | 17 |
| | |    a. Preparation | 17 |
| | |    b. Presentation | 18 |
| | |    c. Summary | 18 |
| | |    d. Application | 18 |
| | |    e. Evaluation | 18 |
| | | 2. Teaching Methods | 18 |
| | |    a. Lecture | 18 |
| | |    b. Discussion | 18 |
| | |    c. Demonstration | 19 |
| | |    d. Performance | 19 |
| | |    e. Which Method to Use | 19 |

# PHILOSOPHY, PRINCIPLES, PRACTICES, AND TECHNICS OF SUPERVISION, ADMINISTRATION, MANAGEMENT, AND ORGANIZATION

## MEANING OF SUPERVISION

The extension of the democratic philosophy has been accompanied by an extension in the scope of supervision. Modern leaders and supervisors no longer think of supervision in the narrow sense of being confined chiefly to visiting employees, supplying materials, or rating the staff. They regard supervision as being intimately related to all the concerned agencies of society, they speak of the supervisor's function in terms of "growth," rather than the "improvement" of employees.

This modern concept of supervision may be defined as follows: Supervision is leadership and the development of leadership within groups which are cooperatively engaged in inspection, research, training, guidance, and evaluation.

## THE OLD AND THE NEW SUPERVISION

### TRADITIONAL
1. Inspection
2. Focused on the employee
3. Visitation
4. Random and haphazard
5. Imposed and authoritarian
6. One person usually

### MODERN
1. Study and analysis
2. Focused on aims, materials, methods, supervisors, employees, environment
3. Demonstrations, intervisitation, workshops, directed reading, bulletins, etc.
4. Definitely organized and planned (scientific)
5. Cooperative and democratic
6. Many persons involved (creative)

## THE EIGHT (8) BASIC PRINCIPLES OF THE NEW SUPERVISION

I. Principle of Responsibility
   Authority to act and responsibility for acting must be joined.
   A. If you give responsibility, give authority.
   B. Define employee duties clearly.
   C. Protect employees from criticism by others.
   D. Recognize the rights as well as obligations of employees.
   E. Achieve the aims of a democratic society insofar as it is possible within the area of your work.
   F. Establish a situation favorable to training and learning.
   G. Accept ultimate responsibility for everything done in your section, unit, office, division, department.
   H. Good administration and good supervision are inseparable.

II. Principle of Authority
The success of the supervisor is measured by the extent to which the power of authority is not used.
  A. Exercise simplicity and informality in supervision
  B. Use the simplest machinery of supervision
  C. If it is good for the organization as a whole, it is probably justified.
  D. Seldom be arbitrary or authoritative.
  E. Do not base your work on the power of position or of personality.
  F. Permit and encourage the free expression of opinions.

III. Principle of Self-Growth
The success of the supervisor is measured by the extent to which, and the speed with which, he is no longer needed.
  A. Base criticism on principles, not on specifics.
  B. Point out higher activities to employees.
  C. Train for self-thinking by employees to meet new situations.
  D. Stimulate initiative, self-reliance, and individual responsibility
  E. Concentrate on stimulating the growth of employees rather than on removing defects.

IV. Principle of Individual Worth
Respect for the individual is a paramount consideration in supervision.
  A. Be human and sympathetic in dealing with employees.
  B. Don't nag about things to be done.
  C. Recognize the individual differences among employees and seek opportunities to permit best expression of each personality.

V. Principle of Creative Leadership
The best supervision is that which is not apparent to the employee.
  A. Stimulate, don't drive employees to creative action.
  B. Emphasize doing good things.
  C. Encourage employees to do what they do best.
  D. Do not be too greatly concerned with details of subject or method.
  E. Do not be concerned exclusively with immediate problems and activities.
  F. Reveal higher activities and make them both desired and maximally possible.
  G. Determine procedures in the light of each situation but see that these are derived from a sound basic philosophy.
  H. Aid, inspire, and lead so as to liberate the creative spirit latent in all good employees.

VI. Principle of Success and Failure
There are no unsuccessful employees, only unsuccessful supervisors who have failed to give proper leadership.
  A. Adapt suggestions to the capacities, attitudes, and prejudices of employees.
  B. Be gradual, be progressive, be persistent.
  C. Help the employee find the general principle; have the employee apply his own problem to the general principle.
  D. Give adequate appreciation for good work and honest effort.
  E. Anticipate employee difficulties and help to prevent them.
  F. Encourage employees to do the desirable things they will do anyway.
  G. Judge your supervision by the results it secures.

VII. Principle of Science
Successful supervision is scientific, objective, and experimental. It is based on facts, not on prejudices.
- A. Be cumulative in results.
- B. Never divorce your suggestions from the goals of training.
- C. Don't be impatient of results.
- D. Keep all matters on a professional, not a personal, level.
- E. Do not be concerned exclusively with immediate problems and activities.
- F. Use objective means of determining achievement and rating where possible.

VIII. Principle of Cooperation
Supervision is a cooperative enterprise between supervisor and employee.
- A. Begin with conditions as they are.
- B. Ask opinions of all involved when formulating policies.
- C. Organization is as good as its weakest link.
- D. Let employees help to determine policies and department programs.
- E. Be approachable and accessible—physically and mentally.
- F. Develop pleasant social relationships.

## WHAT IS ADMINISTRATION

Administration is concerned with providing the environment, the material facilities, and the operational procedures that will promote the maximum growth and development of supervisors and employees. (Organization is an aspect and a concomitant of administration.)

There is no sharp line of demarcation between supervision and administration; these functions are intimately interrelated and, often, overlapping. They are complementary activities.

I. Practices Commonly Classed as "Supervisory"
- A. Conducting employees' conferences
- B. Visiting sections, units, offices, divisions, departments
- C. Arranging for demonstrations
- D. Examining plans
- E. Suggesting professional reading
- F. Interpreting bulletins
- G. Recommending in-service training courses
- H. Encouraging experimentation
- I. Appraising employee morale
- J. Providing for intervisitation

II. Practices Commonly Classified as "Administrative"
- A. Management of the office
- B. Arrangement of schedules for extra duties
- C. Assignment of rooms or areas
- D. Distribution of supplies
- E. Keeping records and reports
- F. Care of audio-visual materials
- G. Keeping inventory records
- H. Checking record cards and books

I. Programming special activities
J. Checking on the attendance and punctuality of employees

III. Practices Commonly Classified as Both "Supervisory" and "Administrative"
A. Program construction
B. Testing or evaluating outcomes
C. Personnel accounting
D. Ordering instructional materials

**RESPONSIBILITIES OF THE SUPERVISOR**

A person employed in a supervisory capacity must constantly be able to improve his own efficiency and ability. He represent the employer to the employees and only continuous self-examination can make him a capable supervisor.

Leadership and training are the supervisor's responsibility. An efficient working unit is one in which the employees work with the supervisor. It is his job to bring out the best in his employees. He must always be relaxed, courteous, and calm in his association with his employees. Their feelings are important, and a harsh attitude does not develop the most efficient employees.

**COMPETENCES OF THE SUPERVISOR**

I. Complete knowledge of the duties and responsibilities of his position.
II. To be able to organize a job, plan ahead, and carry through.
III. To have self-confidence and initiative.
IV. To be able to handle the unexpected situation and make quick decisions.
V. To be able to properly train subordinates in the positions they are best suited for.
VI. To be able to keep good human relations among his subordinates.
VII. To be able to keep good human relations between his subordinates and himself and to earn their respect and trust.

**THE PROFESSIONAL SUPERVISOR-EMPLOYEE RELATIONSHIP**

There are two kinds of efficiency: one kind is only apparent and is produced in organizations through the exercise of mere discipline; this is but a simulation of the second, or true, efficiency which springs from spontaneous cooperation. If you are a manager, no matter how great or small your responsibility, it is your job, in the final analysis, to create and develop this involuntary cooperation among the people whom you supervise. For, no matter how powerful a combination of money, machines, and materials a company may have, this is a dead and sterile thing without a team of willing, thinking, and articulate people to guide it.

The following 21 points are presented as indicative of the exemplary basic relationship that should exist between supervisor and employee:

1. Each person wants to be liked and respected by his fellow employee and wants to be treated with consideration and respect by his superior.
2. The most competent employee will make an error. However, in a unit where good relations exist between the supervisor and his employees, tenseness and fear do not exist. Thus, errors are not hidden or covered up, and the efficiency of a unit is not impaired.

3. Subordinates resent rules, regulations, or orders that are unreasonable or unexplained.
4. Subordinates are quick to resent unfairness, harshness, injustices, and favoritism.
5. An employee will accept responsibility if he knows that he will be complimented for a job well done, and not too harshly chastised for failure; that his supervisor will check the cause of the failure, and, if it was the supervisor's fault, he will assume the blame therefore. If it was the employee's fault, his supervisor will explain the correct method or means of handling the responsibility.
6. An employee wants to receive credit for a suggestion he has made, that is used. If a suggestion cannot be used, the employee is entitled to an explanation. The supervisor should not say "no" and close the subject.
7. Fear and worry slow up a worker's ability. Poor working environment can impair his physical and mental health. A good supervisor avoids forceful methods, threats, and arguments to get a job done.
8. A forceful supervisor is able to train his employees individually and as a team, and is able to motivate them in the proper channels.
9. A mature supervisor is able to properly evaluate his subordinates and to keep them happy and satisfied.
10. A sensitive supervisor will never patronize his subordinates.
11. A worthy supervisor will respect his employees' confidences.
12. Definite and clear-cut responsibilities should be assigned to each executive.
13. Responsibility should always be coupled with corresponding authority.
14. No change should be made in the scope or responsibilities of a position without a definite understanding to that effect on the part of all persons concerned.
15. No executive or employee, occupying a single position in the organization, should be subject to definite orders from more than one source.
16. Orders should never be given to subordinates over the head of a responsible executive. Rather than do this, the officer in question should be supplanted.
17. Criticisms of subordinates should, whoever possible, be made privately, and in no case should a subordinate be criticized in the presence of executives or employees of equal or lower rank.
18. No dispute or difference between executives or employees as to authority or responsibilities should be considered too trivial for prompt and careful adjudication.
19. Promotions, wage changes, and disciplinary action should always be approved by the executive immediately superior to the one directly responsible.
20. No executive or employee should ever be required, or expected, to be at the same time an assistant to, and critic of, another.
21. Any executive whose work is subject to regular inspection should, wherever practicable, be given the assistance and facilities necessary to enable him to maintain an independent check of the quality of his work.

**MINI-TEXT IN SUPERVISION, ADMINISTRATION, MANAGEMENT, AND ORGANIZATION**

I. Brief Highlights

Listed concisely and sequentially are major headings and important data in the field for quick recall and review.

A. Levels of Management
Any organization of some size has several levels of management. In terms of a ladder, the levels are:

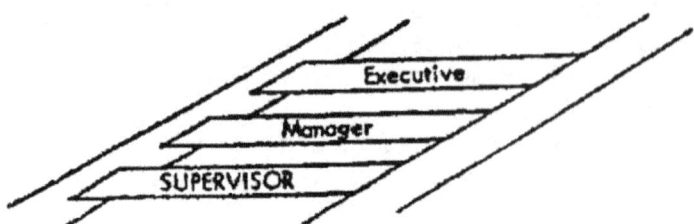

The first level is very important because it is the beginning point of management leadership.

B. What the Supervisor Must Learn
A supervisor must learn to:
1. Deal with people and their differences
2. Get the job done through people
3. Recognize the problems when they exist
4. Overcome obstacles to good performance
5. Evaluate the performance of people
6. Check his own performance in terms of accomplishment

C. A Definition of Supervisor
The term supervisor means any individual having authority, in the interests of the employer, to hire, transfer, suspend, lay-off, recall, promote, discharge, assign, reward, or discipline other employees or responsibility to direct them, or to adjust their grievances, or effectively to recommend such action, if, in connection with the foregoing, exercise of such authority is not of a merely routine or clerical nature but requires the use of independent judgment.

D. Elements of the Team Concept
What is involved in teamwork? The component parts are:
1. Members
2. A leader
3. Goals
4. Plans
5. Cooperation
6. Spirit

E. Principles of Organization
1. A team member must know what his job is.
2. Be sure that the nature and scope of a job are understood.
3. Authority and responsibility should be carefully spelled out.
4. A supervisor should be permitted to make the maximum number of decisions affecting his employees.
5. Employees should report to only one supervisor.
6. A supervisor should direct only as many employees as he can handle effectively.
7. An organization plan should be flexible.

8. Inspection and performance of work should be separate.
9. Organizational problems should receive immediate attention.
10. Assign work in line with ability and experience.

F. The Four Important Parts of Every Job
1. Inherent in every job is the *accountability* for results.
2. A second set of factors in every job is *responsibilities*.
3. Along with duties and responsibilities one must have the *authority* to act within certain limits without obtaining permission to proceed.
4. No job exists in a vacuum. The supervisor is surrounded by key *relationships*.

G. Principles of Delegation
Where work is delegated for the first time, the supervisor should think in terms of these questions:
1. Who is best qualified to do this?
2. Can an employee improve his abilities by doing this?
3. How long should an employee spend on this?
4. Are there any special problems for which he will need guidance?
5. How broad a delegation can I make?

H. Principles of Effective Communications
1. Determine the media.
2. To whom directed?
3. Identification and source authority.
4. Is communication understood?

I. Principles of Work Improvement
1. Most people usually do only the work which is assigned to them.
2. Workers are likely to fit assigned work into the time available to perform it.
3. A good workload usually stimulates output.
4. People usually do their best work when they know that results will be reviewed or inspected.
5. Employees usually feel that someone else is responsible for conditions of work, workplace layout, job methods, type of tools/equipment, and other such factors.
6. Employees are usually defensive about their job security.
7. Employees have natural resistance to change.
8. Employees can support or destroy a supervisor.
9. A supervisor usually earns the respect of his people through his personal example of diligence and efficiency.

J. Areas of Job Improvement
The areas of job improvement are quite numerous, but the most common ones which a supervisor can identify and utilize are:
1. Departmental layout
2. Flow of work
3. Workplace layout
4. Utilization of manpower
5. Work methods
6. Materials handling

7. Utilization
8. Motion economy

K. Seven Key Points in Making Improvements
1. Select the job to be improved
2. Study how it is being done now
3. Question the present method
4. Determine actions to be taken
5. Chart proposed method
6. Get approval and apply
7. Solicit worker participation

l. Corrective Techniques of Job Improvement
Specific Problems
1. Size of workload
2. Inability to meet schedules
3. Strain and fatigue
4. Improper use of men and skills
5. Waste, poor quality, unsafe conditions
6. Bottleneck conditions that hinder output
7. Poor utilization of equipment and machine
8. Efficiency and productivity of labor

General Improvement
1. Departmental layout
2. Flow of work
3. Work plan layout
4. Utilization of manpower
5. Work methods
6. Materials handling
7. Utilization of equipment
8. Motion economy

Corrective Techniques
1. Study with scale model
2. Flow chart study
3. Motion analysis
4. Comparison of units produced to standard allowance
5. Methods analysis
6. Flow chart and equipment study
7. Down time vs. running time
8. Motion analysis

M. A Planning Checklist
1. Objectives
2. Controls
3. Delegations
4. Communications
5. Resources
6. Manpower

7. Equipment
8. Supplies and materials
9. Utilization of time
10. Safety
11. Money
12. Work
13. Timing of improvements

N. Five Characteristics of Good Directions
In order to get results, directions must be:
1. Possible of accomplishment
2. Agreeable with worker interests
3. Related to mission
4. Planned and complete
5. Unmistakably clear

O. Types of Directions
1. Demands or direct orders
2. Requests
3. Suggestion or implication
4. volunteering

P. Controls
A typical listing of the overall areas in which the supervisor should establish controls might be:
1. Manpower
2. Materials
3. Quality of work
4. Quantity of work
5. Time
6. Space
7. Money
8. Methods

Q. Orienting the New Employee
1. Prepare for him
2. Welcome the new employee
3. Orientation for the job
4. Follow-up

R. Checklist for Orienting New Employees

| | | Yes | No |
|---|---|---|---|
| 1. | Do you appreciate the feelings of new employees when they first report for work? | ___ | ___ |
| 2. | Are you aware of the fact that the new employee must make a big adjustment to his job? | ___ | ___ |
| 3. | Have you given him good reasons for liking the job and the organization? | ___ | ___ |
| 4. | Have you prepared for his first day on the job? | ___ | ___ |
| 5. | Did you welcome him cordially and make him feel needed? | ___ | ___ |

|   |   | Yes | No |
|---|---|---|---|

6. Did you establish rapport with him so that he feels free to talk and discuss matters with you? ___ ___
7. Did you explain his job to him and his relationship to you? ___ ___
8. Does he know that his work will be evaluated periodically on a basis that is fair and objective? ___ ___
9. Did you introduce him to his fellow workers in such a way that they are likely to accept him? ___ ___
10. Does he know what employee benefits he will receive? ___ ___
11. Does he understand the importance of being on the job and what to do if he must leave his duty station? ___ ___
12. Has he been impressed with the importance of accident prevention and safe practice? ___ ___
13. Does he generally know his way around the department? ___ ___
14. Is he under the guidance of a sponsor who will teach the right way of doing things? ___ ___
15. Do you plan to follow-up so that he will continue to adjust successfully to his job? ___ ___

S. Principles of Learning
 1. Motivation
 2. Demonstration or explanation
 3. Practice

T. Causes of Poor Performance
 1. Improper training for job
 2. Wrong tools
 3. Inadequate directions
 4. Lack of supervisory follow-up
 5. Poor communications
 6. Lack of standards of performance
 7. Wrong work habits
 8. Low morale
 9. Other

U. Four Major Steps in On-The-Job Instruction
 1. Prepare the worker
 2. Present the operation
 3. Tryout performance
 4. Follow-up

V. Employees Want Five Things
 1. Security
 2. Opportunity
 3. Recognition
 4. Inclusion
 5. Expression

W. Some Don'ts in Regard to Praise
1. Don't praise a person for something he hasn't done.
2. Don't praise a person unless you can be sincere.
3. Don't be sparing in praise just because your superior withholds it from you.
4. Don't let too much time elapse between good performance and recognition of it

X. How to Gain Your Workers' Confidence
Methods of developing confidence include such things as:
1. Knowing the interests, habits, hobbies of employees
2. Admitting your own inadequacies
3. Sharing and telling of confidence in others
4. Supporting people when they are in trouble
5. Delegating matters that can be well handled
6. Being frank and straightforward about problems and working conditions
7. Encouraging others to bring their problems to you
8. Taking action on problems which impede worker progress

Y. Sources of Employee Problems
On-the-job causes might be such things as:
1. A feeling that favoritism is exercised in assignments
2. Assignment of overtime
3. An undue amount of supervision
4. Changing methods or systems
5. Stealing of ideas or trade secrets
6. Lack of interest in job
7. Threat of reduction in force
8. Ignorance or lack of communications
9. Poor equipment
10. Lack of knowing how supervisor feels toward employee
11. Shift assignments

Off-the-job problems might have to do with:
1. Health
2. Finances
3. Housing
4. Family

Z. The Supervisor's Key to Discipline
There are several key points about discipline which the supervisor should keep in mind:
1. Job discipline is one of the disciplines of life and is directed by the supervisor.
2. It is more important to correct an employee fault than to fix blame for it.
3. Employee performance is affected by problems both on the job and off.
4. Sudden or abrupt changes in behavior can be indications of important employee problems.
5. Problems should be dealt with as soon as possible after they are identified.
6. The attitude of the supervisor may have more to do with solving problems than the techniques of problem solving.
7. Correction of employee behavior should be resorted to only after the supervisor is sure that training or counseling will not be helpful.

8. Be sure to document your disciplinary actions.
9. Make sure that you are disciplining on the basis of facts rather than personal feelings.
10. Take each disciplinary step in order, being careful not to make snap judgments, or decisions based on impatience.

AA. Five Important Processes of Management
1. Planning
2. Organizing
3. Scheduling
4. Controlling
5. Motivating

BB. When the Supervisor Fails to Plan
1. Supervisor creates impression of not knowing his job
2. May lead to excessive overtime
3. Job runs itself—supervisor lacks control
4. Deadlines and appointments missed
5. Parts of the work go undone
6. Work interrupted by emergencies
7. Sets a bad example
8. Uneven workload creates peaks and valleys
9. Too much time on minor details at expense of more important tasks

CC. Fourteen General Principles of Management
1. Division of work
2. Authority and responsibility
3. Discipline
4. Unity of command
5. Unity of direction
6. Subordination of individual interest to general interest
7. Remuneration of personnel
8. Centralization
9. Scalar chain
10. Order
11. Equity
12. Stability of tenure of personnel
13. Initiative
14. Esprit de corps

DD. Change

Bringing about change is perhaps attempted more often, and yet less well understood, than anything else the supervisor does. How do people generally react to change? (People tend to resist change that is imposed upon them by other individuals or circumstances.

Change is characteristic of every situation. It is a part of every real endeavor where the efforts of people are concerned.

1. Why do people resist change?
   People may resist change because of:
   a. Fear of the unknown
   b. Implied criticism
   c. Unpleasant experiences in the past
   d. Fear of loss of status
   e. Threat to the ego
   f. Fear of loss of economic stability

2. How can we best overcome the resistance to change?
   In initiating change, take these steps:
   a. Get ready to sell
   b. Identify sources of help
   c. Anticipate objections
   d. Sell benefits
   e. Listen in depth
   f. Follow up

II. Brief Topical Summaries

   A. Who/What is the Supervisor?
      1. The supervisor is often called the "highest level employee and the lowest level manager."
      2. A supervisor is a member of both management and the work group. He acts as a bridge between the two.
      3. Most problems in supervision are in the area of human relations, or people problems.
      4. Employees expect: Respect, opportunity to learn and to advance, and a sense of belonging, and so forth.
      5. Supervisors are responsible for directing people and organizing work. Planning is of paramount importance.
      6. A position description is a set of duties and responsibilities inherent to a given position.
      7. It is important to keep the position description up-to-date and to provide each employee with his own copy.

   B. The Sociology of Work
      1. People are alike in many ways; however, each individual is unique.
      2. The supervisor is challenged in getting to know employee differences. Acquiring skills in evaluating individuals is an asset.
      3. Maintaining meaningful working relationships in the organization is of great importance.
      4. The supervisor has an obligation to help individuals to develop to their fullest potential.
      5. Job rotation on a planned basis helps to build versatility and to maintain interest and enthusiasm in work groups.
      6. Cross training (job rotation) provides backup skills.

7. The supervisor can help reduce tension by maintaining a sense of humor, providing guidance to employees, and by making reasonable and timely decisions. Employees respond favorably to working under reasonably predictable circumstances.
8. Change is characteristic of all managerial behavior. The supervisor must adjust to changes in procedures, new methods, technological changes, and to a number of new and sometimes challenging situations.
9. To overcome the natural tendency for people to resist change, the supervisor should become more skillful in initiating change.

C. Principles and Practices of Supervision
1. Employees should be required to answer to only one superior.
2. A supervisor can effectively direct only a limited number of employees, depending upon the complexity, variety, and proximity of the jobs involved.
3. The organizational chart presents the organization in graphic form. It reflects lines of authority and responsibility as well as interrelationships of units within the organization.
4. Distribution of work can be improved through an analysis using the "Work Distribution Chart."
5. The "Work Distribution Chart" reflects the division of work within a unit in understandable form.
6. When related tasks are given to an employee, he has a better chance of increasing his skills through training.
7. The individual who is given the responsibility for tasks must also be given the appropriate authority to insure adequate results.
8. The supervisor should delegate repetitive, routine work. Preparation of recurring reports, maintaining leave and attendance records are some examples.
9. Good discipline is essential to good task performance. Discipline is reflected in the actions of employees on the job in the absence of supervision.
10. Disciplinary action may have to be taken when the positive aspects of discipline have failed. Reprimand, warning, and suspension are examples of disciplinary action.
11. If a situation calls for a reprimand, be sure it is deserved and remember it is to be done in private.

D. Dynamic Leadership
1. A style is a personal method or manner of exerting influence.
2. Authoritarian leaders often see themselves as the source of power and authority.
3. The democratic leader often perceives the group as the source of authority and power.
4. Supervisors tend to do better when using the pattern of leadership that is most natural for them.
5. Social scientists suggest that the effective supervisor use the leadership style that best fits the problem or circumstances involved.
6. All four styles—telling, selling, consulting, joining—have their place. Using one does not preclude using the other at another time.

7. The theory X point of view assumes that the average person dislikes work, will avoid it whenever possible, and must be coerced to achieve organizational objectives.
8. The theory Y point of view assumes that the average person considers work to be a natural as play, and, when the individual is committed, he requires little supervision or direction to accomplish desired objectives.
9. The leader's basic assumptions concerning human behavior and human nature affect his actions, decisions, and other managerial practices.
10. Dissatisfaction among employees is often present, but difficult to isolate. The supervisor should seek to weaken dissatisfaction by keeping promises, being sincere and considerate, keeping employees informed, and so forth.
11. Constructive suggestions should be encouraged during the natural progress of the work.

E. Processes for Solving Problems
1. People find their daily tasks more meaningful and satisfying when they can improve them.
2. The causes of problems, or the key factors, are often hidden in the background. Ability to solve problems often involves the ability to isolate them from their backgrounds. There is some substance to the cliché that some persons "can't see the forest for the trees."
3. New procedures are often developed from old ones. Problems should be broken down into manageable parts. New ideas can be adapted from old one.
4. People think differently in problem-solving situations. Using a logical, patterned approach is often useful. One approach found to be useful includes these steps:
    a. Define the problem
    b. Establish objectives
    c. Get the facts
    d. Weigh and decide
    e. Take action
    f. Evaluate action

F. Training for Results
1. Participants respond best when they feel training is important to them.
2. The supervisor has responsibility for the training and development of those who report to him.
3. When training is delegated to others, great care must be exercised to insure the trainer has knowledge, aptitude, and interest for his work as a trainer.
4. Training (learning) of some type goes on continually. The most successful supervisor makes certain the learning contributes in a productive manner to operational goals.
5. New employees are particularly susceptible to training. Older employees facing new job situations require specific training, as well as having need for development and growth opportunities.
6. Training needs require continuous monitoring.
7. The training officer of an agency is a professional with a responsibility to assist supervisors in solving training problems.

8. Many of the self-development steps important to the supervisor's own growth are equally important to the development of peers and subordinates. Knowledge of these is important when the supervisor consults with others on development and growth opportunities.

G. Health, Safety, and Accident Prevention
1. Management-minded supervisors take appropriate measures to assist employees in maintaining health and in assuring safe practices in the work environment.
2. Effective safety training and practices help to avoid injury and accidents.
3. Safety should be a management goal. All infractions of safety which are observed should be corrected without exception.
4. Employees' safety attitude, training and instruction, provision of safe tools and equipment, supervision, and leadership are considered highly important factors which contribute to safety and which can be influenced directly by supervisors.
5. When accidents do occur, they should be investigated promptly for very important reasons, including the fact that information which is gained can be used to prevent accidents in the future.

H. Equal Employment Opportunity
1. The supervisor should endeavor to treat all employees fairly, without regard to religion, race, sex, or national origin.
2. Groups tend to reflect the attitude of the leader. Prejudice can be detected even in very subtle form. Supervisors must strive to create a feeling of mutual respect and confidence in every employee.
3. Complete utilization of all human resources is a national goal. Equitable consideration should be accorded women in the work force, minority-group members, the physically and mentally handicapped, and the older employee. The important question is: "Who can do the job?"
4. Training opportunities, recognition for performance, overtime assignments, promotional opportunities, and all other personnel actions are to be handled on an equitable basis.

I. Improving Communications
1. Communications is achieving understanding between the sender and the receiver of a message. It also means sharing information—the creation of understanding.
2. Communication is basic to all human activity. Words are means of conveying meanings; however, real meanings are in people.
3. There are very practical differences in the effectiveness of one-way, impersonal, and two-way communications. Words spoken face-to-face are better understood. Telephone conversations are effective, but lack the rapport of person-to-person exchanges. The whole person communicates.
4. Cooperation and communication in an organization go hand in hand. When there is a mutual respect between people, spelling out rules and procedures for communicating is unnecessary.
5. There are several barriers to effective communications. These include failure to listen with respect and understanding, lack of skill in feedback, and misinterpreting the meanings of words used by the speaker. It is also common

practice to listen to what we want to hear, and tune out things we do not want to hear.
6. Communication is management's chief problem. The supervisor should accept the challenge to communicate more effectively and to improve interagency and intra-agency communications.
7. The supervisor may often plan for and conduct meetings. The planning phase is critical and may determine the success or the failure of a meeting.
8. Speaking before groups usually requires extra effort. Stage fright may never disappear completely, but it can be controlled.

J. Self-Development
1. Every employee is responsible for his own self-development.
2. Toastmaster and toastmistress clubs offer opportunities to improve skills in oral communications.
3. Planning for one's own self-development is of vital importance. Supervisors know their own strengths and limitations better than anyone else.
4. Many opportunities are open to aid the supervisor in his developmental efforts, including job assignments; training opportunities, both governmental and non-governmental—to include universities and professional conferences and seminars.
5. Programmed instruction offers a means of studying at one's own rate.
6. Where difficulties may arise from a supervisor's being away from his work for training, he may participate in televised home study or correspondence courses to meet his self-development needs.

K. Teaching and Training
1. The Teaching Process
Teaching is encouraging and guiding the learning activities of students toward established goals. In most cases this process consists of five steps: preparation, presentation, summarization, evaluation, and application.

   a. Preparation
   Preparation is two-fold in nature; that of the supervisor and the employee. Preparation by the supervisor is absolutely essential to success. He must know what, when, where, how, and whom he will teach. Some of the factors that should be considered are:
   1) The objectives
   2) The materials needed
   3) The methods to be used
   4) Employee participation
   5) Employee interest
   6) Training aids
   7) Evaluation
   8) Summarization

   Employee preparation consists in preparing the employee to receive the material. Probably the most important single factor in the preparation of the employee is arousing and maintaining his interest. He must know the objectives of the training, why he is there, how the material can be used, and its importance to him.

b. Presentation
In presentation, have a carefully designed plan and follow it. The plan should be accurate and complete, yet flexible enough to meet situations as they arise. The method of presentation will be determined by the particular situation and objectives.

c. Summary
A summary should be made at the end of every training unit and program. In addition, there may be internal summaries depending on the nature of the material being taught. The important thing is that the trainee must always be able to understand how each part of the new material relates to the whole.

d. Application
The supervisor must arrange work so the employee will be given a chance to apply new knowledge or skills while the material is still clear in his mind and interest is high. The trainee does not really know whether he has learned the material until he has been given a chance to apply it. If the material is not applied, it loses most of its value.

e. Evaluation
The purpose of all training is to promote learning. To determine whether the training has been a success or failure, the supervisor must evaluate this learning.
In the broadest sense, evaluation includes all the devices, methods, skills, and techniques used by the supervisor to keep himself and the employees informed as to their progress toward the objectives they are pursuing. The extent to which the employee has mastered the knowledge, skills, and abilities, or changed his attitudes, as determined by the program objectives, is the extent to which instruction has succeeded or failed.
Evaluation should not be confined to the end of the lesson, day, or program but should be used continuously. We shall note later the way this relates to the rest of the teaching process.

2. Teaching Methods
A teaching method is a pattern of identifiable student and instructor activity used in presenting training material.
All supervisors are faced with the problem of deciding which method should be used at a given time.

   a. Lecture
   The lecture is direct oral presentation of material by the supervisor. The present trend is to place less emphasis on the trainer's activity and more on that of the trainee.

   b. Discussion
   Teaching by discussion or conference involves using questions and other techniques to arouse interest and focus attention upon certain areas, and by doing so creating a learning situation. This can be one of the most

valuable methods because it gives the employees an opportunity to express their ideas and pool their knowledge.

    c. Demonstration
The demonstration is used to teach how something works or how to do something. It can be used to show a principle or what the results of a series of actions will be. A well-staged demonstration is particularly effective because it shows proper methods of performance in a realistic manner.

    d. Performance
Performance is one of the most fundamental of all learning techniques or teaching methods. The trainee may be able to tell how a specific operation should be performed but he cannot be sure he knows how to perform the operation until he has done so.
As with all methods, there are certain advantages and disadvantages to each method.

    e. Which Method to Use
Moreover, there are other methods and techniques of teaching. It is difficult to use any method without other methods entering into it. In any learning situation, a combination of methods is usually more effective than any one method alone.

Finally, evaluation must be integrated into the other aspects of the teaching-learning process.

It must be used in the motivation of the trainees; it must be used to assist in developing understanding during the training; and it must be related to employee application of the results of training.

This is distinctly the role of the supervisor.